JOURNAL FOR THE STUDY OF THE NEW TESTAMENT
SUPPLEMENT SERIES
225

Executive Editor
Stanley E. Porter

Editorial Board
Elizabeth A. Castelli, David Catchpole, Kathleen E. Corley,
R. Alan Culpepper, James D.G. Dunn, Craig A. Evans,
Stephen Fowl, Robert Fowler, George H. Guthrie,
Robert Jewett, Robert W. Wall

CLASSICS IN BIBLICAL AND THEOLOGICAL STUDIES
SUPPLEMENT SERIES
2

Selected and Edited by
Craig A. Evans and Stanley E. Porter

Sheffield Academic Press

Trinity Academic Press

Essays in Biblical Criticism and Exegesis

William Sanday

Selected and Edited by
Craig A. Evans and Stanley E. Porter
with the assistance of Scott N. Dolff

Journal for the Study of the New Testament
Supplement Series 225

Classics in Biblical and Theological Studies
Supplement Series 2

Copyright © 2001 Sheffield Academic Press
Published by Trinity Academic Press, a wholly
owned imprint of Sheffield Academic Press

Sheffield Academic Press
Mansion House
19 Kingfield Road
Sheffield S11 9AS
England
www.SheffieldAcademicPress.com

Printed on acid-free paper in Great Britain
by Bookcraft Ltd,
Midsomer Norton, Bath

British Library Cataloguing-in-Publication Data

A catalogue record for this book is available
from the British Library

ISBN 1-84127-281-7

CONTENTS

PART II LANGUAGE

PART III EXEGESIS

The editors are pleased to present this volume as the first in the series, Classics in Biblical and Theological Studies, under the imprint of Trinity Academic Press and as part of the JSNT Supplement Series of Sheffield Academic Press.

The scholar William Sanday is not nearly so well known today as he once was, and as he deserves to be. Born on 1 August 1843 in Nottingham, he was educated at Repton, and then Balliol and Corpus Christi Colleges at the University of Oxford, being placed in the first class in Honours Moderations in 1863 and Literae Humaniores in 1865. He was also awarded the D.D. and LL.D. degrees by Oxford and the Litt.D. by Cambridge. Sanday was a Fellow of Trinity College in 1866 and a Lecturer in 1866–69, while being ordained in the Anglican Church in 1867. Sanday served a number of churches from 1869–76, before becoming Principal of Bishop Hatfield's Hall in Durham, from 1876–83, while also being Examining Chaplain to Bishop J.B. Lightfoot in Durham from 1879–81. He then became Dean Ireland Professor of Exegesis of Holy Scripture from 1883–95, and then Lady Margaret Professor of Divinity and Canon of Christ Church, from 1895–1919, at the University of Oxford. He was also a Fellow of the British Academy and Chaplain in Ordinary to the King. He died on 16 September 1920.

Today Sanday is perhaps best known for his work with A.C. Headlam on *A Critical and Exegetical Commentary on the Epistle to the Romans* (International Critical Commentary; Edinburgh: T. & T. Clark, 1895), and for his editorship of the important collection of essays, *Studies in the Synoptic Problem: By Members of the University of Oxford* (Oxford: Clarendon Press, 1911), in which there are important contributions by such scholars as J.C. Hawkins, B.H. Streeter, and W.C. Allen, among others. Less well known today are the numerous other books that Sanday authored. These include: *The Authorship and Historical Character of the Fourth Gospel: Considered in Reference to the Contents of the Gospel Itself* (London: Macmillan, 1872); *The Gospels in the Second Century: An Examination of the Critical Part of a Work Entitled 'Supernatural Religion'* (London: Macmillan, 1876); with J. Wordsworth and H.J. White, *Portions of the Gospels According to St Mark and St Matthew, from the Bobbio MS (k)* (Oxford: Clarendon Press, 1886); *Appendices ad Novum Testamentum Stephanicum* (Oxford: Clarendon Press, 1889); *The Oracles of God: Nine Lectures on the Nature and Extent of Biblical Inspiration and on the Special Significance of the Old Testament Scriptures at the Present Time* (London: Longmans, Green, 1890); *Two Present-Day Questions.* I. *Biblical Criticism.* II. *The Social Movement. Sermons Preached before the University of Cambridge on Ascension Day and the Sunday after Ascension Day* (London: Longmans, Green, 1892); *Inspiration: Eight Lectures on the Early History and Origin of the Doctrine of Biblical Inspiration* (Bampton Lectures for 1893; London: Longmans, Green, 1896); with W. Lock, *Two Lectures on the 'Sayings of Jesus' Recently Discovered at Oxyrhynchus* (Oxford: Clarendon Press, 1897); *Sacred Sites of the Gospels: With Illustrations, Maps and Plans* (assisted by P. Waterhouse; Oxford: Clarendon Press, 1903); *Outlines of the Life of Christ* (Edinburgh: T. & T. Clark, 2nd edn, 1905), which is an expanded reprint of his article on 'Jesus Christ', in J. Hastings (ed.), *Dictionary of the Bible* (5 vols.; Edinburgh: T. & T. Clark, 1898–1904), II, pp. 603-53; *The Criticism of the Fourth Gospel* (Morse Lectures; Oxford: Clarendon Press, 1905); *The Life of Christ in Recent Research* (Oxford: Oxford University Press, 1907); *Christologies Ancient and Modern* (Oxford: Clarendon Press, 1910); *Personality in Christ and in Ourselves* (Oxford: Clarendon Press, 1911); *The Primitive Church and Reunion* (Oxford: Clarendon Press, 1913); *Divine Overruling* (Edinburgh: T. & T. Clark, 1919); plus a number of church-related books and pamphlets, as well as a number of articles and chapters in books. A bibliography of Sanday's writings can be found in A. Souter, 'A Bibliography of Dr Sanday', *Journal of Theological Studies* 22 (1921), pp. 193-205.

Many of Sanday's books are still of value and merit reading, especially as they combine interest in exegetical, church-historical and theological matters. Especially worth noting are his books on Jesus, but his volumes on the Fourth Gospel and on Inspiration are also significant. Although some are difficult to find, many libraries still have them readily available, if one knows to search them out. Less easy to find are a number of Sanday's many articles and papers. The editors were fortunate to come into possession of two privately bound volumes (1923) of Sanday's papers, one called 'Papers and Bibliography' and the other 'Miscellanea'. These volumes had at one time belonged to C.H. Turner, who had apparently come into the possession of Sanday's papers sometime after his death, and they had then been placed in the library of Trinity College, Oxford, perhaps after Turner's death in 1930. We have used this collection, as well as other works that we have found through various means, as the basis of this volume. In this volume, the first of two volumes of Sanday's papers that we intend to publish, we have collected a selection of what we consider his most important essays in the areas of biblical criticism and exegesis. They cover matters of method, language, and exegesis. Even among the most technical of his papers, one senses that for Sanday the topics discussed go far beyond the academic arena. This combination of scholarship and piety provides a breath of fresh air compared to much contemporary scholarship.

The full publication details for each essay are given on the first page of the individual chapter. Sanday's work is here reproduced essentially as it was first published, but the style of presentation has been made in places to conform to the publisher's house style (e.g. conforming biblical and other references, changing some capitalization). We have also made attempts to complete the pertinent bibliographical data for works mentioned by Sanday, often by adding footnotes where appropriate in the text. Anyone with experience of attempting to trace nineteenth- and early twentieth-century references will know that finding all of such references is a near impossibility, especially when only vague and imprecise references are given. We have not attempted to create or fill out additional notes that Sanday did not provide, or to find data for every scholar mentioned, so that his discussion remains in terms of the scholarship of the time. We have also silently corrected a number of other infelicities.

Craig A. Evans   Stanley E. Porter
Trinity Western University   McMaster Divinity College
Langley, B.C.   Hamilton, ON

PART I METHOD

Chapter 1

BIBLICAL CRITICISM: THE FULNESS OF REVELATION IN THE NEW TESTAMENT*

When I undertook to read a paper in the very attractive subject proposed to me, my first thought was to utilize the opportunity mainly by inviting attention to what I believe to be the two most important events in the history of Christian thought within our Church since last year's Congress—the delivery of Mr Illingworth's Bampton Lectures, on 'The Personality of God', in the spring of the present year, and the posthumous appearance, about last Christmas, of Dr Hort's Hulsean Lectures for 1871, 'The Way, the Truth, and the Life'.

The two books—for I may be allowed to speak of Mr Illingworth's lectures as a book, as I understand that they are very shortly to be published in book form—have this in common, that both deal very much with first principles, and both take a bold and exceedingly high view of the claims of Christianity.

If I am not mistaken, Mr Illingworth's lectures will be found to mark the beginning of a new phase in the religious thought of our time—a phase in which philosophy will once more take its proper place on supplying a broad foundation for other branches of theological study, and, at the same time, quickening them with new life. Philosophy is, after all, still the queen of the sciences. Its influence is felt in every department of human thought, especially the highest. And it seems that at last, if my judgment does not deceive me, we have a Christian philosophy which is on essentially right lines—a philosophy on which we can take our stand, strongly and confidently, and from which we can each go forward to that branch of study which has a call for us. Of course, it is as yet early days to speak before the lectures have gone through the ordeal of criticism. I can only say that I found in Mr Illingworth's lectures, as I listened to them, what seemed to me an admirably clear and strong

* This is a paper read at the Church Congress in Exeter, in October 1894.

expression of thoughts to which I believe that others also are gravitating. It remains to be seen how far they will hold good; but, in any case, there are many of us who will owe to the Bampton lecturer for 1894 a deep debt of gratitude.

You will ask how a course of lectures on so abstruse a subject as 'The Personality of God' could be connected with the topic specially proposed to me today. I reply that, with the 'fulness of revelation in the New Testament', they have, undoubtedly, a close connection. I may be allowed, perhaps, to state the case in a way which has been impressing itself upon me more and more as the years wear on. If we believe in a real God, we shall believe also in a real Christ, and a real Atonement, and a real Bible, and, I will venture to say, also in a real Church—by which I mean not so much a body which has this or that definite circumscription (in regard to which another set of considerations comes in), but a body which has an organic life, and is animated by real spiritual forces—a body which is really 'fitly joined together and compacted' with its Head.

On this side lies what I conceive to be the great value of Dr Hort's Hulsean Lectures, published so long after they were delivered, and published, we grieve to think, not by the hand that wrote them. If I were to speak of Dr Hort's lectures in the same kind of terms in which I have spoken of Mr Illingworth's, I might convey a misleading impression. The book is not quite one for which everyone would care, or through which everyone would find his way. There are some things in it, especially in the notes and aphorisms at the end, which I could not yet say that I understood myself, and more which I should not be sure that I could altogether appropriate. Still, it is a noble book, written in a noble spirit, with, perhaps, the loftiest conception of the search for truth which I have ever seen in print, and full of profound and far-reaching thoughts. I have said that it is not a book for which everyone could be expected to care; but those who do care for it, who are not afraid of grappling with difficulties and of living in a high and somewhat rarefied air, will I think prize it very much indeed.

There would be still less difficulty in this case than in the other in establishing a connection with the 'fulness of revelation in the New Testament', and I should have liked to spend the rest of my twenty minutes in doing what I could to expound some of the leading ideas in Dr Hort's book from this point of view; but I should have had some qualms of conscience, derived not from the special subject assigned to me, but from the general subject of this session—Biblical Criticism. It is remarkable that a work proceeding from one whom most of us know chiefly as a Biblical critic, should have so very little to do with criticism in the narrower and proper sense of the term. I hope to be forgiven for straining a point to say as much as I have said about two works, neither of which is in the strict sense critical, though both are such as ought to be brought to the notice of this Congress, and both find a natural place under the subject with which I am entrusted.

At first sight it might not seem as if there was any exact relation between Biblical criticism in the technical sense and the 'fulness of revelation'. It might be thought that this subject belonged rather to the head of exegetical or constructive theology. There is, however, I suppose, an impression abroad that the practise of criticism has had a tendency to weaken the hold upon doctrinal Christianity. On this point it may be desirable for me to say a few words.

I may take for my text a conversation which I had a short time ago with one of our leading Nonconformists. I had not mentioned the Church Congress, though I confess that I had it in my mind when I put to him a question which drew from him in reply what was practically a direct negative of the impression of which I am speaking. He said that in his experience—which is an exceptionally wide one—the Nonconformist ministers of the present day, as compared with those of twenty years ago, were more critical, but had a stronger hold on doctrine. Twenty years ago the tendency was to vagueness and indefiniteness of belief; there was considerable impatience of anything like dogma. Now that impatience has largely disappeared, and the tendency to looseness of belief along with it.

I have not the slightest doubt that this statement is true, though, again, I can quite imagine that it will run counter to a prevailing impression. We have all heard of a 'down-grade' in Nonconformist theology. But partly that 'down-grade' consisted in the adoption of critical views in regard to the Bible as a literature, which is admitted; and partly its existence was due to the teaching of men whose training for the ministry went back some twenty years or more—the generation which is in the front of the stage, not that which is just entering upon it.

I think we shall see very much the same thing in our own communion. If we each of us interrogate our own experience, I do not think we shall say that the adoption of critical views has led to any real loosening of the hold upon doctrine, but rather the contrary. The critical movement of the present day is quite a different thing from the theological liberalism of twenty or thirty years ago. The two things may be connected; the one may, in many cases, have grown out of the other. But still they are distinct in their methods, and distinct also in their results.

The liberalism of the time of which I am speaking had some good points. It had a great wish to be honest, and to see things as they are. It had a strong moral sense. But its criticism lay very much upon the surface of things, and it was not really scientific. It had a specially imperfect conception of history. Its intellectual equipment consisted mainly of a certain number of common-places, the key-notes of most of them being liberty, toleration, and the superior wisdom of the nineteenth century. But it was by no means patient or severe in its methods of study. It reached its conclusions long before it had proved them. It read its own rather small stock of ideas into the facts which it professed to study; and then, as a natural consequence, it claimed the support of the facts for its ideas.

Since that time 'another race hath been, and other palms are won'. The one conspicuous change has been the growth of a stricter conception of scientific method, the determination to let the facts tell their own tale, not to anticipate conclusions or to impose upon the facts conclusions drawn from outside them.

You may imagine what has been the inevitable result of applying this stricter conception of scientific method to the Bible and to early Church history. It has been the discovery that the facts are not really what the rather shallow liberalism of which I have spoken supposed them to be. The mystery of things is not to be unlocked by a few plain and easy formulae. In not a few instances it has been remarkable how a closer and more disinterested study has led back to a position of things, which has far more in common with that which was supposed to be old-fashioned and out of date.

I must not do what I have just been deprecating, and allow myself to convey an impression which is not strictly suggested by the facts. I am speaking chiefly of England and of those workers in the field of criticism with whom I am best acquainted. Of course, there is such a thing as a rationalistic criticism, in which criticism is used as an instrument to arrive at what are really foregone conclusions. To my thinking, that is not a legitimate use for criticism to be put to. It ceases to be criticism if the path which it shall go is marked out for it beforehand. A genuine criticism may attempt to distinguish between what is of the essence of a doctrine and what is not; but it will do so by objective, and not merely subjective, standards. And when the doctrine is seen to be really there, in well authenticated texts, and belonging to the vital structure of the writer's thought, a criticism that is true to itself will not deny or explain it away. It will rather try its utmost to get at the reality which lies behind it—to understand and feel what it really means.

With the caution, then, that you must take the experience of a single worker for what it is worth, I will proceed to give a few examples in which I have myself found criticism, or critical study, tend to strengthen, and not to weaken, the hold on fundamental doctrine. I will take four doctrines which, if any, may be called fundamental: the doctrine of the Trinity; the doctrine of the Logos, or Divine Word; the doctrine of the Atonement; and the doctrine of the union of the Christian with Christ.

It is natural to think of the doctrine of the Trinity as a later growth. So, in one sense, it is. It is not complete until we come to the enlarged form of the Nicene Creed and the Council of Chalcedon, in AD 451. But all that is essential in the doctrine—the main lines—were already laid down when Paul wrote his first two groups of epistles, in the years 52, 53, and 57–58. In the very earliest of all his extant letters, Paul solemnly addresses the Thessalonian Christians as being 'in the fellowship of God the Father and the Lord Jesus Christ', placing the two Names in the closest juxtaposition, and giving to them an equal weight of authority. And from the date of his second epistle to the same Church onwards, he invokes 'grace and peace' also 'from God the Father and the Lord Jesus Christ', making them the one conjoint source of Divine blessing.

And if it is urged that this is but the first stage in the history of the doctrine, we have only to turn to the Second Epistle to the Corinthians, written, in any case, within a year or two of AD 57, and we have there the familiar benediction at the end of the epistle, in which the Name of the Holy Spirit is associated on equal terms with that of God the Father and God the Son; while in the body of the epistle, as in the two almost contemporary epistles—1 Corinthians 12 and Romans 8—the doctrine of the Holy Spirit has already received a considerable development. I say a development, but only in the sense that the doctrine comes to us as a new one. Paul himself does not teach it as if he were teaching something in itself wholly new. He assumes it as already substantially understood and known. Does not this cast back a light upon, and does not it supply an extraordinary confirmation of, what the Gospels tell us of the promise of the Comforter, and what the Acts tell us of the fulfilment of that promise? When we are brought so near in time to our Lord's own ministry upon earth, can we help referring this rapid growth of a doctrine, which seems to us so difficult, to intimations received directly from Him? But, indeed, the greatest difficulty in the doctrine of the Trinity was already over, and the foundation stone of the doctrine was already laid, the moment that it was distinctly realized that there was walking upon the earth One who was God as well as Man. If the Son of God was really there, and if there was, nevertheless, a Godhead in the heavens, then, in the language of men, we must needs say that there were two Persons in the Godhead; and if two, then it was a comparatively easy step to say that there were three. The doctrine of the Trinity is only one of the necessary sequels of the doctrine of the Incarnation.

The next doctrine which I mentioned was the doctrine of the Logos, or Word of God, as we have it in the prologue to the Gospel of John, and again, in all essentials, before John, in the epistles of Paul. Think, for a moment, what is the place which this doctrine holds in Christian theology now compared with what it was some fifty years ago; and to what else is that changed place due but primarily and mainly to the critical labours of the great Cambridge triumvirate, the commentator on the Epistle to the Colossians, the commentator on the Gospel and Epistles of John and the Epistle to the Hebrews, and the author of 'The Way, the Truth, and the Life'? It would seem to be hardly less than a special dispensation of Providence which brought this doctrine once more to the front just as the comparative study of religions made it, of all others, the most necessary. Let me commend to your notice some weighty words on pages 214 and 215 of the last book I have mentioned—words which embrace a still larger outlook than even that which is required by the comparative science of religions:

> The Word was early perceived by that part of the Church which most fully comprehended the completeness of revelation and of redemption. There was a danger on that side—the danger of the truth becoming no more than a philosophy, and the faith in the Son which was needed to sustain the faith in the Word was in the end substituted for it. But the old faith in the Word must be revived if the Creed is to stand—if Christianity is to be a knowledge. It was the definiteness and personality given to the Word by its identification with the Son that differenced it from previous doctrines of a word or words; and now fifteen centuries have so firmly fixed the idea of

Sonship that there can be no risk that the Church itself should ever merge Him in the Word. Truth at the last is the word or speech of God.[1]

On the doctrine of the Atonement we have all been lately reading a paper which presents many aspects of the doctrine with much impressiveness and force. If I differ at all from Mr Gladstone, it would be only in a direction which not a few would call retrogression. I should be prepared to lay rather more stress on the forensic element in the Atonement, and the doctrine of justification which goes with it. The central term in the latter doctrine, δικαιοῦσθαι, is essentially forensic, and nothing else. It means, not 'to be made righteous', but 'to be pronounced or declared righteous' as by a judge. The language of Paul also certainly implies what we call 'imputation'. It certainly implies a great sacrificial act, which Paul himself described as propitiatory. I might be able to say something if I had time in mitigation of the difficulties which are thus caused, but I could not profess wholly to remove them. Some of Mr Gladstone's remarks are admirable on this head. I have only referred to the subject because, if I know my own mind, any opinions which I hold upon it are due almost entirely to a study of Paul which I have tried to make as critical as possible. I began with a rather strong sense of the difficulties, and a wish if I could to avoid them. But I have come to the conclusion that they are not to be avoided, but must be faced, at least by those who take their theology from the Apostles. What convinced me of this was not any work on dogmatic theology, but the work of exegetes, such as Meyer. It is a significant fact that many German critics who have departed some way from the views of their own reformers on other points are much nearer to them on this. And even where they break away on this, too, it is with the frank admission that Paul himself meant something very like what is attributed to him.

I mentioned last that profound doctrine which Paul states so powerfully in Romans 6, the union of the Christian with the crucified and risen Christ. Where shall we find this doctrine expounded with the greatest freshness and insight? Again, I should be inclined to say not in any of our professed theologians, so far, at least, as my knowledge goes, but in Matthew Arnold's 'S. Paul and Protestantism', and in a very striking lay sermon by the philosopher, T.H. Green, entitled 'The Witness of Faith'. It is perfectly true that in both these works there is much that I for one could not accept. Both writers apply a criticism

1. F.J.A. Hort, *The Way the Truth the Life* (Hulsean Lectures, 1871; London: Macmillan, 1893), pp. 214-15.

which seems to me to be very questionable as criticism. But that only throws into the stronger relief the workings of the *anima naturaliter Christiana* on the matter congenial to it.

I may be reminded, on the other side, that a little more than a year ago we had imported from Germany, by Mrs Humphry Ward, an article of Harnack's, impugning certain portions of the second article of the Apostle's Creed. I only hope that those who have read this will also read the reply to it—not less scrupulously critical—in Dr Swete's recently published lectures. I do not contend that the results of the critical process are all in places equally favourable. The evidence may be somewhat weakened in one direction, but only to be strengthened in another. Of this, I think, we may be quite sure, that no criticism fairly applied to the New Testament can ever give us an Arian or Socinian Christ. To obtain such a result as this, we must go behind the New Testament.

The first question which we have to ask ourselves where criticism is involved is, What of the criticism itself? Is that sound, and has it the marks of permanence? Or is it merely a passing phase of the *Zeitgeist*? No doubt, criticism is an edged tool; it must be used with a careful and considerate hand. But it has been the will of God that at this century of the Church's history it should play a larger part than it has ever played before. The process is quite inevitable. We might as well try to stop the Atlantic as to stop it. But I think that it is a matter for the thankfulness that in this country, at least, the first essays have been made in so careful and reverent a spirit. The future must show whether they will be sustained with a corresponding thoroughness and patience.

Chapter 2

METHODS OF THEOLOGY: THE HISTORICAL METHOD[*]

Enough will have been said in the preceding paper on the nature of the historical method as before all things an appeal to fact. Christianity is so much bound up with history that the first duty of the student is to ascertain, as nearly as may be, what were the historical facts. He will do so by the same methods by which he would ascertain the data in any other branch of historical enquiry. So far there is no difference between sacred history and profane. Only one caution must be given, and that has already been brought out with sufficient clearness. The historical method must not be employed as a covert means of getting rid of the supernatural. Wherever it has been so used, the use is wrong. It is no longer really the historical method. In itself that method is just as applicable to supernatural facts as to facts which are not supernatural. It is concerned with them only as facts. On the question of the cause of the facts it does not enter. To reject that for which the evidence is otherwise good, merely because it is supernatural, is a breach of the historical method; and where this is done the cause is sure to be ultimately traceable to that which is the direct opposite of this method, viz., philosophical presupposition.

These main points, I may assume as dealt with by the last reader. I may assume that every care has been taken to find out the facts, and I may go on to the next step, which is to put the facts so ascertained into relation to other contemporary facts, and to construct a living picture of the whole.

Here comes in the difference between the newer methods and the old as applied to the Bible. The old asked at once, What is the permanent significance of the Biblical record? The newer method also asks, What is its permanent significance? but as an indispensable preliminary to this, it asks, What was its immediate significance at the particular place and time

---

[*]   This is a paper read at the Church Congress in Nottingham, in September 1897.

to which each section of the history belongs? Clearly here, there are different points of view which will need some adjustment, and I think that it may be best for me to take a concrete case in which the difference comes out rather conspicuously. I will take the case of prophecy.

It will be instructive to cast back a glance over the treatment of this subject in recent years. One who is not a specialist on the Old Testament can only profess to give what seems to him to be the main landmarks, and those only in relation to the present subject. Thus regarded, it would seem that the turning point in the study of prophecy during the present century was the work of Heinrich Ewald. Ewald's leading works were being translated during the latter part of the sixties, and throughout the seventies (*History of Israel;*[1] *Prophets of the Old Testament*[2]).

Ewald had a vivid imagination and penetrating insight; he threw himself back into the position of the prophets, and he sought to present to us the message which they delivered to their own age. He is allowed on all hands to have done this with very considerable success. The prophets became once more living figures, who spoke directly to us because they spoke directly to the men of their own day. In England, the popularizing of Ewald's methods begins with Dean Stanley's 'Lectures on the Jewish Church', the first volume of which appeared in 1863.[3] But this accomplished writer caught rather the picturesque externals than the real heart of the matter. A more thorough grasp was apparent in Robertson Smith's lectures on the 'Prophets of Israel and their Place in History'—a significant addition—first published in 1882, and in a new edition with an introduction by Dr Cheyne in 1895.[4] In the meantime (1877), an English translation had appeared of Kuenen's *Prophets and Prophecy in Israel*.[5] Of all Kuenen's works this is the one which some of us find it hardest to forgive. No doubt he was a great scholar and a man of wide learning; nor need we dispute the claim which some of his friends make for him to have had also a calm judgment in matters of

1. H. Ewald, *The History of Israel* (ed. R. Martineau; 8 vols.; London: Longmans, Green, 1869–86).

2. H. Ewald, *Commentary on the Prophets of the Old Testament* (trans. J.F. Smith; 8 vols.; London: Williams & Norgate, 1875–81).

3. A.P. Stanley, *Lectures on the History of the Jewish Church* (3 vols.; ed. T.K. Cheyne; London: John Murray, 1889).

4. W.R. Smith, *The Prophets of Israel and their Place in History to the Close of the Eighth Century, B.C.: Eight Lectures* (Edinburgh: A. & C. Black, 2nd edn, 1895).

5. A. Kuenen, *The Prophets and Prophecy in Israel: An Historical and Critical Enquiry* (trans. A. Milroy; London: Longmans, Green, 1877).

criticism. But in this work he deliberately sets himself to prove that the words of the prophets were in every sense their own, and not, as they asserted and believed, the word of God; the conclusion being that there was no real converse between God and the human soul. This Kuenen set himself to prove; and the book in which he did so was as thoroughly an *ex parte* statement as one could easily see out of the law courts. That was certainly not an application of the historical method. The most searching answer to Kuenen was a work entitled, *Der Offenbarungsbegriff des Alten Testamentes* ('The Conception of Revelation in the Old Testament'), by Dr E. König, now Professor at Rostock. In this, Kuenen's thesis was directly grappled with, and it was maintained with much boldness and force, but not without some crudity and exaggeration, not only that the prophets were really moved by the Spirit of God, but also that when it said that 'God spake', and that the prophet heard or saw in a vision, there were actual sounds audible by the bodily ear and actual sights seen with the bodily eye.

It is one of the great merits of the Germans that they seldom let an idea drop when once they have taken it up. They test and criticize it, and go over the ground again and again, until they have reduced it to some more workable shape. This has now been done for König's leading idea by Dr Giesebrecht, of Greifswald, who contributed a paper to a volume of Greifswald essays, which he has since reissued in an enlarged form as a monograph under a title which we might paraphrase 'The Prophetic Inspiration' (literally 'the endowment of the prophets for their office', *Die Berufsbegabung der Alttestamentlichen Propheten*).[6] This seems to me to be a treatise of great value, Dr Giesebrecht belongs to the critical school, but he has handled his theme with a candour and openness of mind which I should call really 'historical' in the sense of which we are speaking.

Two points especially concern us. One is that he insists strongly on the reality of the prophetic inspiration. The belief of the prophets that they were moved to speak by God is to him no mere delusion, but a real objective fact. And the other point is that he also contends for the reality of the gift of prediction; not of unlimited prediction, but of a power specially given at particular times, and for the accomplishment of special Divine purposes. This, I think, will mark the lines of the answer to a

---

6.   F. Giesebrecht, *Die Berufsbegabung der Alttestamentlichen Propheten* (Göttingen: Vandenhoeck & Ruprecht, 1897).

question which will inevitably arise when we consider the application of the historical method to such a subject as prophecy.

I have said that the historical method seeks to place the facts which it discovers in relation to their surroundings. It takes the prophet as primarily the preacher, teacher, and guide of his own day and generation. But does it therefore refuse to him the gift of prediction? Does it confine the range of his message to the particular society to which it was given? It cannot do so if it is true to itself. It cannot be denied that the prophets were thought by their contemporaries to predict events, and that the power was considered so important a part of their divine commission, that special regulations are laid down for its exercise (Deut. 18). It cannot be denied that they themselves believed themselves to possess the power (e.g., Jer. 28). It cannot be denied that many—though not all—of the events which they predicted came true, the non-fulfilment of certain prophecies being due, in part at least, to the conditional nature of prophecy (Jer. 26.3, 13, 19). These are the facts to which a sound historical method must do justice. To attempt to get rid of them is not to explain, but to explain away. And such facts supply a touchstone by which to distinguish between a true application of the historical method and a false. An instance of the former, i.e., of a right application, may be seen in a writer of our own, Dr Driver's *Sermons on the Old Testament*.[7]

I am not prepared to say that the subject of prophetic prediction has been exhausted. The last word has not yet been said. The different kinds of prophetic outlook need to be classified and considered separately. But I do believe that, after some aberrations, the enquiry as it now stands is on right lines.

Another question may arise in connection with the characteristic of the historical method to present each successive stage and phase of revelation in relation to its surroundings. It may be asked whether there is not danger in this of explaining it away as revelation. I reply as before that any theory or mode of presentation which seeks not only to explain but to explain away, is not the historical method. To explain without explaining away might be taken as the motto of that method. When, therefore, we see, as may be seen, in commentaries on the New Testament an increasing number of parallels from Jewish sources— especially from the Apocalyptic and other literature of the centuries on

7.   S.R. Driver, *Sermons on Subjects Connected with the Old Testament* (London: Methuen, 1892), pp. 107-13.

each side of the Christian era: the *Book of Enoch*, the *Fourth Book of Ezra*, the *Apocalypse of Baruch*, the Psalms of Solomon, the *Book of Jubilees*, the *Assumption of Moses*, nearly all of which have recently been made so much more accessible in good editions than they were— when we see copious quotations from such books as these, it must not be supposed that an attempt is being made to reduce the New Testament writings themselves to no higher level. And I may remark in passing that, although they vary somewhat among themselves, the level of the books I have mentioned is not really low. They at least come within the 'sphere of influence' of the Old Testament revelation. When compared with the New Testament they show the point of departure, the ideas that were in men's minds, ideas which it was impossible to ignore and which were taken up; some to be added to and developed, some to be corrected, some to be denounced and opposed. Even in the case of our Lord Himself, this connection with the current teaching is very noticeable. He puts new meanings into words, but the words that He uses are not new. Take for instance such leading conceptions as those of the 'Kingdom of God' or of 'Heaven', his own title 'the Son of Man'. His teaching as to the Fatherhood of God, the Second Coming and the Judgment. In all these instances he starts from the current language, though he recasts it and puts it to new uses.

The recognition of this is one of the leading principles in the study of the New Testament, as it is being prosecuted at the present time. And do we not all feel that it has gained greatly in richness, fulness, and reality? The more we can set before our minds in concrete shape the way in which Christianity affected the actual men and women of the generation to which it was addressed, the more we shall understand the message which it has for other ages, including our own, because it speaks to us through those permanent elements in human mature which are the same in all ages and connect the remote past with the present.

My own belief is that at this moment the conditions of Biblical study are more favourable than ever they have been, and that just because it is being more and more upon the lines of that historical method which we are invited to consider. The historical method itself is being better understood and perverse applications of it are being discarded. On the Continent of Europe for some fifty years, the dominant theory which was supposed to cover the history of the Church in the first two centuries, was that which took its name from the University of Tübingen. This theory, although those who held it passed for representatives of the best science of their time, was the reverse of historical. It was really a product of the Hegelian philosophy; it went on the assumption that all progress proceeds by a certain law—the law of affirmation, negation, and reconciliation, or synthesis. This formed the scheme into which the facts were compelled to fall, whether they did so naturally or not. I do not say that the theory has done no good. It has thrown into relief certain groups of facts which are not likely in future to be lost sight of. To set against this was the arbitrary way in which it treated a great number of the data, deciding upon the conclusion before it had settled the premises, and as a consequence, manipulating the premises to suit the conclusion. But whatever the balance of good or evil in the Tübingen theory, as a theory it is now dead, and its epitaph has been written in the striking preface to Professor Harnack's last great work on the *Chronology of Early Christian Writings*. It is true that this deals primarily with the chronology, and true also that Dr Harnack holds a number of opinions in which many of us would not agree with him. But his book was important as a sign of the times, and as a return to a sounder method of enquiry.

In England there had always been great reluctance to admit the Tübingen inferences, but there had not been the same skill in formulating principles. Now this is practically done in what we call the historical method. To study the facts as they really were by patient weighing of the evidence, to approach them in a teachable spirit, ready to catch the least hint which they give spontaneously from within, and careful not to force upon them conclusions brought from without; this is a method which carries with it a promise of sound advance. Not least among its merits is this, that by its help we may hope to acquire a better understanding of the supernatural. Not crudely rejecting it as too many have done, and not crudely accepting it, as if the simple pronouncing of the name rendered any further explanation unnecessary, but reverently studying the laws by which it acts, we shall be enabled in some degree to enter into the counsels of God, and obtain some further insight into the method of his dealings with men.

Chapter 3

THE ESCHATOLOGY OF THE NEW TESTAMENT[*]

My time is short, so that I shall try to compress what I have to say into a series of connected propositions as condensed as I can make them.

1. The first is that the Jews of our Lord's day had an elaborate doctrine of the 'last things' mapped out in clear divisions and successive stages. First, there were to be the Signs of the end; then the Woes—a period of trouble, war and famine and pestilence; then the appearance of the Messiah, whom they certainly thought of as a supernatural Being; then the Judgment, with a separation of good and bad; then the reign of the saints and the great Transformation—a new heaven and a new earth.

2. That is the first point; and the second point is that the Gospels also appear to share this doctrine. I say 'the Gospels', leaving it for the moment an open question whether that means those who wrote the Gospels, the disciples and the Church, or whether it meant our Lord himself.

3. What are we to say on that all-important question? It is difficult to speak quite decidedly. Where men had their minds so full of the doctrine, they would have been almost sure to ascribe it to our Lord, whether his language really implied it or not. Many German scholars think that they have succeeded in showing that the chapter which has the most direct bearing on this subject, Mark 13, with the parallel portions of the other Gospels, is largely made up of what they call a 'little apocalypse', really of Jewish origin, which came to be incorporated in the text of Mark, and was so passed on to the other Gospels. It is interesting to see from the lately-published fragment by Dr Hort on the first three chapters of the Apocalypse of John, that he had considered this theory and rejected it.[1] And I have always thought myself that it is one thing to be able to mark off certain portions of the chapter that *might* be Jewish, and another

*   This is a paper read at the Church Congress, in Manchester, October 1908.
1.   F.J.A. Hort, *The Apocalypse of St John, I–III* (ed. P.H.L. Brereton; London: Macmillan, 1908).

thing to prove that they really were Jewish. Because certain verses are separable, it does not follow that they ought to be separated. It would perhaps ease the problem a little to think that our Lord himself did not speak the whole of that chapter, but it would not remove or solve it.

4. For myself, on the whole I am inclined to think that our Lord himself really did use not a little distinctly apocalyptic language. I think so largely on the evidence of the epistles, because it is quite clear that not only Paul, but the other Apostles as well, began by expecting that the end of the world was very near, and that the Son of Man would return upon the clouds with power and great glory.

5. You will observe that one consequence of this is that our Lord certainly thought of himself as the Messiah—i.e., as a supernatural Being endowed with extraordinary powers, which were to be one day put forth on a vaster scale than ever they were during the period of what we call his Incarnation. For all the extreme humility which he, the meek and lowly of heart, assumed as man, he knew that at any moment he could have been surrounded by more than 'twelve legions of angels', or whatever supreme investiture and command of power that expression implies. Let us bear this momentous fact in mind, that our Lord certainly believed himself to be the Messiah; and the picture of him in the Gospels is not that of one who would be likely to cherish a mere delusion.

6. But if our Lord did take to himself and use this apocalyptic language, then it was of the nature of prophecy and subject to the laws of prophecy. One of those laws we might call 'the law of *receding horizons*'. If we look at the Old Testament, there was hardly any prophecy which people did not think was going to be fulfilled long before it was. The date of fulfilment was being constantly postponed.

7. Another law is what I might perhaps describe as 'the law of *unforeseen fulfilments*'. Few prophecies have been fulfilled precisely in the way that was expected. Our Lord himself fulfilled a number of prophecies; but how many were prepared for just *such* a fulfilment? The *when* and the *how* of prophecy, except in a few cases of precise prediction, have as a rule been left largely uncertain.

8. It is instructive to observe how the greatest Apostles, Paul and John, dealt with these prophecies. We can trace the process most clearly in the case of Paul. He evidently began by taking the prophecies quite literally. Along with the whole Church, he was deeply imbued with the expectation of the near approach of the coming of the Son of Man. He does not speak of it as his *second* coming, but simply as his coming; it is

the one coming of the Messiah as the Messiah—i.e., in full Messianic glory. This coming he regarded as very near at hand. The earliest epistles (1 and 2 Thessalonians and 1 Corinthians) are full of it. But as time went on and the coming was delayed, little by little the expectation seems to subside. It is not relinquished altogether, but it becomes much less intense. Other topics come to the front.

9. Among these topics the chief is the teaching as to the work of the Holy Spirit. It is not a new doctrine; it had been there all the time—it is clearly marked in the earliest epistles as well as in the later; but in the later epistles it assumes a new degree of prominence. Indeed, it becomes one of the foundational stones of the Apostle's preaching. I need only remind you of Romans 8. There seems to be a sort of proportional or complementary relation between these two cycles of teaching—the teaching as to the Holy Spirit and as to the Last Things. We note a significant change in the language used as to the kingdom of God. 'The kingdom of God' is originally and strictly an eschatological phrase; it is something future and supernatural. It is used repeatedly in this sense in the earlier epistles—e.g., 1 Cor. 6.9, 10: 'Or know ye not that the unrighteous shall not inherit the kingdom of God?' etc. But that does not exclude a present sense, and this present sense tends to become more prominent—e.g., Rom. 14.17: 'For the kingdom of God is not eating and drinking, but righteousness and peace and joy in the Holy Ghost'. These are present things, and belong to a present state, which (it will be seen) is within the sphere of the working of the Holy Ghost.

10. When John wrote his Gospel the time of transition was passed, and, accordingly, the teaching about the Holy Spirit fills the foreground, especially the last discourses (Jn 14–16). But there is just one little point to which I should like to call your attention as showing that there is no inconsistency between this teaching as it appears in the Fourth Gospel and the teaching of the Synoptic Gospels. The most prominent function of the Holy Spirit in the Synoptic Gospels is to stand by and defend the disciples after their Master is gone—e.g., Mk 8.11: 'And when they lead you to judgment, and deliver you up, be not anxious beforehand what ye shall speak... for it is not ye that speak, but the Holy Ghost', etc. But it is precisely this function which is brought out in the title 'Paraclete', which is characteristic of the Fourth Gospel. Paraclete means advocate or (as we should say) counsel—counsel for the prisoner at the bar, who makes his defence for him.

11. When, then, we go on to ask whether there is evidence that this teaching as to the Holy Spirit that we find in Paul and John goes back in the last resort to our Lord himself, our answer is that it certainly does. Note how one of the last things in the Gospel of Luke is the assurance: 'Behold, I send forth the promise of My Father upon you' (Lk. 24.49). And one of the first things to be taken up in the Acts is the command to wait for the fulfilment of this promise (Acts 1.4).

12. Then we may further ask whether the teaching as to the Holy Spirit as it fell from our Lord's lips is fitted to take the place of the eschatological teaching as it apparently does in Paul and John. And here again I think we may answer in the affirmative. The connecting link between the two groups is supplied by that phrase of which we have been speaking, and which stands out so conspicuously in the Synoptic Gospels—'the kingdom of God'. What does 'the kingdom of God' ultimately mean? It seems to me that it must mean, and does mean, God's assertion of his sovereignty in the world at large and in the hearts of men. But that is just the special work of the Holy Spirit. In Biblical language it is the Holy Spirit which brings home the power of God to the heart. When, therefore, our Lord is represented as saying, 'Verily I say unto you, there be some here of them that stand by which shall in no wise taste of death till they see the kingdom of God come with power' (Mk 9.1), I believe, and I believe more and more, that the true fulfilment of that prophecy is to be seen in the Day of Pentecost and in the work that we commonly date from the Day of Pentecost. It was not altogether a new work, but a work that on that day entered upon a new phase. It found its most characteristic expression in the enthusiasm which animated the first Christians; but it has been going on from that day until now, and we are encouraged to hope at this moment it is as active as ever it has been.

13. It is perhaps not quite an identical question to ask what our Lord himself meant by his own predictions. We are speaking in this case of the human processes of his human mind. And although we believe that the mind of the Son was in perfect unison with the mind of the Father, still there is room for difference between the truth of things absolutely as they are and the truth of things humanly apprehended—i.e., apprehended under the conditions and limitations of humanity. We might perhaps put it this way: that the mind of the Father was expressed in facts—in the actual course of history as determined by him, whereas the mind of the Son—the Incarnate Son—was expressed even to himself in

words. But in words there may well be an element of type and symbol; and to say precisely how far this element of type and symbol extended in the case of our Lord may perhaps be beyond our power. Further study may do something, but these are profound questions that perhaps we cannot expect wholly to fathom.

14. And, lastly, it is important to remember that although the eschatological language was to a greater or less extent laid aside, it has never been repealed. This may well mean that there are realities corresponding to it which still remain unexhausted. Such a verse as Heb. 9.27, 'It is appointed unto men once to die, and after this cometh judgment', is ratified by our own consciences. And although the imagery in which the judgment is described *is* imagery, and is not to be taken too literally, yet we may be sure that it has a solid foundation in the eternal laws of God's providence and of his dealings with the souls of men.

Chapter 4

THE INTERPRETATION OF THE GOSPELS AS AFFECTED BY THE NEWER HISTORICAL METHODS[*]

I am anxious that what I am going to say should be said quite calmly and, if I may make the suggestion, taken quite calmly. There is a situation that I think we want to look fairly in the face, without exaggeration either on the one side or on the other.

My subject is, of course, somewhat narrowed down. It deals, not with the New Testament as a whole, but only with the Gospels. At the same time, the Gospels are so very much the most vital part of the whole New Testament, that what applies to them will *a fortiori* apply to the rest, and will even affect the whole Christian position.

From the point of view of the subject assigned to me it may be said that we here in England have entered upon a new period, roughly speaking, with the beginning of the new century. We may take as a landmark the publication in English of Harnack's lectures, known to us under the title, *What is Christianity?* in 1901.[1] The same year saw the appearance of volume 2 of *Encyclopaedia Biblica* (through the accident of the alphabet there had been nothing of great importance for our subject in volume 1);[2] and that work has now, as you know, been completed. With the present year we have a new volume of the

[*] This is a paper read at the Church Congress, in Bristol, 1903 and reprinted as Appendix I in *Outlines of the Life of Christ* (Edinburgh: T. & T. Clark, 2nd edn, 1906), pp. 243-51.

1. A. von Harnack, *What is Christianity? Lectures Delivered in the University of Berlin During the Winter-Term 1899–1900* (trans. T.B. Saunders; London: Williams & Norgate, 1901).

2. T.K. Cheyne and J.S. Black (eds.), *Encyclopaedia Biblica: A Critical Dictionary of the Literary, Political, and Religious History, the Archaeology, Geography, and Natural History of the Bible* (London: A. & C. Black, 1899–1907).

'Theological Translation Library', Wernle's *Beginnings of Christianity;*[3] and we have also had translations of two rather noticeable pamphlets on the Virgin Birth, by Lobstein[4] and Soltau.

The general effect of these publications may be said to be that the English public has been placed more completely on a level with the more advanced criticism on the Continent than it has ever been before. And this applies especially to the particular subject on which I am asked to speak. I have little doubt that the ablest of all the articles on New Testament subjects in the *Encyclopaedia Biblica* are those by Professor P.W. Schmiedel, of Zürich. To him have fallen the articles, 'Gospels', 'John, son of Zebedee', 'Mary', 'Resurrection-and-Ascension Narratives'; and he has treated these crucial subjects with great fulness and thoroughness. The article, 'Nativity', has fallen to another distinguished German scholar, Professor Hermann Usener, of Bonn. All these articles are significant in the history of German as well as of English theology, for I do not think that the views expressed had ever been stated in quite so trenchant a manner. Since the great works of Keim and Weizsäcker there had been rather a lull in the more penetrating criticism of the Gospels. Here in Great Britain I may point to Dr Hastings's *Dictionary of the Bible,*[5] Dr Swete's *St Mark,*[6] and Sir John C. Hawkins's *Horae Synopticae,*[7] and other works[8] as proof that British scholars have not been idle. But it would be true to say that their efforts have been

3.   P. Wernle, *The Beginnings of Christianity* (2 vols.; London: Williams & Norgate, 1903–1904).

4.   P. Lobstein, *The Virgin Birth of Christ: An Historical and Critical Essay* (Crown Theological Library, 2; trans. W.D. Morrison; London: Williams & Norgate, 1903).

5.   J. Hastings, *A Dictionary of the Bible; Dealing with its Language, Literature, and Contents, Including the Biblical Theology* (5 vols.; Edinburgh: T. & T. Clark, 1898–1904).

6.   H.B. Swete, *The Gospel According to St Mark: The Greek Text with Introduction, Notes, and Indices* (London: Macmillan, 1898).

7.   J.C. Hawkins, *Horae Synopticae: Contributions to the Study of the Synoptic Problem* (Oxford: Clarendon Press, 1899).

8.   A. Plummer, *A Critical and Exegetical Commentary on the Gospel According to St Luke* (International Critical Commentary; Edinburgh: T. & T. Clark, 1896); A. Menzies, *The Earliest Gospel: A Historical Study of the Gospel According to Mark, With a Text and English Version* (London: Macmillan, 1901); and J. Moffatt, *The Historical New Testament, Being the Literature of the New Testament Arranged in the Order of its Literary Growth and According to the Dates of the Documents* (London: Hodder & Stoughton, 1901).

directed primarily to the literary criticism and analysis of the Gospels rather than to the criticism of their subject matter; it was generally felt that analysis of the documents ought to go further before the greater and more fundamental questions were raised.

Perhaps the time had come for the next step to be taken. But, whether that is so or not, in any case it has been taken; we are directly face to face with the whole problem, or series of problems, that the Gospels raise for us.

It should not be supposed that the writers I have mentioned, or their English and Scotch sympathizers, are in all respects simply radical and destructive. The erratic fancies of the Dutch school (represented in *Encyclopaedia Biblica* by Professor Van Manen) find no favour in their eyes. Harnack, in particular, is on most points of literary criticism decidedly conservative. Apart from a certain difference of tone in his latest utterances about the Fourth Gospel, there would not be a wide interval between his views and those that are largely held in this country. Neither are Schmiedel or Wernle extreme in literary criticism, strictly as such. But in the treatment of the subject matter of the Gospels there are some common characteristics that run through all this recent literature. I will try to state these briefly.

1. There is a great tendency to narrow down the gospel to the actual teaching of our Lord. Hitherto we have most of us been in the habit of describing by that name the sum of the teaching of the whole New Testament. In the hands of the critics it is reduced to something less than the whole teaching of the Gospels; the Fourth Gospel is practically put aside, and considerable deductions are made from the other three.

2. It is another aspect of the same thing, that the apostolic writers outside the Gospels are criticized with the utmost freedom. For instance, Wernle says in his preface: 'Fidelity to the Christian conscience implies the clearest and most unflinching criticism of all that contradicts it, even though it be received upon the authority of a S. Paul or a S. John, i.e., the Gospel is to be employed practically as the canon and standard for all its later historical accretions'. At the outset of his lectures Harnack promised to make use of the apostolic writings to supplement the data supplied by the Gospels; but he never adequately made good this promise.

3. In particular, he did not use these writings as the Christian Church has been in the habit of using them, to complete his estimate of the Person of Christ. The distaste for dogma characteristic of the school

reaches its highest under this head. Full value is given to the recognition of our Lord as Son of Man, but it could not be said that equally full value is given to the recognition of him as Son of God.

4. In the treatment of the Gospel narrative we observe a general tendency (1) to the denial of the Virgin Birth; (2) to the restriction of miracles to the miracles of healing; (3) to the adoption of some form of the vision-theory of the Resurrection.

On the whole, it must be said that the Christianity of these writers is greatly reduced in its contents; and we are not surprised to find that the criticism which is so freely exercised on the more outlying portions of the New Testament does not spare even that central nucleus from which it takes its start—the teaching of our Lord Himself.

Now the question that will be asked is, How far are these results the natural and logical outcome of the 'newer historical methods'? Are they really so scientific as they claim to be, and are very often supposed to be? I venture to think that they are not. It seems to me that they rest on too narrow a basis. The assumption with which they start—that essential Christianity is confined to the teaching of Christ—is, after all, only an assumption, and, I believe, not a valid assumption.

No great movement can rightly be judged only by its initial stages, or apart from the impression left by it upon the highest contemporary minds.

It is a peculiar advantage that we have in the New Testament the impression made by Christ upon minds endowed with an extraordinary genius for religion. There may be in the writings (e.g.) of Paul and John a certain element that is derived from the current ideas of the time, but behind and beneath this element we can see a fresh and vivid impression that comes straight from the facts.

Hitherto Christians have thought that they could not do better than try to reproduce in themselves an attitude of mind like that which they observe in these great Apostles. And there is much reason to doubt whether any other attitude—and in particular the attitude of the modern critics—can have equal value from the point of view of religion.

Further, we have the advantage of being able to study the experience of other eminent Christians all down the centuries. I conceive that this double study, in the first place of the experience embodied in the New Testament, and in the second place of the like experience carried through eighteen additional centuries of Christian history, is a real induction, and an induction that rests on the widest basis possible.

If we ask ourselves which describes most adequately the total effect of all this experience—the language hitherto held by the whole Christian Church and expressed in its Creeds, or the language now used by a group of critics—we cannot hesitate a moment for the answer.

The critics of whom I have been speaking seem to me to be in too great haste to rationalize the Gospel history. They are too eager to make the narrative of the Gospels conform to the conditions of other narratives, and to make the Life described in it conform to the standard of other lives. I do not think that there is anything, at least in the sounder part of modern historical methods, that compels us to do this.

It is one thing to 'read the Bible like any other book', and another thing to assume that we shall only find in it what is found in other books. Unique spiritual effects require a unique spiritual cause, and we shall never understand the full significance of that cause if we begin by denying or minimizing its uniqueness.

I have always considered the ideal temper the one that renders to Caesar the things that are Caesar's, and to God the things that are God's; in other words, that gives to criticism all that properly belongs to it, and yet leaves room for the full impression of that which is Divine. What we want to do is to keep a perfectly open mind towards that which transcends our experience as well as towards that which falls within it. I am well aware that this is not an easy thing—that to determine the exact relations of human and Divine in the Gospels is a task at once difficult, delicate, and responsible. I am far from thinking that the last word has yet been said by anyone; and I distinctly recognize that writers from whom I differ very widely may yet be really suggestive and helpful. But at the same time I very much hope that we shall hold our ground in reference to them; I very much hope that we shall not model our beliefs on the pattern of *Encyclopaedia Biblica*.

There is an important warning of Dr Hort's: 'Criticism is not dangerous except when, as in so much Christian criticism, it is merely the tool for reaching a result not itself believed on that ground but on the ground of speculative postulates'.[9] It is these 'speculative postulates' that really need to be closely cross-examined. We all have our postulates; and for all of us they affect the whole course of our reasoning; but it is important that we should see exactly what they are and where they are leading us.

9. F.J.A. Hort, *The Way the Truth the Life* (Hulsean Lectures, 1871; London: Macmillan, 1893), p. 177.

In the case of the writers to whom I have been referring, the postulates are not only speculative or philosophical; there are postulates of another kind that have exercised a deeper influence over their work than the writers perhaps themselves are aware. They all start with the same kind of religious ideal, an ideal which is the more powerful because it is latent rather than expressed, taken for granted rather than explicitly argued. And this ideal is rather peculiar; it is certainly not common to all Christians; I do not think that it would be very largely shared in the Church of England.

A short time ago, in writing of Harnack's lectures, I could not help remarking that 'there are three things of which he rarely speaks without some disparaging epithet. They are the Church, Doctrine, and Worship.' We might say the same thing with yet greater emphasis of Wernle, and I suspect also in a more latent form of Schmiedel. The religious ideal of all three appears to reduce those three things—Church, Doctrine, and Worship—to an absolute minimum. I sometimes wonder what the ideal would be like carried out in practice. It could hardly be that of ordinary Lutheranism. One is almost inclined to suppose that there must be in Germany a sort of professorial religion which exists rather in the air, in a religious Cloud-Cuckoo-Town, and does not correspond to that of any actual religious body.

I have said that this ideal is taken for granted and not explicitly argued. And that is the serious part of it; because the ideal is constantly being invoked, and is constantly affecting the judgment though it is nowhere distinctly stated and compelled to give an account of itself.

I should not be surprised if Harnack and Wernle (I would rather not speak so definitely of Schmiedel) were under the impression that their own views reflect the teaching of the Gospels, and were even taken from them. But if they do think this, I feel sure that they are very much mistaken. The inference is not sound. It is, I believe, far too roughly and inconsiderately drawn. But in any case, I have little doubt that this is where the weak point in the argument lies—in the religion of presuppositions. It is the presuppositions which need a far more serious testing than they have ever received.

The truth is that all these writers represent a reaction—and, as I am convinced, an excess of reaction—against the historical tradition of the Church. The true solution, I feel sure, is to be sought more on Church lines, i.e., with more regard for historical continuity, with a firmer faith that the Divine guidance of the Church throughout all these centuries has not been really, and even fundamentally, wrong.

Chapter 5

The Conditions under which the Gospels were Written, in their Bearing upon Some Difficulties of the Synoptic Problem[*]

We assume what is commonly known as the 'Two Document Hypothesis'. We assume that the marked resemblances between the first Three Gospels are due to the use of common documents, and that the fundamental documents are two in number: (1) a complete Gospel practically identical with our Mark, which was used by the Evangelists whom we know as Matthew and Luke; and (2) a collection consisting mainly but not entirely of discourses, which may perhaps have been known to, but was probably not systematically used by Mark, but which supplied the groundwork of certain common matter in Matthew and Luke.

The first document contains 661 verses, the length of our Mark in the Revised Text. We can measure this exactly, because the document itself has come down to us as our Second Gospel. All but at most some 50 verses, out of 661, have been actually incorporated in the other two Gospels. The other document we cannot measure exactly, because in its original form it has perished. We may take provisionally the estimate of Sir John Hawkins,[1] who assigns to this document some 191 (of 218) verses of Matthew and 181 (of 208) verses of Luke. For the purpose of this essay it is indifferent whether we accept this reconstruction of the document or the alternative put forward by Mr W.C. Allen in the present volume.[2] I also keep an open mind as to the possibility of to

---

[*]   This chapter first appeared in W. Sanday (ed.), *Studies in the Synoptic Problem: By Members of the University of Oxford* (Oxford: Clarendon Press, 1911), pp. 3-26.

1.   J.C. Hawkins, *Horae Synopticae: Contributions to the Study of the Synoptic Problem* (Oxford: Clarendon Press, 2nd edn, 1899), p. 110.

2   W.C. Allen, 'The Book of Sayings Used by the Editor of the First Gospel', in Sanday (ed.), *Studies in the Synoptic Problem*, pp. 235-86.

some extent combining the two theories by adding to the common matter of Matthew and Luke some of the sections peculiar to the First Gospel which may have been omitted by the author of the Third. The common matter of Matthew and Luke is a fixed nucleus in both theories, though the nature and history of the document are differently conceived. We call the second document in Sir John Hawkins' reconstruction (which is shared by many other scholars) Q; in Mr Allen's special reconstruction we shall perhaps do well to call it L. But as I have said, for the purpose of this essay the distinction need not be considered.

The above may be taken as a rough outline of the documentary theory of the origin of the Synoptic Gospels.

It will be obvious that this theory explains easily and naturally the multitude of resemblances which the Three Gospels present to each other. But after all this is only half the problem. The real difficulty of the Synoptic problem arises, not from the resemblances only, nor yet from the differences only, but from the remarkable combination and alternation of resemblance and difference. The strong point of the documentary theory is the satisfactory way in which it accounts for the resembances; its weak point—or at least the point at which the strain upon it is most felt—is when we come to deal with the differences. And the main purpose of the present essay is to suggest that in the particular direction which I am going to follow is to be found the simplest and most satisfactory solution of a group of difficulties which on a comparison of the Three Gospels are raised by the points in which they differ.

The opposite of a documentary theory of the origin of the First Three Gospels would be an oral theory: in other words, the view that our Gospels as we have them are not based upon earlier written documents, but that until the time at which they were committed to writing the substance of them had been transmitted orally.

Now, just as it is the strong point of the documentary theory to account for agreements, so also is it the strong point of the oral theory to account for differences. And it is true that the differences between the Three Gospels are of such a kind as to suggest oral transmission. This has been hitherto the chief stumbling-block in the way of the acceptance of the documentary hypothesis. And it is a testimony to the strength of the arguments for the use of written materials that the majority of scholars accept that use in spite of all apparent indications to the contrary. It is, however, not enough to do this; we cannot really rest until all the phenomena are accounted for, not one set alone but both sets, however much they may seem to be opposed.

Our first duty, then, will be to try to form an idea of the nature of the differences which subsist between the Gospels. When we have done this, we may go on to consider how they may best be explained.

1. *The Characteristic Forms of Difference between the First Three Gospels*

No one has described more exactly or classified more successfully these phenomena of difference than Sir John C. Hawkins,[3] and I shall use his data freely in what follows. The most significant cases of difference are not those in which the divergence is complete, but those in which it is only partial. Sir John points out that 'we not infrequently find the same, or closely similar, words used with different applications or in different connections, where the passages containing them are evidently parallel'. And then he naturally and rightly remarks that it is not at all difficult to see how variations such as these might have arisen in the course of oral transmission. Particular words 'might linger in the memory, while their position in a sentence was forgotten: and in some cases they might become confused with other words of similar sound'.

The kind of facts that we meet with are these.

a. *The same or similar words are used in different senses or with a different reference.*
For instance: in Mk 11.3 (corrected text) the two disciples who are sent on before to fetch the ass which our Lord was to ride on his entry into Jerusalem are told that, if they are questioned as to what they are doing, they are to answer, 'The Lord hath need of him; and straightway he will send him back hither': meaning that the ass would very soon be returned. In Mt. 21.3 the version is, 'The Lord hath need of them (i.e. the ass and the colt): and straightway he (i.e. the owner) will send them': meaning that the owner would at once let them go. In the one case it is the Lord who will send the ass back: in the other case it is the owner who will send the ass[es] without delay.

In Mk 4.19 there are the words εἰσπορευόμεναι, 'entering in', and συμπνίγουσι, 'choke': 'the cares of the world...entering in choke the word' (cf. Mt. 13.22 sing.). In Lk. 8.14 the same words are used of the

---

3.   Hawkins, *Horae Synopticae*, pp. 67-80.

men represented by the seed sown among thorns: these as they go on their way—i.e. in course of time—συμπνίγονται, 'are choked' by the cares.

In Mk 12.20 the word ἀφῆκεν is used of the woman married to seven brothers, the husband dying '*leaves* no seed'; in Mt. 22.25 the husband, having no seed, 'leaves' his wife.

b. *Sometimes the same or similar words are assigned to different speakers.*
For instance: in Mk 4.14, Mt. 14.2, Herod himself says that John the Baptist was risen from the dead; in Lk. 9.7 others say it in his hearing.

In Mk 10.21 Jesus says to the young ruler, 'One thing thou lackest' (ἕν σε ὑστερεῖ: cf. Lk. 18.22 ἔτι ἕν σοι λείπει); in Mt. 19.20 the ruler puts it as a question, 'What do I lack?' (τί ἔτι ὑστερῶ;).

In Mk 15.36 it is the man who offers our Lord the sponge soaked in vinegar who says 'Let be; let us see whether Elijah cometh to take him down'; in Mt. 27.49 it is not the man who says this, but the crowd of bystanders.

c. *In one Gospel we sometimes have in the form of a speech what in another is part of the narrative, and in one Gospel we have a question where in another there is a direct statement.*
For instance: in Mk 5.30 the Evangelist writes, 'And straightway Jesus, perceiving in himself that the power proceeding from him had gone forth, turned him about in the crowd, and said, Who touched my garments?' In Lk. 8.46 Jesus says, 'Some one did touch me: for I perceived that power had gone forth from me'.

In Mk 14.1 the Evangelist states that 'after two days was the feast of the Passover', whereas in Mt. 24.1, 2 Jesus says to his disciples, 'Ye know that after two days the Passover cometh'.

In Mk 14.49 'This is done that the scriptures might be fulfilled' are words of Christ; in Mt. 26.56 it is a comment of the Evangelist's.

The question in Mk 4.21, 'Is the lamp brought to be put under the bushel?' becomes in Lk. 8.16 the statement 'And no man, when he hath lighted a lamp, covereth it with a vessel'.

The question (Mk 6.37), 'Shall we go and buy two hundred pennyworth of bread, and give them to eat?' disappears in the condensed paraphrase of the other Gospels, and is fused with the previous suggestion 'Send them away, that they may…buy themselves somewhat to eat'.

Mk 8.12, 'Why doth this generation seek a sign? verily I say unto you, There shall no sign be given unto this generation,' corresponds to Mt. 16.4, 'An evil and adulterous generation seeketh after a sign; and there shall no sign be given unto it, but the sign of Jonah'. But the Matthaean version is really a conflation of two distinct documents.

d. *Other conspicuous examples of diverse application.*
In Mt. 3.5, 'All the region round about Jordan' (i.e. the inhabitants of the region) went out to Jesus; in Lk. 3.3 Jesus 'came into all the region round about Jordan'.

In Mk 6.19, 20 Herodias desired to kill John but could not, because Herod feared him; in Mt. 14.5 Herod desired to kill John but feared the multitude.

In Mk 6.3 we read 'Is not this the carpenter, the son of Mary?'; in Mt. 13.55 'Is not this the carpenter's son? Is not his mother called Mary?'

In Mk 10.18 (= Lk. 8.19), 'Why callest thou me good?' becomes in the best text of Mt. 19.17 'Why asketh thou me concerning that which is good?' The Markan version is undoubtedly the more original; the Matthaean appears to be due to the First Evangelist.

e. *A special class of variations is formed by the cases of inversion of order, which are somewhat frequent.*
For instance: in Mt. 4.5-10, Lk. 4.5-12, there is a transposition of the second and third Temptations, the pinnacle of the temple and the high mountain.

Mt. 12.41, 42, Lk. 11.31, 32: 'The men of Nineveh' and the 'queen of the south' change places.

In the most probable text of Lk. 22.17-19, the cup is represented as given before the Bread, and not as in Matthew and Mark.

On transpositions in general see especially Mr Streeter.[4]

The above are all examples—many of them striking examples—of the freedom with which the Evangelists reproduced the matter that lay before them. In all the cases in which Mark is involved we believe his version to be the original, and the variants in the other Gospels are deviations from the original. And these deviations are so free that we cannot be surprised if they have been often thought to point to oral

4. B.H. Streeter, 'On the Original Order of Q', in Sanday (ed.), *Studies in the Synoptic Problem*, pp. 141-64.

transmission. It is true that they do point to just that kind of unconscious or semi-conscious mental action—lapses of memory, rearrangement of details, and the like—which is characteristic of oral transmission. But it would, I think, be a mistake to draw from these data the sweeping inference that, prior to our present Gospels, the substance of their contents had been transmitted not otherwise than orally. The conclusion would be too large for the premises. We shall see presently what I believe to be the right conclusion. In the meantime we will note these examples of free reproduction as a difficulty in the way of the Two-Document Hypothesis with which we started. In any case they are phenomena which, upon that hypothesis, require to be satisfactorily accounted for.

And then, besides this general difficulty, there are two particular difficulties, which also appear to conflict with the hypothesis.

1. The first is the problem of *secondary or divergent features in Mark*. For a long time past the existence of these features has been a leading crux of the Synoptic Problem. It is very generally agreed that the 'most assured result' of the investigations which have been going on for the best part of a century, and with concentrated energy for the last fifty or sixty years, has been the proof of what is commonly called 'the priority of Mark'; in other words, the proof that our Mark actually lay before the authors of the First and Third Gospels and was used by them in the construction of their own works. The assumption that this was the case explains the whole phenomena far better than any other hypothesis that has been suggested.

At the same time it must not be thought that the phenomena are perfectly homogeneous. There is a great preponderance of data pointing towards the conclusion just stated; but, after all, it is a *preponderance* of evidence and not a compact mass of details pointing all the same way. There still remains a residuum of cases in which the usual relation of the documents to each other is not sustained. And this residuum of cases it is which constitutes the difficulty of which I am speaking.

In the first place there are a few rather prominent examples in which the text of Mark as we have it does not appear to be prior to that of one or both of the two companion Gospels.

For instance, the saying 'I was not sent but unto the lost sheep of the house of Israel' (Mt. 15.24) has nothing corresponding to it in Mark; and yet on internal grounds the presumption would be strongly in favour of its genuineness. In other respects, too, the section in which these words occur is somewhat peculiar.

Again, in Mt. 24.29, '*Immediately* after the tribulation of those days,' the word 'immediately' is not found in the parallel text Mk 13.24; and yet we may be pretty sure that it is original, because it would seem to be contradicted by the event.

But apart from these few and rather special cases, there are a number of expressions in which the two presumably later Gospels (Matthew, Luke) combine together against the presumably earlier (Mark). This inverts the usual relationship, and may well seem at first sight to be inconsistent with the priority of Mark altogether.

Sir John Hawkins[5] has collected twenty or twenty-one rather notable examples of this phenomenon; and Dr E.A. Abbott has printed in full the whole collection, numbering in all about 230 examples, as an appendix to his book *The Corrections of Mark*.[6] These lists, especially the longer, are perhaps subject to some deductions, of which we shall speak later. But in any case the instances are too numerous to be entirely the result of accident.

2. Another question arises as to *omissions*. In particular, why has Luke omitted a rather long section of Mark (Mk 6.45–8.26)? A common view is that this section is omitted by Luke because it contains duplicates—a second Feeding, a second Storm at Sea—as well as in part discussions (like that about eating with unwashen hands) which would not interest Luke's Gentile readers. Dr Plummer[7] notes in reply to the first point that there are various places in which Luke has not avoided duplicates, so that some further explanation seems to be required.

These still outstanding difficulties of the Synoptic Problem, and more particularly of the Two-Document Hypothesis, have been described so far in a way that is of course quite summary. We will try to state them with a little more precision before we have done. I would only ask the reader to bear in mind the general character of these difficulties, in order that he may be in a position to judge how far the explanations which are about to be offered can really be said to meet them.

---

5.   Hawkins, *Horae Synopticae*, pp. 210-11.

6.   E.A. Abbott, *The Corrections of Mark Adopted by Matthew and Luke* (*Diatessarica*, 2; London: A. & C. Black, 1901).

7.   A. Plummer, *A Critical and Exegetical Commentary on the Gospel according to St Luke* (ICC; Edinburgh: T. & T. Clark, 1896), p. xxxviii.

I would venture to lay it down that explanations, in order to be satisfactory, should be simple. And the chief recommendation of those which I am going to submit is that they are, I hope, both simple and real—*verae causae,* not drawn from a state of things that is purely imaginary, but from the actual conditions under which we have strong reason to believe that the Gospels were written. When we speak of 'conditions' we have in view conditions of two kinds: (1) those consisting in the mental or psychological attitude of the writer towards his task; and (2) those consisting in the external circumstances in which his task had to be discharged.

2. *The Conditions under which the Synoptic Gospels were Written*

a. *Psychological Conditions*

We are concerned at present, not with the individual Evangelists, but with the Evangelists as a class. The characteristics of the individual writers will come up for consideration in other parts of this volume.[8] Our present inquiry has to do with the Gospels, and more particularly the Synoptic Gospels, as a group by themselves. And our first duty is to correct an impression that may easily be formed in regard to this group.

We are so accustomed to a close comparison of the Synoptic texts, and those texts do in fact often present so close a resemblance to each other, that we are apt to think of the writers as though they were simply transcribing the documents which lay before them. But that was not the way in which they thought of themselves.

1. *The Evangelists are not copyists but historians.* The Evangelists thought of themselves not merely as copyists but as historians. They are not unconscious of a certain dignity in their calling. They are something more than scribes, tied down to the text which they have before them. They considered themselves entitled to reproduce it freely and not slavishly. They do not hesitate to tell the story over again in their own words.

At the same time, when we describe them as historians, we must think of them as belonging to a naïve and not very highly developed literary type. Historical writing varies according to the scale on which it is planned and the complexity of the authorities of which it takes account.

8. See especially B.H. Streeter, 'The Literary Evolution of the Gospels', in Sanday (ed.), *Studies in the Synoptic Problem*, pp. 209-27.

We must put aside altogether an ideal constructed in view of the abundant materials of modern times. More often than not an Evangelist would only have a single authority before him. We may believe that the author of the Fourth Gospel was acquainted with the works of all his predecessors, though he did not deliberately base his own work upon theirs, and though his attitude towards them was quite independent. But the Gospel of Mark was a first attempt in its own particular kind. In this case we may believe that the writer knew of the existence of a previous document (Q), and allowed his work to be in some degree shaped by this knowledge. This seems to be the best way of explaining the comparatively summary character of the opening paragraphs; and it would also account for the preponderance of narrative over discourse— if the earlier document consisted mainly of discourse, the later writer would naturally wish to supplement its contents rather than to repeat them. There is reason to think that the tradition is true which represents him as deriving his own material chiefly from the public preaching of Peter. Besides this, he would doubtless be affected by the body of floating tradition which circulated amongst all the greater Churches. This tradition would be for the most part oral; whether Mark made use of any written document may remain, at least for our present purpose, an open question.[9] In the case of Matthew (i.e. our present First Gospel), the two chief constituent elements are Mark's Gospel and Q. These sometimes overlap each other, with the effect of producing the phenomenon known as 'Doublets'.[10] If any further written sources need be assumed in addition to these, they were probably not extensive. If we study the First Evangelist's treatment of Mark, it resolves itself for the most part into (a) free rearrangement for the sake of effectiveness of teaching, and (b) simple abridgement. Luke has rather more peculiar matter, and with him the peculiar matter is rather more considerable and rather more important. As an historical work his Gospel is a degree more elaborate than those of his companions. Accordingly, there is perhaps in his case a little more of the blending or fusion of different authorities. He has a somewhat higher ambition in the matter of style. In a word, he approximates rather more nearly to the ancient secular historian; and he shows that he is conscious of doing so, partly by the language of his preface, and partly by such features of his Gospel as his

9.   See the essay by N.P. Williams, 'A Recent Theory of the Origin of St Mark's Gospel', in Sanday (ed.), *Studies in the Synoptic Problem*, pp. 389-421.

10.   On which see Hawkins, *Horae Synopticae*, pp. 80-107.

attempts to connect the events which he narrates with the larger framework of the world's history (Lk. 2.1, 2; 3.1, 2, etc.). In this respect, however, he should not be judged by too severe a standard. He had not the advantages that (e.g.) Josephus had of living at the centre of the empire in personal intercourse with the court, and with access to the best authorities. Even with the help of public inscriptions and the like, it cannot have been an easy matter for a provincial like Luke to fix exact synchronisms. It is something to be able to say that in recent years, especially through the investigations and influence of Sir W. M. Ramsay, his credit has steadily risen.

2. *And yet the Gospels are not exactly histories.* Luke is thus most nearly akin to the secular historians. It was very much their ideals which guided his hand. But even he to some extent, and his companions still more, had a further object in view. They were not content to narrate facts simply as facts. They all three—or we may say all four, for the statement is true most conspicuously and avowedly of the Fourth Gospel (Jn 20.1)—had an eye not only to the facts but to something to be believed as growing out of the facts. Even Luke has an eye to this retrospectively; he writes to strengthen the confidence of his patron Theophilus in the truths in which he had been instructed. Mark indicates his object when he calls his work 'the gospel of Jesus Christ, the Son of God'; and this would still hold good, even if with a small but early group of textual authorities (ℵ*, Irenaeus 1/3 Origen *pluries* Basilides) we were to omit the last clause, which only defines more explicitly the meaning of that which precedes; 'the gospel of Jesus Christ' is the good news of One who is believed in as Son of God. Matthew indicates his object when he so frequently points out the fulfilment of ancient prophecy. The purpose of the Evangelists is thus in part homiletic, though it is embodied in an historical form, and though the story is left as a rule to have its own effect.

I refer to the point here, chiefly in order to give a complete and not misleading impression of the frame of mind in which the Evangelists approached their task. For the more immediate bearings of this essay, it is of less importance. Our direct concern is with the difficulties of the Synoptic Problem; and in regard to these, the attitude of the writers comes in as a determining factor so far as it explains the nature and degree of the freedom with which they reproduced their documents. What has been said will perhaps go some way to explain this freedom. It shows us the Evangelists, not as painfully transcribing the older texts on which they relied (such as Mark and Q), or feeling themselves in any way called upon to reproduce them verbally, but as setting to work in a spirit independent and yet on the whole faithful, not punctilious and yet not wilfully capricious and erratic, content to tell their story very much as it came, sometimes in the words of their predecessors and sometimes in their own. This is the kind of picture that we should be led to form for ourselves from a combined study of the antecedent probabilities of the case and of the facts as we have them. It happens that we are in an exceptionally favourable position for this part of our inquiry. For the whole of the Triple Synopsis all three documents are extant—not only the two later Gospels, but the original which the writers worked up into their own compositions; so that we can see exactly what changes they introduced and in most cases can form a shrewd guess as to the reason which led to their introduction. In the net result the Evangelists come out as very human, not as actuated by the Machiavellian motives which at one time it was the fashion to attribute to them, as neither pedants nor yet wantonly careless, influenced a little by their wishes and their feelings, but not to such an extent as seriously to affect their credit. The examples given above of the degree of freedom which they allowed themselves are in this sense extreme that they are at least selected from among the more striking of their kind; and the reader will be able to judge for himself how far the general estimate based upon them is justified.

We have, however, as yet only considered one half of our problem. We must go on to the other half; and, if I am not mistaken, we shall find our results confirmed on another side or sides.

b. *External Conditions*

1. *The writing and use of books, in their bearing upon freedom of reproduction.* We have had to correct one impression which the inexperienced student may subconsciously or semi-consciously form for himself; and now we shall have to correct another impression of the same kind. When we think of composing a book, and still more when we think of compiling a book in the way in which the later Gospels at least were compiled, it is natural to us to picture to ourselves the author as sitting at a table with the materials of which he is going to make use spread out before him, his own book in which he is writing directly in front of him, and the other writings a little further away in a semicircle, each kept open at the place where it is likely to be wanted; so that the

author only has to lift his eyes from his manuscript as he writes to his copy, and to transfer the contents from its pages to his own. In such a case it would be only natural to reproduce what lay before the eye with a considerable degree of accuracy. But it happens that this picture, if it were applied to the writing of the Gospels, would be in almost every feature wrong.

The ancients had tables, but they did not use them for the same miscellaneous purposes that we do. They used them for eating; they used them as a stand for vases or statuary; they used them for paying out money. But I am not aware of any evidence that they were used for other purposes than these.[11]

The ancients had books; but they were not at this time (i.e. when the Gospels were composed) like our own books. They were rolls, and rather lengthy rolls, with the writing in short vertical columns across them, as a rule less than a foot high. They were therefore rather cumbrous, and not quite easy to keep open at a particular place. Again, I am not aware of a single representation of the book-roll so kept open. There are many representations of a writer or student making use of books (i.e. of rolls); but to the best of my belief these are always, or almost always, contained in a sort of round canister (*capsa*) or square box (*scrinium*) which stands upon the ground.[12] Birt lays this down as the all but universal rule,[13] and the exceptions which he notes are hardly exceptions. Under such conditions it is not at all likely that the roll would be taken out and referred to more often than could be helped.

The ancients had desks; but they were not like our desks on a writing table. They were quite small, like the reading desks that we attach to the

---

11.   Cf. T. Birt, *Die Buchrolle in der Kunst. Archäologisch-antiquarische Unter-suchen zum antiken Buchwesen von Theodor Birt* (Leipzig: Teubner, 1907), p. 2. Perhaps as the facts stated in this essay coincide closely with those given in Birt's excellent volume, it may be right to say that the rough draft of the essay was written some years before the book appeared, but of course with help from Birt's older work, *Das antike Buchwesen in seinem Verhaltniss zur Litteratur, mit Beitragen zur Textgeschichte des Theokrit, Catull, Properz, und anderer Autoren* (Berlin: Hertz, 1882), and W. Wattenbach's *Schriftwesen im Mittelalter* (Leipzig: Hirzel, 3rd edn, 1896); also from Dr F.G. Kenyon's *Handbook to the Textual Criticism of the New Testament* (London: Macmillan, 1901), *Palaeography of Greek Papyri* (Oxford: Clarendon Press, 1899), and other recent literature. But I have been glad to introduce a few illustrations from Birt's new book, which is the most complete and detailed.

12,   'In allen Darstellungen, die wir kennen gelernt, steht die Buchschachtel am Boden.'

13.   Birt, *Die Buchrolle*, p. 254.

arm of an armchair. As a rule they are affixed to a raised stand, which is independent of other furniture. Sometimes the writer sits at such a desk, more especially in the later examples from the fourth century onwards, when the *codex*, or book proper, had superseded the roll. But in the earlier examples the writer is usually represented with the roll open simply upon his knees. So Virgil,[14] who, however, is not writing but only holding a roll and has a desk at his side. So, more distinctly, an Evangelist in Palaeographical Society, Series I, pl. 44 (where the book is a *codex*). There are several examples of Evangelists at work in Beissel's *Vaticanische Miniaturen*[15] (pll. v, ix, x, xi); and more in the sumptuous reproduction of the copy of the Gospels written for Ada, sister of Charles the Great (*Die Trierer Ada-Handschrift*,[16] pll. 10, 15, 16, 17, 20, 23, 26, 29, 32, 33, 36). Plate 23 of this work, from an Evangeliarium in the Domschatz at Aachen, is reproduced as a frontispiece to the present book.[17]

What is the effect of all this on the problem more immediately before us? It enables us, I think, to realize more exactly the process involved in the construction of a narrative on the basis of older materials. A modern, if he were doing this, would have the document he was using constantly under his eye. There would be hardly any interval of time between the perusal of its text and the reproduction of it in writing. The copy would be followed clause by clause and almost word by word. Given physical accuracy of sight and an average power of attention, the rest of the process would be almost mechanical. With the ancient writer it would be otherwise. He would not have his copy before him, but would consult it from time to time. He would not follow it clause by clause and phrase by phrase, but would probably read through a whole paragraph at once, and trust to his memory to convey the substance of it safely from the one book to the other.

We see here where the opening for looseness of reproduction comes in. There is a substantial interval between reading and writing. During that interval the copy is not before the eye, and in the meantime the brain is actively, though unconsciously, at work. Hence all those slight rearrangements and substitutions which are a marked feature in our texts as we have them. Hence, in a word, all those phenomena which

14. *Ap.* Birt, *Die Buchrolle*, p. 78.

15. S. Beissel, *Vaticanische Miniaturen* (Freiburg i. B.: Herder, 1893).

16. P. Corssen (ed.), *Die Trierer Ada-Handschrift* (Leipzig: Durr, 1889).

17. Sanday (ed.), *Studies in the Synoptic Problem*, facing the title page.

simulate oral transmission. There is a real interval during which the paragraph of text is carried in the mind, though not a long one. The question may be not one of hours or days but only of minutes. We cannot indeed lay down a rigid rule to which all use of books would strictly conform. We must leave a margin for the habits of the particular writer. One man would trust his memory, and run the risk of trusting his memory, for a longer period than another. All we need assume is that there would be some interval, some period; enough to account for, or to help to account for, the phenomena of free reproduction which, as a matter of fact, we find. The cause we are considering is elastic within certain limits. I believe that it will be found to meet all that we want.

The phenomena of variation (as between Mark and the succeeding Gospels) in the texts that have come down to us do not require for their explanation any prolonged extension of time or diffused circulation in space; they might be described in homely phrase as just so many 'slips between the tip and the lip'.

2. *The copying and transmission of texts in their bearing upon the agreements of Matthew and Luke against Mark.* The question as to the agreements of Matthew and Luke against Mark in the Triple Synopsis takes us into another region, but still a region connected with the production and transmission of books.

This question of the coincidences between Matthew/Luke in places where Mark is extant is of great importance. There is a complete collection of these coincidences at the end of Dr E.A. Abbott's *The Corrections of Mark*, which is a valuable basis for study. It has been already said that the examples (many of them simple, but many also complex) given by Dr Abbott number in all about 230. These examples, as constituting a problem in regard to the relation between Mark and his successors, are doubtless subject to some reduction. It may be questioned whether in all the cases the writers are even professing to reproduce the same text.

Mr C.H. Turner has recently called attention to two other causes which will account for some of the examples besides that of which we are about to speak.[18] It might well be thought that some of the agreements are so slight and easy to account for that they might be set

18. C.H. Turner, 'Historical Introduction to the Textual Criticism of the New Testament. II. The Contents of the Canon of the New Testament: (A) The Four Gospels', *Journal of Theological Studies* 10 (1909), pp. 161-82, esp. pp. 175ff.

down as accidental, that they are obvious corrections of Mark arising in each of the two later Gospels independently of each other. And then, allowance may also be made for the possibility (on which Mr Turner specially enlarges) that we have not yet got back to the true text of one or other of the Gospels, and that when we have done so, the double coincidence against Mark will be found to disappear. Besides these, there is yet a third cause to which I should be inclined to ascribe some of the most complex of the examples noted by Dr Abbott. The later Evangelists certainly used Mark; but they also used the second document Q; and I suspect that in some of the cases there has been an overlapping of the two documents. This overlapping of documents is a phenomenon that certainly happened sometimes. It is by means of it that I should account for some cases of marked divergence between Matthew and Luke in places where both Evangelists were using Q. The simplest way of explaining the divergence (as compared with the no less marked identity in other places) is to suppose that the same passage occurred not only in Q but in Luke's special source (or in one of his sources) in a somewhat different form. Luke will then have preferred the form in his own source to that of Q. A conspicuous example would be the treatment of the Beatitudes. The same sort of thing may well have happened in the case of the parallels to Mk 3.19-21, 23-26; 4.30-32; 6.7-13, 31-34; 8.12, 29; 9.19, and a few others.

But I believe that by far the greater number of the coincidences of Matthew/Luke against Mark are due to the use by Matthew/Luke not of an *Ur-Marcus* or older form of the Gospel, but—*of a recension of the text of Mark different from that from which all the extant manuscripts of the Gospel are descended.*

I reject the idea of an *Ur-Marcus,* or older form of the Gospel, because the great majority of the coincidences seem to me to belong to a later form of text rather than an earlier. And I call this form of text a recension, because there is so much method and system about it that it looks like the deliberate work of a particular editor, or scribe exercising to some extent editorial functions.

This appears to come out clearly from Dr Abbott's classification of the corrections. We may give this in Dr Abbott's own words:

> They are, almost entirely, just such modifications of Mark's text as might be expected from a Corrector desirous of improving style and removing obscurities.
>
> (i) In about twelve instances Matthew and Luke adopt corrections defining subject or object. For example, where Mark omits the subject

(leaving it to be understood as 'they', 'people', &c.) Matthew and Luke supply 'the disciples', &c...

(ii) In about fifteen instances they correct in Mark the abrupt construction caused by the absence of a connecting word...

(iii) In about thirteen instances they correct Mark's historic present. This number does not include the corrections of Mark's use of 'says' applied to Jesus (see (v)).

(iv) In about twelve instances they substitute the participle (e.g. 'saying') for the indicative with 'and' (e.g. 'and he says'), or for the relative and for the subjunctive, e.g. 'whosoever has', which is changed to 'those having', &c.

(v) In about twenty-three instances they substitute for Mark's 'says (λέγει)' the word 'said (εἶπεν)', or correct Mark's imperfect 'used to say' or 'began to say' (ἔλεγεν, more rarely ἤρξατο λέγειν)...

(vi) In at least thirty instances Matthew and Luke agree in adopting the idiomatic Greek connecting particle (δέ)—commonly and necessarily (though most inadequately) rendered by the English 'but'—instead of the literal translation of the Hebrew 'and', i.e. καί...

(vii) Another class of corrections includes improvement of Greek construction or style, by softening abruptness of a different kind from that mentioned above...changing interrogatives into statements, introducing μέν...δέ, ἀλλά, or other particles, and altering Hebraic or vernacular words or phrases. In a few instances the correction may be made in the interests of seemliness, rather than of style...

(viii) In some cases, and notably in the use of the exclamatory 'behold', Matthew and Luke appear to agree in returning to the Hebrew original.[19]

The number and the recurrence of these phenomena is evidently due to design, and not to accident. What appears to have happened is something of this kind. Neither our present Gospel, even in the best text, nor the copies used by Matthew and Luke were exactly what Mark wrote. All our extant copies, whether of the Received Text or of those constructed upon the most highly critical principles, are descended from a single copy which, although very near to Mark's autograph, is not to be identified with it. A few mistakes or slight modifications had already crept in. In like manner, the copies used by Matthew/Luke were not Mark's autograph. Into them too changes had been introduced, and that with considerable freedom. And it happens that, while these two copies—the copies used by Matthew/Luke—were closely allied to each other, indeed we may say probably sister manuscripts, they belonged to a different family or different line of descent from that other important copy from which the great mass of other extant authorities is descended.

19. Abbott, *The Corrections of Mark*, pp. 300-304.

This is easily exhibited in the form of a diagram.

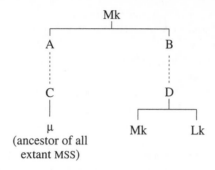

The question may be asked how it came about that these copies which were used by Matthew and Luke have not (like the A group) left descendants that have survived to the present day. It is never difficult to account for a manuscript of this period perishing, and perishing without offspring. The books of this date were almost all written upon papyrus, and papyrus is a fragile material; and the Christian book must have been much used and exposed to accidents of many kinds. But there was a special reason why those two copies should perish unregarded. The moment the two longer Gospels of Matthew and Luke were written, the shorter Gospel of Mark was at a discount. In early times it was always the Gospel least used and least quoted. The two longer Gospels incorporated the greater part of Mark; and therefore the possessor of either of them possessed practically the substance of Mark as well: and so that Gospel fell into comparative, though of course not complete, disuse.

We can form two interesting inferences as to the divergent families or lines of descent derived from Mark's autograph. One is, as I have just said, that the parent of our extant authorities was very near to the autograph, and represents it closely. The other is, that on the line of perhaps four or five copies intervening between Mark's autograph and the copies used by Matthew/Luke one at least must have been the work of a person with literary tastes and habits, who did not hesitate to improve the text before him and make it more correct and classical. This process of improvement went so far that I have ventured to call it a 'recension'. It was a recension perpetuated into just those two copies, but which after giving birth to them came to an abrupt end.

It is a remarkable fact that those two copies should have been so like each other, and it puts us upon questions which we are not able to answer. There is every reason to think that tradition is right in placing the origin of Mark's Gospel at Rome. But, apart from this curious connecting link, we know of nothing that would naturally bring the authors of the First and Third Gospels together. It is natural to suppose that the First Gospel was written not far from the outskirts of Palestine, at such a place, say, as Damascus or Antioch. And it is equally natural to associate Luke's Gospel with that part of the mission field in which the Evangelist seems to have been most at home—from Greece in the West to Antioch in the East. Is it possible that after the death of Paul and the destruction of Jerusalem, Luke made his way once more to Caesarea, where he had spent the two years of Paul's captivity, or to Antioch? Two sister copies of Mark's Gospel might quite easily have been brought thither, or from Luke's copy another copy may have been made, which fell into the hands of the compiler of the First Gospel. It is, however, well to remember that at this time all roads led to Rome.

3. *The copying and transmission of texts in their bearing upon the omission by Luke of Mk 6.45–8.26.* There remains only the little puzzle about the omission by Luke of the contents of Mk 6.45–8.26. Sir John Hawkins has written at length about this.[20] Perhaps I may be allowed to say that, so far as my judgment goes, I agree entirely with his conclusions. He has stated, as I conceive, very happily the reasons which led Luke to omit this particular section—that is, always assuming that he found that he had to omit something.

It is only on this last point that I have one small remark to offer, which falls strictly within the subject of this essay. The Gospels were written each on a separate roll of papyrus. These rolls were, roughly speaking, of the same kind of average length. This became a general rule for literary compositions dating from the Alexandrian critics of the second century BC. There was a sort of recognized average length for a book, i.e. for the whole of a small composition or for a subdivision of a larger one.[21] The so-called 'books' of the *Iliad* and *Odyssey,* of Herodotus and Thucydides, were conventional divisions imposed upon the ancient poems and histories by the scholars of Alexandria after the fact.[22] But

20. J.C. Hawkins, 'Three Limitations to St Luke's Use of St Mark's Gospel: 2. The Great Omission by St Luke of the Matter Contained in St Mark 6.45–8.26', in Sanday (ed.), *Studies in the Synoptic Problem*, pp. 61-74.

21. 'Fur verschiedene Litteraturgattungen waren verschiedene Buchmaxima oder Formate üblich oder obligat' (Birt, *Das antike Buchwesen*, p. 288).

22. Birt, *Das antike Buchwesen*, pp. 443ff.

the later works, written after their time, were usually composed 'to scale'. The reason was that the materials for writing, the blank rolls of papyrus, were cut into convenient lengths, ranging within certain accepted limits. This was the meaning of the word τόμος, which in its origin had nothing to do with 'ponderous tomes'; it meant simply a 'cut' or 'length' of papyrus.[23]

Now, if we take Westcott and Hort's text, which is not encumbered with footnotes, we observe that Matthew occupies about 68 pages, Mark (without the last 12 verses) not quite 41, Luke about 73, John about 53 (not including the *pericope adulterae*), while the Acts occupies very nearly 70 pages. Dr Kenyon has calculated that the Gospel of Mark would take up about 19 feet of an average-sized roll, that of John 23 feet 6 inches, Matthew 30 feet, the Acts and Luke's Gospel about 31 or 32 feet. The last figures are larger than those for any of the existing manuscripts mentioned (Hyperides 28 feet; *Iliad* 25 feet; *Mimes of Herodas* about the same; *Odyssey* 24 feet.[24] I have little doubt that Luke was conscious of being pressed for space, and that he felt obliged to economize his materials. Something had to be omitted, and for the motives which led to the choice of this particular section I cannot do better than refer the reader to Sir John Hawkins' paper.

The suggestions made in this essay are all very simple. It is just their simplicity which has had the chief attraction for me: as a rule, the simpler the cause, provided it is adequate, the more likely it is to be true. And I cherish the hope that the connections of effect and cause propounded may have the advantage of being, within their limits, adequate as well as simple. The essay will have served its purpose if it enables any of its readers to form for themselves a more exact conception of the processes which gave shape to time Gospels as we have them, and of the influences of various kinds to which they were due.

---

23. τόμος = 'abgeschnittene *charta papyracea*' (Birt, *Das antike Buchwesen*, p. 35). 'Denn es ist hervorzuheben, dass gerade er (τόμος) klarer und schärfer als alle anderen die Papyrusrolle und nur sie allein bezeichnete' (*ibid.*).

24. Kenyon, *Handbook to Textual Criticism*, p. 29.

Chapter 6

THE NEW TESTAMENT BACKGROUND[*]

The Gospels

We call this little book *The New Testament Background*. If it is asked, 'Background of what?' the answer, in accordance with the general title of this series, must be 'of Common Prayer'. The reading of the Bible enters into and plays an important part in our Common Prayer, and the knowledge of the Bible is the most important knowledge that a Christian can possess for purposes of religion. We might, if we liked, call our book the 'Background (so far as it is found in the New Testament) of Christian Belief'.

We are writing for the plain man and the plain woman, the plain boy and the plain girl, who desire to look at things just as they are without any assumption for which a reason is not given. In the past it has been the custom to dole out information about the Bible with a rather sparing hand. A great process of study and inquiry has been going on; and until this process had settled down to fairly clear and definite results, it was perhaps natural that what the teacher had to say should be partial and not very coherent or well thought out; he could not give more than he had been able to take in and digest himself. But now the time seems to have come when an attempt should be made to present the new knowledge in as connected a form as possible. This does not mean that the results obtained, or that seem to be obtained, are fixed and final; but a point has been reached at which it is possible to look round and take stock of what has been gained. We can only promise to do this according to the best of our ability and the best light that we have from without. Both method and results may be improved in the future; and

*   This chapter is taken from the parts that Sanday wrote in W. Sanday and C.W. Emmet, *The New Testament Background* (Tracts on Common Prayer, 4; London: Oxford University Press, 1918), pp. 1-34 on the Gospels, and pp. 56-58 on approximate chronology.

yet we may feel that there is solid ground beneath our feet and that we are not likely to find ourselves very far wrong. And there will be at least this advantage: that we are not knowingly suppressing anything or keeping back anything, and that we do not claim any monopoly on knowledge, but only ask to have our conclusions believed so far as they can be proved by the ordinary methods of human reason.

Our endeavour will be to carry the reader as far as we have been able to go ourselves; to help him to see what are the questions that arise, and what they look like in relation to such other knowledge as we possess of the times and circumstances to which they belong. It is necessary to remember that in many ways these differ very considerably from our own, and that allowance has to be made for the difference. A case in point meets us at the outset. Not many years ago the question was seriously raised whether our Lord Jesus Christ had ever lived at all. The one fact which made such a question possible for a single moment was that the century in which he lived, and in particular the part of the century in which he lived, is a time about which our knowledge of details is very limited. We are apt unconsciously to judge it by the standards of our own day when the knowledge of what is going on all over the world comes pouring in upon us every morning, when the printing presses are sending out newspapers and books in great profusion from almost every country under the sun. Under such conditions as these it would be strange if an important series of events escaped without mention. But the chances of mention must always be in proportion to the amount of literature in which an allusion to the events might be looked for. In view of the conditions which prevail now, it may well be difficult for us to realize what they must have been in a century of which all the literature that has come down to us might be got on to a single small bookshelf, and all the historical literature into quite the half of that. The first century of our era happens to be rather specially meagre in this respect. The century before was much more prolific, and a much larger proportion of the works that it produced has been preserved.

In the non-Christian literature of the first century AD there is only one clear and unambiguous reference to the founding of Christianity. But it happens that this one reference is very clear and direct, and satisfactory so far as it goes; and it agrees well with all that we know from Christian sources. The Roman historian Tacitus, in speaking of the great fire at Rome in 64 AD, says that the suspicion of having caused it was thrown by Nero upon the unpopular sect of Christians; and he adds that Christ, the founder of the sect, had been put to death by the procurator Pontius Pilate in the reign of Tiberius.

That distinctly corroborates our Christian books, and is enough corroboration for them. But, apart from this, the Christian books bear their own witness to themselves. It is often possible to tell, without going outside it, whether a book is telling a true story or not. The early epistles of Paul are specially of this character. Take for instance the two Epistles to the Corinthians. No one could read these without seeing that they describe a bit of real life and very intense life. It is no fancy picture. Some parts of it are rather sordid. The Corinthian converts have just the weaknesses that men lately converted might be expected to have. Among them Paul appears as a very earnest shepherd of souls. We see him becoming all things to all men in order that he might by all means save some. He does not in the least gloss over his failures. We see him at work; and we see the immense difficulties of his work (1 Cor. 2.3-5; 4.11-13; 2 Cor. 1.5-10; 4.7-18; 6.3-10; 11.23-33; 12.20-21). There can be no doubt that all this is a chapter of real testimony.

If these two epistles stood alone we could reconstruct a great deal of what Christianity is from them. As Paul stands behind his converts so the figure of Christ his Master stands behind his own. We see there where he got his motive and his inspiration. Indeed the whole workings of the apostle's mind are laid bare to us with extraordinary clearness. Even about Christ himself we learn much; we learn what was the kind of impression that he made upon men (2 Cor. 11.1); we learn about his crucifixion and the place which it held in the apostolic teaching (1 Cor. 1.13, 23; 2.2); we learn in full and close detail about his resurrection (from the famous passage 1 Cor. 15.1-9). And then we can see how even at this early date—less than thirty years after his death—a whole 'theology', as we should call it, had been built up round his Person (1 Cor. 1.23-24; 2.2; 8.12; 10.16-17; 11.26; 12.13; 15.1-4, 16-19, 22-26, 28, 57; 2 Cor. 3.17-18; 4.5-6, 14; 5.10, 14-15, 17-21; 13.4, 14).

We must be thankful for what we have; and it is a great deal to have that the chief of missionaries, and perhaps the chief of saints, should have left us all this wealth of material from his own hand. How we wish that it had pleased Almighty God that his Blessed Son, the Captain of our Salvation, should do the same—that he too should allow us to converse with him directly at first hand and not through any medium!

This privilege has not been granted to us; what we know of his words has come to us through a medium; we have not the absolute guarantee of their authenticity that we should have had if they had come to us with his own signature. Still it is much that we should know what we do of his words and of his life through the agency of others.

What are we to think and to say about the Gospels? We no longer take them for infallible records. We no longer think that any record that comes to us at second or third hand can be infallible. But, short of infallibility, a record may come to us with great weight of trustworthiness and authority. And, at least as regards the words of our Lord, the record in the Gospels does come to us with this. The claim may be made for the words, more completely than for the record of the acts, on the one broad and simple ground that the words as they come to us are, speaking roughly and approximately, beyond the reach of invention. In this general sense, they hang together so well that we may take them in the main with a high degree of confidence. We cannot say quite so much for the record of the acts. The writers of the Gospels do indeed, we may believe, set them down as they had received them. But it is doubtful whether we have any single account (unless it is perhaps the narrative of the Healing of the Centurion's Servant, Mt. 8.5-13; Lk. 7.2-10, and another small incident, Mt. 12.22-24), even at one degree removed, directly from an eyewitness of the actual event. It is conceivable that this narrative may come as nearly as this from the apostle Matthew. It is also conceivable that the evangelist Mark may have been a distant spectator of the crucifixion. But it would be hazardous to say more than this. And it should further be remembered that those who wrote the Gospels did so, not in the spirit of what we should call critical historians, but with their minds full of the ideas current among the Jews of that generation. Allowance has to be made for this.

It is well to take the first three Gospels together, and separately from the Fourth. The reason for this strikes us at once when we come to examine the relation in which the three Gospels stand to each other. That relation is soon found to be very peculiar. If we take the main body of the narrative as it stands in the Gospel of Mark, cutting off the first two chapters of Matthew and Luke and comparing the rest of the Gospels with each other, we find that there is a great amount of resemblance between them. Beginning (as the Gospel of Mark begins), with the account of the ministry of John the Baptist and the Baptism of our Lord, and following the main thread of the narrative to the discovery of the empty tomb (Mk 16.1-8), it appears that nearly the whole of this material is reproduced in the other two Gospels. The most probable explanation of this is that the writers of those Gospels had before them the actual Gospel of Mark and made use of its contents to supply a framework for the story as they tell it themselves. The incidents which they choose to relate are substantially the same. At least two out of the three Gospels usually go together; in the earlier portion of the history, where Matthew somewhat diverges, Mark and Luke agree, and in the later portion of the history, where Luke somewhat diverges, Matthew and Mark agree. In other words, Mark is the connecting link or common foundation of the three Gospels. And the same observation holds good for the substance and wording of the successive sections of narrative that holds good for their order. The larger proportion of the common material is found in Mark; where Matthew differs, Luke very often agrees; and where Luke differs, Matthew very often agrees.

The inference that we draw from this rather strange relation of the three writings is that the other two evangelists both had access to a Gospel that was practically identical with our Mark, and made use of this Gospel independently of each other. In this way almost the whole of the substance of the Second Gospel became incorporated in the First and Third. The writers of these Gospels reproduced, not slavishly but freely, what they had before them in the work of their colleague. Mark in this respect comes first in order of time; the other evangelists are both later and base their work upon his.

This seems to be the account that ought to be given of the matter that is common to all three Gospels. It comes in the first instance from our Mark. There are some very small differences to be accounted for; but they practically do not affect the main proposition. We observe, however, that each of the other Gospels is considerably longer than Mark's. They each contain other matter that has no parallel in his. This non-Markan matter is found on examination to be of two kinds. In respect to some of it there is substantial agreement between Matthew and Luke. Speaking generally, the double matter that is found in these two Gospels and not on the third may be said to be mainly of the nature of discourse. It consists for the most part of more or less scattered *Sayings* of our Lord. It contains the nucleus of what we call the Sermon on the Mount, of a considerable portion of the Charge to the Apostles, of the Discourse on John the Baptist and other similar discourses. The only complete incident, in which there is as much of narrative as of discourse, is the Healing of the Centurion's Servant in Mt. 8.10 and Luke 7. The simplest way of explaining this group of facts is to suppose that the First and Third evangelists had access to a second writing that was not used by Mark.

But, besides this double material in the two longer Gospels, each of them has a good deal of matter peculiar to itself, and therefore presumably the special property of the single writer who has it. The first two chapters of Matthew and Luke would come under this head. The rest of the peculiar matter in the two Gospels has something of a common character running through it in each case, and may therefore have a common origin, written or oral. Luke's peculiar sections seem to have three noteworthy features about them: (1) that they include a number of Parables (the Good Samaritan, the Importunate Friend, the Rich Fool, the Fig Tree, the Prodigal Son, the Unjust Steward, the Rich Man and Lazarus, the Unjust Judge, the Pharisee and the Publican); (2) that not only the Parables but several incidents relate specially to the Samaritans; (3) that the source from which they are derived seems to have stood in some special connection with the court of the Herods. The peculiarities in Matthew, or at least some of them, have more the look of having been handed down by word of mouth. To these (such as the details in Mt. 27.19, 51-52, 62-66) a high value cannot be attached. Others (like the sections without parallel in Mt. 25), which appear to rest on a more solid basis, are of deeper import.

Thus it would seem that our first three Gospels, when analysed into their component parts, are made up of material of three kinds: first there is the Gospel of Mark, which at once forms a Gospel to itself and also served as a common basis and framework for Matthew and Luke; then there is that other primitive writing, which did not enter into the substance of Mark, but contributed a number of Sayings sometimes lightly prefaced by narrative by the two Gospels; and, lastly, there is the residuum of unparalleled matter in Luke and Matthew.

The succession and relative dates of these different strata are important. There can be no doubt that the oldest to be committed to writing was the little discourse-document which has been mentioned second on the list. This was just a brief manual for missionaries, put together in Palestine and taking its shape from its surroundings, laying stress upon the ministry of the Baptist and his relation as forerunner and witness to our Lord because in Palestine his followers were still frequently to be met with. It also gave an outline of the Master's teaching, in contrast to that of the Pharisees and Jewish Rabbis with whom his disciples were often brought into collision. And it further maintained his authority as the expected Messiah and was careful to indicate the many ways in which he fulfilled the prophecies that pointed to him. A writing like this clearly belongs to the first phase of missionary effort, dating from the time when the disciples were dispersed by the persecution which led to the death of Stephen (Acts 8.1-5). It might be placed approximately in the decade 40–50 AD, in other words, not more—or hardly more—than twenty years after the Crucifixion.

Next in order would come the Gospel of Mark. There is good reason to think that this Gospel was written under quite different conditions, not in Palestine among Jews, but among Gentiles at Rome, somewhere about the middle of the decade 60–70 AD. An express statement has come down to us which is worthy of credence, that Mark wrote his Gospel on the basis of the preaching of Peter, though not until after Peter's death and in any case without direct assistance from him. This Gospel is much more like a Life of our Lord, written for the instruction of those who knew little or nothing about him. In Palestine where he had worked, and within the first twenty years after his death, this kind of information would not be needed. But at Rome, in the far West, the whole story had to be told. A special stress was laid on the circumstances of the Passion and Resurrection which were leading points in the apostolic teaching. On the other hand it was less necessary to enlarge on the ethical and religious teaching of Christ, which had been already summarily described in writing, and could so be put into the hands of converts.

The impulse given by the Gospel of Mark soon gave rise to more extended works, such as we have specimens of in the Gospels of Matthew and Luke. Both of these might be called expansions of Mark by combining with the substance of his Gospel, more or less abbreviated, the main substance of the other earlier writing, and any other stray documents or traditions that the later evangelists in the course of their wanderings could find. We may well believe that the additional material in the Gospel of Luke was collected by that writer during the two years in which he would seem to have been in the company of Paul at Caesarea (Acts 24.27). Caesarea was the regular seat of the Roman government, and it would be easy to acquire information here about the Herodian dynasty. The Gospel of Luke corresponds quite well with what might have been expected from 'the beloved physician', the companion of Paul. It is not likely that it was written considerably earlier. It is right to mention that in recent years the opinion has gained ground among scholars that the book of Acts was written about the time when its narrative breaks off (i.e. about the year 64 AD). A good many questions that may be raised would be satisfactorily answered if that were so; the chief difficulty on the other side is that the antecedent processes involved, especially in the composition and publication of the Gospel of Mark, would have to be somewhat compressed and hurried.

What the Gospel of Luke was for the later first or second generation of Gentile converts, that the Gospel known to us as Matthew's would seem to have been for the second generation of Jewish converts—more probably of the Dispersion than of Palestine. One of the nearer cities of mixed population like Damascus, or possibly the more distant Antioch, would suit the conditions. If the author of the Third Gospel was a cultivated and liberal-minded Gentile, the author of the First Gospel might be described as a liberal-minded Jew who was also well read in the sacred books of his fathers. We might call his Gospel a developed and enlarged edition of the missionary tract which opened the series. The considerations which help us to fix a date for this Gospel are not certain; but they would suggest a date not very long after 70 AD.

Such would seem to be in broad outline, so far as it can be recovered, the kind of history which we may believe lies behind three out of the four books which we call the Gospels. The important question for us to ask is, What sort of guarantee does such a history give for the general truth of the record as it has come down to us? There is a rather different measure for Words and for Deeds. We shall have probability with us if we say that the more important Words of our Lord Jesus Christ became fixed in writing within an interval of thirty to forty years after they were done. Different people may estimate differently the exact amount of assurance that this will give them. But we may be thankful on the whole that it is not less than it is.

There is one further consideration that ought to be mentioned. In all testimony as to facts there is always a double element: there is what the mind receives through the senses and what it gives out from itself. Every statement of fact involves something also of interpretation. The fact must be related to other facts and at the same time to a certain attitude towards those facts. As this varies in different ages so will the resultant conception of the facts vary. Now in the first century of our era the dominant influence in Jewish circles came from the Old Testament; there was an antecedent tendency to think of religious events happening at the time, so far as they were at all parallel to events recorded in the Old Testament, more and more in language modelled upon the Old Testament description. The picture called up by the older narrative presented itself before the mind of the later narrator and helped to shape the forms of his own description. In our present century quite different influences are at work. The scientific habit has become widespread, and it is natural to think of everything as happening in accordance with the laws of science. Hence the difficulty arises when we have to translate, as it were, a story told under one set of conditions into a language suited to the other set of conditions.

The evidence is decisive that wonderful things happened in connection with the ministry on earth of our Lord Jesus Christ and his disciples. We cannot doubt that spiritual forces were at work in those days in a higher degree than they have ever been at work either before or since. And yet we are justified in believing that, in the light of the further revelation that God has given us to his own ways and methods of working, events would present themselves to us in a manner somewhat different from that in which they presented themselves to the forefathers of our faith nearly nineteen hundred years ago. They described things in one way, and we (if we could change places with them) should describe them in another. The events were the same; and in either case their general effect was the same—viz. to bring home to the minds of men that divine forces were at work in a special and peculiar degree. But we should describe the operation of these forces under certain restrictions and cautions which did not exist for those who originally bore witness to them. We should do our best to tell over and over again the story of the Gospels; but we should not tell it in quite the same way.

If what has just been said applies to the first three Gospels, it applies still more strongly to the Fourth. The studies of nearly a century have affected the view that is taken of this Gospel. In any case it is considerably later than the other Gospels, and it was written under different conditions. It has become difficult to think of it as the actual work of the son of Zebedee. There were two Johns who played a prominent part in the Church of the first century, one in the middle, and the other (who may have been a disciple of the first) at the end. This second John was a reverend figure which loomed large in the sight of the generations of Christians who followed him. He would seem to have carried on the tradition of the 'beloved disciple'; but that tradition blended with and was absorbed in the thoughts of his own. These thoughts belong, not to the early preaching of the Gospel, but to the time when largely under the influence of Paul, a more mature and penetrating theology was forming. The problem was how to find the deepest expression for that which was Divine in the Person of Christ. Paul had been in search of this; and he gave the result of his search most fully in the passage Col. 1.12-20. This passage is the most complete; but it had been led up to by many briefer hints in the earlier epistles; and the author of the Epistle to the Hebrews had been working upon similar lines in Heb. 1.2-4. In both these cases the writer had the Life of Christ behind him, and put upon it the best interpretation that he could, suggested by the richest philosophy of his day. The writer of the Fourth Gospel must have done much the same thing; but he reverses the method of presentation. He begins from the philosophy as applying a key to the Life. He grasps this key with a firm hand, and he uses it in developing his sketch on the Life. The solemn and impressive phrases with which the Gospel opens embody the maximum of truth that the deeper thinkers of that day could understand and assimilate. They culminate in the announcement that the Word (i.e. the expressed Mind of God) became flesh, and tabernacled among us (and we beheld his glory, glory as of the only begotten from the Father), full of grace and truth (Jn 1.14). This is the concise formula in which the evangelist describes what we call the Incarnation. To see it in its full setting, it should be taken with the verses which precede. The philosophy from which the language is taken is no longer exactly in vogue; and yet to this day the sentences as they follow each other are wonderfully illuminating.[1] We do not go to the Gospel so much for new facts as to help us to find the meaning of the facts. What the writer gives us is a series of pictures—dissolving views, we might call them—as he himself saw them, and taking their colour from his inward vision.

The earlier Gospels are a simpler product, but not so profound. As compared with the Fourth Gospel, they give the portrait of the Christ 'in his outward habit as he walked'. It is such a portrait as would serve best to represent him to us now. They help us to see him as nearly as we can by the shore of the lake, teaching on the hillside, going about doing good. They too (the earlier Gospels, or at least two out of the three) have their own way of bringing out his Divine nature. The First Gospel and the Third each devote two chapters to the Nativity and Infancy of the Lord; both stories must be regarded as poetry and not prose.[2] Both

1.   To appreciate this, the reader would do well to take the opening verses as they stand in the Poet Laureate's Anthology *The Spirit of Man*—a book which is now to be found in many households—No. 42, along with the note on the passage and in connexion with the other pieces which precede and follow (R.S. Bridges, *The Spirit of Man: An Anthology in English and French from the Philosophers and Poets, Made by the Poet Laureate in 1915 and Dedicated by Gracious Permission to his Majesty the King* [London: Longmans, Green, 1916]).

2.   The psalm that we know as the *Magnificat* is modelled upon the Song of Hannah in 1 Sam. 2.1-10. It is hardly possible to think of it as an impromptu arising

are attempts to come a little nearer to the expressing of the inexpressible—the entrance of Deity into manhood. The Matthean version centres in the prophetic phrase, 'Immanuel; God with us' (Mt. 1.23). The Lukan version culminates in the verse which describes that operation of the Holy Ghost whereby the Holy Thing which was to be born should be called the Son of God (Lk. 1.3).

If we are asked what warrant we have for our belief in this Divine Birth, our answer must be that our ultimate warrant and our best warrant is that our Lord Jesus Christ believed in it himself, he has not indeed anywhere defined or described the process by which this Incarnation, or embodying of Godhead in the form of manhood, took place. He speaks of it by the result, which appears in his own consciousness of Sonship. We look on from without, but we are permitted to see what was within. The secret of his being—the central point of consciousness which dominated all his life as man—was his sense of standing in a unique relation to God, the relation which he expressed both to himself and others by the word 'Son'. We have just said that this sense of Sonship dominated the whole course of his human life. We are given a glimpse of it in the one anecdote that has come down to us from his childhood (Lk. 2.49). Already as a boy, going up to worship with his parents in the Temple, he felt that the place where he communed with his Father had a unique claim upon him. His communing was not intermittent and distant like that of others, but intimate and constant in a supreme degree. We are never left in any doubt that he who trod the soil of Palestine was truly and fully Man. But we are no more left in doubt that he was at the same time and all the

directly out of the events just narrated. The song of Hannah itself (as may be seen from the reference to 'the king' in 1 Sam. 2.10) was not originally composed for the place in which it is found. And there is much reason to think that the whole group of Canticles in Luke 1, 2, though earlier and more primitive than the rest of the Gospel, was not composed until long after the date with which they are associated. The collection came to Luke probably in writing, and gives a beautiful and essentially true picture of the kind of atmosphere and circumstances which surrounded the Birth of our Lord; but it cannot be taken as literally accurate history, as history would be written now. Much the same must be said of the first two chapters of Matthew; it is more likely that the contents of these came to the evangelist orally than in writing. The free introduction of the ministry of angels and of supernatural communication by means of dreams are further indications that these narratives cannot be incorporated with our own beliefs simply as they stand. In idea and spirit they aim at expressing a profound truth; but the forms in which they are worked up belong to that day, and not to ours.

time of the same essence with his Father in heaven. Once and again this pervading consciousness is confirmed by some special revelation, as at the Baptism (Mk 1.11, etc.), at the Transfiguration (Mk 9.7, etc.); and the same consciousness enters into the last scene and last words of all (Lk. 23.46). We are certainly meant to infer that the filial trust of the Son in the Father was unclouded and unbroken from the beginning to the end; even the cry of agony in Mk 15.34, etc. does not mark any real severance.

In a human life we must needs think of human feeling as uppermost. At the same time, in the Gospels, we get the impression that there is always a vaster consciousness waiting to break through. We are always being prepared for the message sent to the disciples through the Magdalene, 'I ascend unto my Father and your Father, and my God and your God' (Jn 20.17). The immortal Spirit 'cabin'd, cribb'd, confined' in its house of clay looks forward to an infinite expansion. While it is in the flesh it is checked and restrained, but a boundless range of activity lies before it.

Another great belief came in to supply matter for the sense of Sonship to work upon. How was the Son of God to employ himself? What was to be his mission? What use was he to make of this unique endowment of his—so much in him of God, so much in him of Man? Could it not be made a blessing to the whole human race? There was no need to seek for an answer; it lay close at hand.

Under the influence of their spiritual leaders there had grown up among the people a hope which had hardened into an expectation. Some day there would arise a perfect King, a perfect Prophet, a perfect Priest. The common name which embraced these different aspects was the Messiah or Anointed One, that is, one specially endowed and commissioned by God, one empowered to represent the people before God and God before the people. The Messiah bore the name of Son. Hence it was an easy step that one who felt himself to be pre-eminently the Son should also feel that he united in his own Person the complex mission of the Messiah. He felt that he was called to do God's work in the world on a scale on which it had never been done before. And—paradox of paradoxes—this work was to be done primarily by a supreme humiliation. The Lord of all the world was to take upon himself the very extreme of indignity, suffering and death.

Here was a new element added, a new and unheard of characteristic of the Messiah. One drawback to the Messianic Idea, as it came down to our Lord with the imprint of the past upon it, was that it was so closely bound up with the fortunes of the Jewish people. Sometimes that people itself seemed to be invested with the character of the Messiah. When that was so, it was the people as triumphant, as leading the way for all other peoples to God. Small and insignificant as the Jewish people was, it never lost its high self-consciousness. In spite of all its misfortunes it never let go the proud confidence that it would one day tread upon the necks of its enemies. This confidence repeatedly inspired the fierce insurrections in which it turned round upon its oppressors. The first two centuries of our era are full of them.

This was just the time when the Christian Messiah was born, and lived and died. But from the first and always, he cut himself off from this side of the Jewish expectation. He in fact gave it an altogether different turn. In a sense Jesus of Nazareth was the Jews' Messiah; but he was the Jews' Messiah with a large slice of his characteristics taken out and a wholly different character substituted for them. This explains why it is that there should be so much controversy as to the Messiahship of Jesus even to the present day. In one sense he was the Messiah because he inherited so much that was most essential in the functions and vocation of the Messiah. But in another sense he held aloof from that which the Jews themselves regarded as most distinctive of the Messiah.

This ambiguity called for a new name. And our Lord himself, while he accepted the designation of Messiah, preferred to use another name. It was not wholly new. It was a recognized, though subordinate, synonym for the Messiah. Our Lord rarely spoke of himself as the Messiah. And, while he often spoke of God as 'My Father', he would also seem to have avoided referring to himself as 'Son of God'. The title that he preferred to use was 'Son of Man'. This title, in the original Greek, is rather irregular and peculiar in its form. But there can be little doubt that it was the favourite name by which our Lord spoke of himself. And the reason evidently was because it brought out and emphasized that aspect of his character and mission which was new and most clearly distinguished him from the Messiah of the Jews' expectation. The name Son of Man laid stress upon all that he had in common with man. 'He made Himself of no reputation.' So far from making claims, he rather suppressed them. He was content to go through life as a homeless wanderer, mingling chiefly with the common people, and rather courting hardship and suffering than avoiding it. He did this because 'it behoved him in all things to be made like unto his brethren, that he might be a merciful and faithful high priest in things pertaining to God, to make propitiation for the sins of the people' (Heb. 2.17). This is only a more theological expression for the words of the Gospel: 'the Son of Man came not to be ministered unto, but to minister, and to give his life as a ransom for many' (Mk 10.45).

This changed emphasis in the idea of the Messiah goes far to explain and to set in its right place what may be called the latest phase in the study and criticism of the Gospels. For some time past this phase has seemed to have a rather unsettling effect; but the excitement which it caused at first is now subsiding, and—as on so many previous occasions—when the balance of results comes to be struck, it is found that new light is thrown upon the facts and we are enabled to see them in juster proportions. Soon after the beginning of this century it came to be observed, more than it had been before, that the language of the Gospels and their chief centre of interest lay more in the future than had been supposed. The treatment of the Gospels had in the past been what is often called 'static': that is, it took them as something fixed and final; it did not allow for much movement. In the newer view we get this sense of movement, of an onward march of events towards a goal. There is to be a great consummation, the end of one age of the world's order and the beginning of another.

What about times and seasons? The Lord himself frankly confessed that he did not know (Mk 13.3c). As Son of Man, identified as he was with all that is human, he was in this too made like unto his brethren. He came to earth to fulfil a certain ministry; but the temporal and cosmic conditions of the fulfilment of that ministry were kept by the Father in his own power.

There is a great and fundamental distinction between the outward 'shows of the world', which are shifting and variable, and the deep inner realities which, if they move, move by a law of their own which is not apparent upon the surface. It is like the clouds drifting over a landscape and imparting to it the play of light and shade and the more permanent features of the landscape itself. So in history: there is the region of atmosphere, of fleeting shapes and shadows; then there is also the region of hidden forces, which come not with observation. The 'timesetting' belongs to the first and not to the second, and the mind of man is always seeking to penetrate through the one to the other. It never, in this dispensation, wholly succeeds; but little by little it approaches nearer than before.

It may help us perhaps to think of what is written about the Second Coming of our Lord Jesus Christ on some such lines as these. The subject certainly falls within the limits of that which is shifting and variable, where the

> ...margin fades
> For ever and ever as we move.

But beneath this world of passing clouds and fading margins there is another which has to do more with the essence of things that do not pass and fade. The mistake that people have made has been that of confounding the two. When attention was first called to the extent to which the language of the Gospels has been affected by the current doctrine about future things, and especially by the doctrine of the near approach of the end, some students fell into the error of supposing that the basis of morality must needs be changed. They began to talk about 'interim' morals, which only held good for the interval between the First and the Second Coming supposed to be near at hand. And it is true that there is one passage in the writings of Paul, 1 Cor. 7.25-40, in which the apostle does distinctly contemplate a change in the balance of expediency as affecting certain relations of life; but he was far from regarding this as involving any revolution in the fundamental ideas of right and wrong. Perhaps if Paul had been as severely logical as some thinkers aim at being, he might have been equally misled to his own undoing. But it has been well pointed out that the real effect upon him of contemplating the nearness of the end was just the opposite of this. The moral that is drawn at the close of the great chapter 1 Corinthians 15, in view of the thought that 'we shall not sleep, but we shall all be changed', is to be increased steadiness and concentration: 'Wherefore, my beloved brethren, be ye steadfast, unmoveable, always abounding in the work of the Lord, forasmuch as ye know that your labour is not in vain in the Lord'. And this is the general teaching of the New Testament: e.g. 1 Thess. 5.6; 2 Thess. 3.11-12; 1 Pet. 4.7-9; 2 Pet. 3.11-13. It is characteristic of the new heavens and the new earth that 'therein dwelleth righteousness' (2 Pet. 3.13), and that everything that runs counter to righteousness is severely excluded (Rev. 21.7-8, 27; 22.14-15). If such was the goal, such was bound to be also the way to the goal, whether short or long. At no point or period of time could there be any weakening or suspension, but only an intensification, of ordinary morals.

And yet Christianity has its own special note. When the Lord Jesus Christ announced that the Kingdom of God was at hand, and when he taught his disciples to pray that the Kingdom of God might come, he was careful to explain that he was not content with the current conception of the kingdom. He was not come to relax the current ideal, but rather to strengthen and deepen it (Mt. 5.17-20); the righteousness of his disciples was worthless, if it did not exceed that of the scribes and Pharisees, the recognized religious leaders of the day. The first requirement was that the Christian righteousness should be something more real and inward, something more genuinely religious, not an external round of practices and ceremonies, but a movement of the heart and conscience. Where such a movement was at work, the self-complacent attitude of the Pharisee became impossible; it must needs find expression in humility, like that of the Publican in the parable. It involved a change, a change of heart, which could not rest upon the surface. Hence the demand for Repentance and Conversion, the mark of which was to be a spirit like that of a little child. And though, in laying down this as a law for his followers, the Master was not called upon to include himself, yet his own character corresponded to it in type. It was not at random that Paul appealed to the 'meekness and gentleness of Christ' (2 Cor. 1.10). The old law left open the rule of retaliation; the new law laid down the command, Love your enemies.

Even at that time there was something in all this of a counsel of perfection. The disciples of Christ were a small minority, who aimed at something higher than the world around them. And to this day the ideal as an ideal abides, though it would necessarily be much longer before what was a law for the Christian could be made a law for all mankind. Hence the difficulty and dilemma in which the Christian is apt to find himself placed. More especially when might is pitted against right he cannot be content to be passive and neutral.

It follows that the Christianity of the Gospels cannot in all respects be consistently carried out so long as the world remains as it is. We must rather think of it as a leaven working and destined to work 'until the whole be leavened'. There is truth in the view that the Christian rule of turning the cheek to the smiter, as at first promulgated and even till the present day, cannot be universally acted upon but must be taken with a limited application to the methods by which Christianity itself is to be spread and propagated. We can only hope that the worst infringements of this rule, like the present war, may prove the strongest impulse towards its acceptance.

Going back to the Person of our Lord himself: when at last he set his face to go down into the valley of the shadow of death, it is difficult for us to form an exact picture of what was in his mind. We cannot easily distinguish between words that were actually his own and words attributed to him by his disciples and the Early Church. There was a similar ambiguity in the language of the Church and his disciples. All minds were looking forward—eagerly and hopefully forward; but they did not know which of the roads open before they should follow. They did not know how far they ought to choose what was called the language of apocalyptic about the Messiah descending upon the clouds of heaven and how far they ought to throw the stress upon what is described in the Fourth Gospel as the mission of the Holy Spirit, the Comforter. But there was no doubt that something great was coming. There was no doubt that a new era was about to begin. There was something in common between the state of things then and the state of things in respect to the fate of nations now. We also feel that vast changes are before us; but it is beyond our power to guess what form they will take. We may be sure that our Lord knew that the future turned upon him. But it was another thing to forecast that future in definite terms of concrete history; and we are not in a position to say how he did so far forecast it in his own mind. No clear saying of his on the subject has come down to us in terms that we can verify as His. We must be content with the same kind of vague and cloudy outlook of which we have just spoken; but the essential point in our own outlook, as in so much as we are able to reconstruct of his own words, is that whatever the future had in store would certainly centre in him.

The crisis came. The Son of Man died, by voluntary submission, upon the cross. It was the last and crowning evidence of his complete and absolute self-surrender to the will of the Father. For the moment it seemed as though his mission had failed. His disciples were scattered or in hiding. His work seemed brought to nought. He himself slumbered in the grave. And then suddenly, within the four-and-twenty hours of a single day, all was changed. Not as in one form of the tradition (Mt. 28.2-4) by any great earthquake and dazzling apparition from heaven, but in the quietest of ways; now here and now there; first one individual or small group and then another found the Master they had lost in their midst or at their side. And similar experiences were repeated more than once over some time.

It is a very subordinate question to ask 'In what body did he come?'. Different conceptions of resurrection and the resurrection-body were current in the apostolic age; and it is rather strange that the idea which has had the widest diffusion—that of the resuscitation of the dead body—should be specially characteristic of the Pharisees. This, however, does not appear to be the idea which underlies the great chapter 1 Corinthians 15.

We can afford to leave this question unanswered. What is really important for us to grasp is that the belief in the Resurrection was no mere imagination of excited minds but an epoch-making Divine act, the assurance of triumph over death: 'I am he that liveth, and was dead: and behold, I am alive for evermore, Amen, and have the keys of hell and death' (Rev. 1.18).

In the Old Testament period there had grown up the idea (which seems to have come originally from Babylonia) that the career of an eminent saint or man of God ought not to end in death but in some sort of preternatural translation. The oldest example is that of Enoch: 'Enoch walked with God: and he was not; for God took him' (Gen. 5.24); the most conspicuous, the assumption of Elijah in 2 Kings 2. This idea was shared by the early disciples; and it is therefore not surprising that in the shaping of the narrative of the Life of Christ by oral tradition it should have been rounded off by a visible Ascension (Acts 1.9). There may have been some feature in the last appearance of the Risen Christ which suggested this. In any case the story, though not to be taken literally, has spiritual truth as marking the final Return to the Father.

Approximate Chronology

The main object of this sketch is to give a general idea of the relation of the literature to the events, and so of the kind of evidence on which our knowledge of primitive Christian history rests.

It is not possible to date many of the events exactly. At the same time the researches of the last fifty years enable us to put approximate dates to most of them. The table given below represents the rough results of a collation of the evidence and the views of modern scholars. Where the dating is given without qualification or comment it may be assumed that it is not likely to be wrong by more than a year or two on one side or the other. Where the margin of error exceeds five years the date is always given with a query (?).

Events are printed in ordinary type, literature in italics, Roman emperors in small capitals. In one or two cases where an alternative view to that preferred is held with substantial support, it is given in square brackets.

AUGUSTUS, emperor of Rome	27 BC–14 AD
HEROD THE GREAT, King of Judæa	37–4 BC
BIRTH OF OUR LORD JESUS CHRIST	8–6 BC
Herod Antipas, tetrarch of Galilee	4 BC–39 AD
TIBERIUS, emperor	14–37
Pontius Pilate, Roman governor of Judæa	26–36
PUBLIC MINISTRY OF CHRIST	27–29
THE CRUCIFIXION AND RESURRECTION	29
CALIGULA, emperor	37–41
Paul at Damascus (Acts 9.19-25; 2 Cor. 11.32, 33)	37–40
Oldest Christian writing, a collection chiefly of	
Sayings of our Lord, attributed to Matthew	40–50?
CLAUDIUS, emperor	41–54
First draft of Luke 1–2	50?
Conference at Jerusalem (Acts 15)	49–50
Paul at Corinth for more	
than eighteen months (Acts 18.1, 11, 18)	50–52
Earliest group of Epistles: [Galatians], 1, 2 Thessalonians	49–52
NERO, emperor	54–68
Paul at Ephesus	52–55
Second group of Epistles:	
[Galatians], 1, 2 Corinthains; Romans	55–56
Paul's arrest at Jerusalem	56
Paul at Rome (Acts 28.16)	59–61
Third group of Epistles:	
Philippians, Colossians, Ephesians, Philemon	60–61
Pastoral Epistles (1, 2 Timothy, Titus)	61–64?
Epistle of James	60?
1 Peter	62?
Burning of Rome and Neronian Persecution	64
Death of Paul	64–65
Death of Peter	64–65
[Harnack's date for Mark, 60; and Acts, 62]	
Gospel of Mark	65
Epistle to the Hebrews	65?
CIVIL WARS: GALBA, OTHO, VITELLIUS	68–69
Alternative date for *Revelation*	69?
VESPASIAN, emperor	69–79
Siege and fall of Jerusalem	70
Gospel of Matthew	70

PART II LANGUAGE

Chapter 7

THE LANGUAGE SPOKEN IN PALESTINE AT THE TIME OF OUR LORD[*]

Let me preface the few remarks I have to offer upon Dr Roberts's recent series of papers in *The Expositor*, by saying that I have no wish to obtain a merely controversial victory. The subject is worthy of being discussed for its own sake, and as a question of scholarship or history should be, *sine irâ et studio*. There seem to me to be some serious gaps and defects in Dr Roberts's train of reasoning. But if these can be removed—if the case can be made good to the satisfaction of competent judges—I think I can engage not to hold the ground a moment after it becomes untenable. To one who has the truth of things really at heart, there is no disgrace in such defeat. He does not profess to know all about the matter in hand, but certain objections occur to him, and he states them. If they are satisfactorily answered, he makes his bow and walks away. The fact remains upon a firmer basis than before.

And, first, to define somewhat more nearly the point at issue. The difference between the two opposing views is not really so very great. There is no question that the Jews of our Lord's time were practically bilingual. The only question would be as to the proportion in which the two languages were spoken. Dr Roberts maintains that Greek was spoken more and Aramaic less, and that our Lord himself habitually spoke Greek and occasionally Aramaic. I should only wish to invert the qualifying expressions in this statement, and to say that Aramaic was spoken more and Greek less, and that our Lord used Aramaic habitually and Greek only occasionally.

No fairly well-read scholar would deny that Greek was largely spoken in Palestine at the time of our Lord. Greek was the language of universal

* This chapter originally appeared as W. Sanday, 'The Language Spoken in Palestine at the Time of our Lord', *The Expositor* 7 (1878), pp. 81-99. Sanday wrote in response to A. Roberts, 'That Christ Spoke Greek', *The Expositor* 6 (1877), pp. 81-96, 161-76, 285-99, 307-83.

intercommunication, just as, and even more than, Latin was in the Middle Ages. Many nations owned it as a second tongue. There are several causes which made it specially prevalent in Palestine. One main cause would be commerce. The Jews were, then as now, and at home as well as abroad, a very active commercial people. In Galilee especially, which was then densely populated and much better cultivated than it is at present, a thriving trade was driven in corn and oil with Phoenicia and Syria. This trade brought wealth, and wealth brought luxury, and luxury again encouraged trade: imports naturally balanced exports. Thus arose a large commercial class, who in their dealings with the foreigner would naturally speak Greek. Another cause, equally important, would be the constant intercourse with foreign Jews, occasioned by their coming up to attend the great religious feasts. To such an extent was this carried that, at the last Passover before the outbreak of war, the number of people in Jerusalem is said to have reached the almost incredible total of three million. Many of these would not be able to speak Aramaic. Hence both in Jerusalem itself, and in the main roads which led to it, especially from the west, Greek would be spoken. There were also permanent synagogues in Jerusalem for the use of these foreign Jews, and very probably at Caesarea and elsewhere. A third cause would be the direct influence of the dynasty of the Herods, who were especially addicted to Greek manners and customs. Foreigners themselves, they all courted the favour of Rome, and showed but slight sympathy for Judaism. Herod Agrippa I was the only exception to this. His short career (AD 41–44) was enough to win for him the enthusiastic regard of the people as the one truly patriot king. Herod Agrippa II tried, but not quite successfully, to combine the two things. To the house of Herod was due the construction of wholly Greek towns such as Caesarea, Stratonis, and Tiberias. The court and surroundings of Herod the Great and Archelaus at Jerusalem, and of Herod-Antipas in Galilee, would be centres of Hellenizing influences. Something must also be allowed for the influence of heathen colonies like Decapolis. The scattered cities that formed this confederation were founded by the Romans on their conquest of Syria in BC 65. No exact particulars have come down to us as to the language spoken by them. Isolated from each other as they were, and exposed to the influences of the neighbouring populations, we should naturally expect them to be bilingual, only in different proportions from the Jews. Many of the first inhabitants would probably be Syrians, who spoke a dialect of Aramaic very similar to that of Palestine. They would be therefore quite as likely to adopt Aramaic as Greek.[1] We must add, lastly, the influence of a few individuals like Gamaliel and Josephus, wiser and more liberal than the rest of their countrymen, who made a special study of the Greek learning.

But in spite of all these Hellenizing influences, the great kernel of the nation remained true to its traditions. Jewish life was made up of violent contrasts. If there was one current setting strongly in the direction of Hellenizing, there was another setting just as strongly in the opposite direction. The fury which burst out in the great rebellion against Rome had long been secretly gathering. The frequent insurrections showed that the old Maccabean spirit was still not extinct. The mass of the nation hated all that was Greek. Along with some expressions of toleration are others which breathe the fiercest spirit of intolerance.

> The later fanatical Rabbis, both before and after the destruction of Jerusalem, and in the death-struggle against Rome under Hadrian, excluded the friends of the foreign literature from eternal life; they laid the same curse upon those who educated their sons in the wisdom of the Greeks (*chochmat jewanit*) as upon the possessors of swine; while others, who were milder, permitted the reading of Homer as the reading of a [private] 'letter'.[2] But the stricter Rabbis merely expressed the national spirit. Not only Origen, but Josephus also—notwithstanding his coquetting with the foreigner—bear witness to the instinctive repugnance of the nation.[3]

1.   Dr Roberts lays too much stress upon the use of the words Ἕλλην, Ἑλληνίς. These must not be pressed as at all necessarily implying the use of the Greek language. The phrase Ἰουδαῖοί τε καὶ Ἕλληνες is constantly used in the New Testament as an exhaustive division of mankind. The word Ἕλλην is frequently (and not in substance wrongly) translated in our version by 'Gentile': e.g., Jn 7.35 ('The dispersed among the Gentiles'); Rom. 3.9 ('Both Jews and Gentiles'); 1 Cor. 10.32 ('Neither to Jews nor Gentiles'), etc.

2.   *Tr. Sanhedrin* (R. Akibha): 'Nec eum participem esse vitae aeternae, qui libros alienigenarum legit. Execrabilis esto, qui alit porcos, execrabilis item qui docet filium suum sapientiam Graecam.' Dr Keim also refers to Gfrörer, *Das Jahrhundert des Heils* (Stuttgart: C. Schweizerbart, 1838), 115; E.E. Herzfeld, III, 254 *et seq.*; I.M. Jost, *Geschichte des Judentums und seiner Secten* (3 vols.; Leipzig: Dorffling & Franke, 1857–59), III, p. 99. For the English reader we may add F.W. Farrar's *The Life of Christ* (2 vols.; London: Cassell Petter & Galpin, 1874), I, p. 91, and *Excursus* iv, p. 461.

3.   T. Keim, *Geschichte Jesu von Nazara in ihrer Verkettung mit dem Gesammtleben seines Volkes, frei untersucht und ausführlich erzählt* (3 vols.; Zürich: Orell, Fussli, 1867–72), I, p. 228 (ET).

This seems to me, I confess, a much truer picture of the real spirit of Judaism than that which is presented to us by Dr Roberts. It is difficult to see how even a party in the nation can have uttered execrations on those who brought up their sons in the Greek learning when Greek was the habitual language of *all* the rest of their countrymen. I know that Dr Roberts (in his larger work) repeatedly asserts that these expressions of violent antagonism belong only to the time of the war (or, I suppose, the two wars) with the Romans. But the whole tenor of Jewish history is decidedly against this. The Jewish character did not change backwards and forwards like a shuttlecock. The hatred of the foreigner and of things foreign was not begotten in a day. The line of Jewish history is marked by a constant succession of risings and struggles, in which national, religious, and social elements were combined, all the way from the death of Herod to the final destruction of the Jewish nationality under Hadrian.

History, however, bears but a secondary place with Dr Roberts. The evidence for his views is chiefly literary. What that evidence is it now remains for us to see.

And here, in pursuance of the principles laid down at the outset, I propose first to put on one side a number of arguments that, trying to weigh them with candour, I cannot regard as decisive. All *a priori* arguments I willingly give up—with just the proviso that arguments drawn from the historical background cannot strictly be called *a priori*. I know that it has been usual to lay stress upon the Aramaic phrases— *Ephphatha, Talitha cumi*, etc.—occurring in the Gospels. These seem to me to be quite as compatible with one hypothesis as with the other. They may represent an exceptional use of Aramaic, or they may represent an habitual use of it. No one can positively say which. Again, I do not wish to contest the possibility that the Syrophoenician woman may have spoken Greek. I think it more probable that she did not, but that may pass. No very great argument can be drawn either way from the inscription on the cross, because it does not mark the proportions in which the different languages were spoken. Dr Roberts has given an ingenious explanation of the surprise of the Roman officer at finding that Paul could speak Greek (Acts 21.37), which is probably the right one. The surprise may have had its ground in the fact that the officer supposed him to be a certain obscure Egyptian. Dr Roberts also seems to me to be suggesting a truth, though not the whole truth, when he makes the address of Paul to the Jews in Aramaic (Acts 21.40) an act of policy intended to remove the prejudice against him as a Greek.

All these concessions I am prepared to make to Dr Roberts. But, on the other hand, I am afraid he will think me rather exacting when I claim to be allowed to put aside as equally indecisive a great number of arguments of his own. Indeed, I can hardly regard any of the arguments that are derived from the New Testament as really very pertinent. Those, for instance, which are drawn from the Epistle to the Hebrews, seem to me to be singularly inconclusive. In the first place, it is very uncertain that it was written to Palestinian Jews at all. The points urged by Dr Roberts in support of this amount to the barest probability, and are obviously quite insufficient to build a further argument upon. Besides, in the case of a letter there are two persons or sets of persons to be considered—not only those to whom it is addressed, but also the person by whom it is written. Now, supposing the author to have been a thoroughly Hellenized Jew, like Apollos or Luke, why should he not write in Greek? On any hypothesis, quite enough of his readers would understand that language to make the letter worth writing. If a non-resident landlord wished to make some communication to a parish in Wales, he would write to the vicar or to his agent in English. But if the person of the writer may be taken to account for the Epistle to the Hebrews, that of the readers accounts for 1 Peter and the Epistle of James. Both these are written expressly to the Jews of the Dispersion, and the only language that most of these would understand would be Greek. James, by his position at Jerusalem, would naturally be brought much in contact with these Hellenized Jews, and would so acquire a more correct Greek style. Or, apart from this, there was nothing to hinder any individual from learning Greek with a greater or less degree of correctness. Peter, it is rather probable, did not write his epistle for himself. A very old tradition, dating back from the early part of the second century, and repeated frequently in that century, says that he took Mark for his dragoman or interpreter (ἑρμηνευτής). Paul, we know, wrote little with his own hand. Not a few of the peculiarities of style in the apostolic writings are probably to be accounted for by the extent to which they made use of amanuenses. A greater amount of latitude was allowed to the scribe sometimes than at others. The Revelation of John is a good example of the kind of Greek that would naturally be written by a native of Palestine. It abounds in solecisms that would jar upon a Greek ear. The Gospel represents the same style, refined by fifteen or twenty years of contact with a Greek-speaking people.

Nor can I attach any real conclusiveness to the arguments derived from the Gospels. All the main points can be explained quite easily on the other hypothesis. One is almost surprised to see an argument like that from the presence of people from Decapolis among the audience of the Sermon on the Mount seriously put forward. Dr. Roberts admits that Aramaic was the vernacular tongue of Palestine.[4] The cities of Decapolis were not collected together in a single district but were scattered over a considerable extent of country. Surrounded, therefore, by the vernacular, they could not fail to be influenced by it. They must have been also more or less bilingual. But supposing the audience to have consisted partly of persons who understood Aramaic well and Greek only imperfectly (as many, if not most, of the Galilean villagers must have done), and partly of people who understood Greek well and Aramaic only imperfectly (as some of the Decapolitans may have done), why should the first class have been sacrificed to the second, any more than the second to the first? But I see that Dr Roberts admits the hypothesis,[5] which is now held by a majority of critics, that the so-called Sermon on the Mount may not really have been delivered upon a single occasion. But if so, how shall we really determine in what way the different parts of it were brought home to the hearers?

Again, Dr Roberts lays much stress upon the fact that the quotations in the Gospels are, for the most part, taken from the Septuagint. But this can only be done by arguing from a series of assumptions, none of which have any certainty. Dr Roberts is doubtless aware that the quotations from the Old Testament in the Gospels are thought almost universally by critics at the present day to be due, in their form at least, to the Evangelists. I know that he himself holds a peculiar view on that point, and that he has indeed peculiar views as to the composition of the Synoptic Gospels generally. I am quite ready to admit the great difficulty of the problem which these Gospels present, and I doubt very much whether it has received as yet the final solution. But I am afraid the theory put forward by Dr Roberts will not bear detailed examination. It would take us too far from our present subject to enter into this here, but I will undertake to give the proof of what is said, in case it should be required. In the mean time it is not easy to see why the ordinary theory

4.   Roberts, 'That Christ Spoke Greek', p. 376.
5.   Roberts, 'That Christ Spoke Greek', p. 164.

does not explain the facts as well as Dr Roberts's. Two, certainly, of the Synoptic Gospels—the second and third—were written, the one by a Gentile, the other by an Hellenist, for Gentile or Hellenistic readers. It is therefore only natural that the Septuagint should be made use of in them. A third Evangelist, Matthew, wrote for Jewish Christians, and here we have the remarkable fact that the quotations from the Old Testament which are peculiar to this Evangelist show a recurrence to the Hebrew text, while those which are common to him with the other Synoptists retain their Septuagint colouring.[6] This would seem to show, precisely what we should have expected, a Hebraizing tendency in the author. In the parts peculiar to himself he goes back to the Hebrew, in those which he has in common with the rest he keeps to the same Hellenized tradition, or draws from the same document. Thus, at the only point where we should have any reason to expect a study of the Hebrew, we find it.

The reason why the Gospels that have come down to us are all in Greek is, that at the time when the Gospels were composed, the immense majority of Christians were either of Gentile or Hellenistic extraction. In hardly any part of the world did Christianity make so little way as among the native Jews. Even in Jerusalem itself, and but a very few years after our Lord's ascension, we already find that foreign Greek-speaking Jews formed an important part of the Church, so much so that a special order had to be appointed to see that justice was done them in the administration of alms. And yet the first Gospel of which we have any record was in Aramaic. No matter what the relation of this Aramaic Gospel to our present Matthew, there certainly *was* such a Gospel, and it was doubtless for a time the Gospel of the Aramaic-speaking Christians. Even the heretical branches of that body had Aramaic Gospels of their own. But, practically speaking, the great war broke up the Church of Judaea. From that time onwards the Palestinian section of the Aramaic Church sank into insignificance, while Christianity passed over from the Jews to the Hellenists and the Gentiles.

So much having been said with a view to clear the ground of what I cannot but think irrelevant matter, we may come now to the positive side of the evidence. This, I venture to think, may really be compressed within small limits. There are two passages of Josephus which seem to

---

6. See H.J. Holtzmann, *Die Synoptischen Evangelien: Ihr Uhrsprung und geschichtlicher Charakter* (Leipzig: W. Engelmann, 1863), p. 259; B.F. Westcott, *An Introduction to the Study of the Gospels* (Cambridge: Macmillan, 1860), p. 211, etc.

me to decide the whole question; but before I come to them, I should be glad to make a few remarks on some other portions of the subject.

To take, first, the New Testament. There are several passages which Dr Roberts thinks do not tell against his opinion, which, however, seem to me to be much more consistent with the view to which he is opposed. The Aramaic language is expressly mentioned more than once in the historical books. In one instance there is an allusion to the particular dialect spoken in Galilee. We are told in Mt. 26.73, Mk 14.70, that Peter was discovered to be a Galilean by his dialect; and in exact accordance with this we learn from the Talmud that the Galileans were taunted by the Jews with their faults of pronunciation. They could not properly distinguish between the gutturals, and pronounced the *sh* with a lisp, and so on.[7] Here, we should have thought, was very fairly conclusive evidence upon the whole case. It seems to prove that Aramaic was the language *commonly* spoken—the vernacular tongue both in Galilee and Judaea. If Greek was spoken, therefore, it must have been as the exception, and not as the rule. Dr Roberts, however, does not seem to admit this. He says, 'Granting that' Peter spoke Aramaic on this occasion,

> it proves nothing against the proposition which I have endeavoured to establish. It is, on the contrary, in closest accordance with the view which has been here exhibited of the relation subsisting between the two languages. It was exactly in such circumstances as those referred to that we should expect the vulgar tongue of the country to be employed; and it is surely nothing strange that the dialect of it which Peter was accustomed at times to speak in Galilee should now be stated to have been found somewhat different from that generally prevalent in Jerusalem.[8]

Dr Roberts just saves himself by inserting the words 'at times'. If he had said, 'which Peter spoke habitually in Galilee', that would be all for which I should contend. But—I must needs ask the question—*Is* 'the vernacular language', 'the vulgar tongue' of a country (as Dr Roberts himself calls Aramaic in Palestine), spoken only *at times*? Is not the *vernacular* language of a country *the* language? Was the language of England, after the Norman Conquest, French or English? Is the language of Wales, at the present day, English or Welsh? To come

---

7.   See A. Meyer, *Jesus Muttersprache: Das galiläische Aramäisch in seiner Bedeutung für die Erklarung der Reden Jesu und der Evangelien überhaupt* (Freiburg: Mohr, 1896), *ad loc.*

8.   Roberts, 'That Christ Spoke Greek', pp. 366, 367.

exactly to the point at issue, can we suppose that our Lord himself habitually used any other language than the vernacular? If the field of his ministry had not been Palestine, but Wales, or the highlands of Scotland, as they are now, would he have habitually spoken English?

Again, we read in Acts 1.19, that the death of Judas 'became known unto all the dwellers at Jerusalem; insomuch as that field is (rather "was") called in their proper tongue (τῇ ἰδίᾳ διαλέκτῳ αὐτῶν) Aceldama, that is to say, The field of blood'. The word 'Aceldama' is Aramaic. We therefore naturally argue that Aramaic was 'the proper tongue' of Jerusalem: again, all for which I should contend. Dr Roberts has not (I think) noticed this passage in his papers in *The Expositor*. He has, however, in his larger work.[9] He there explains it by saying that the words belong to the speech of Peter, and are not an added note or comment by Luke. He goes so far, indeed, as to argue that Peter himself is speaking Greek, because he introduces the Aramaic word as belonging to a tongue distinct from that in which he is speaking. All turns upon the point whether the words are really those of Peter. In form I do not deny that they are—in fact they can hardly be. Dr Roberts must be aware that it is frequently the custom of the New Testament writers to mingle their own comments with the discourses they are recording, without any clear mark of distinction. This is especially the case in the Gospel of John. And so here, though the words in point of form are attributed to Peter, in substance they must really belong to the historian. The disciples could not need to be told of a fact which was already known to all Jerusalem, and which had happened only a few days before to a former member of their own body. Nor is it likely that such a fact could really have become known to all Jerusalem in so short a time, or that the Apostle could allude to the name given to the field as a past historical fact (κληθῆναι, aorist, 'was called'). Common-sense considerations like these must be taken account of in exegesis, especially with writers so little bound by the laws of formal literary composition as the Evangelists. The undistinguished mixture of narrative and comment is simply a crudeness of style.[10]

9.   A. Roberts, *Discussions on the Gospels: In Two Parts: Part I: On the Language Employed by Our Lord and Disciples: Part II: On the Original Language of St Matthew's Gospel, and on the Origin and Authenticity of the Gospels* (Cambridge: Macmillan, 2nd edn, 1864), p. 305.

10.   So the 'majority of commentators', according to Dr H.B. Hackett in his very sound and judicious commentary on the Acts (*A Commentary on the Original Text of the Acts of the Apostles* [Boston: J.P. Jewett, 1852]). Dr Roberts, while quoting

I have already said that Dr Roberts's explanation of Paul's address to the Jews in Aramaic (Acts 21.40), and their consequent attention, seems to me to be a part of the truth. They did expect to be addressed in Greek, and it was therefore an act of policy in the Apostle to speak to them in their native Aramaic, and so show that he was not a foreigner or a teacher of foreign doctrines. But their very repugnance to foreign doctrines extended also to foreign speech. We shall see this proved from other sources, but it might naturally be inferred from the present passage. The increased attention of the Jews was probably due at once to their satisfaction at hearing the Apostle speak in their own tongue, and also to the greater intelligibility of what was said. Still, as this cannot be proved for certain, I shall not press it against Dr Roberts.

Of Talmud and Targums I shall say little, for two reasons; first, because I am no Rabbinical scholar myself, and should be obliged to collect all I had to say at second-hand; and, secondly, because I know (from the larger work)[11] that Dr Roberts attaches only a slight weight to these sources. Yet I cannot but think that this is a mistaken estimate, and I doubt whether we shall ever have a satisfactory scientific statement of the case until the references in the Talmud have been more thoroughly examined and sifted, and the antiquity and antecedents of the Targums more fully ascertained. What is needed, in fact, is an examination of the whole Jewish literature, beginning with the fragments of Aramaic embedded in the canonical Books of Daniel and Ezra, extending over the whole of the Apocrypha (and many of these books, though now preserved only in Greek, appear to have had undoubtedly Hebrew, i.e., Aramaic, originals),[12] and ending with the final elaboration of the Jerusalem Talmud and the committing to writing of the Jerusalem

---

Alford in support of his view, forgets to notice that both Alford and Meyer (whom Alford loosely follows) regard the two phrases, τῇ ἰδίᾳ διαλέκτῳ αὐτῶν and τουτ' ἔστιν χωρίον αἵματος, as *inserted into the speech* ('zwei eingewobene Erläuterungen': Meyer) by Luke.

11. Roberts, *Discussions on the Gospels*, p. 297.

12. The Book of Ecclesiasticus is expressly stated in the prologue to have been translated from the Hebrew. The same statement is made in regard to the *Book of Jubilees*, by Jerome. The best scholars assign a similar origin to the books of *Judith* ('procul dubio', Fritzsche), *1 Maccabees* ('constat', Fritzsche), *Psalms of Solomon* ('satis certum', Fritzsche). The reason why these books have come down to us in a Greek form is because they have been transmitted through Christian or Hellenistic channels. The Jewish nationality was practically destroyed in the two great rebellions and in the persecutions by the Christian successors of Constantine.

Targum. If this were done, and all the allusions, direct and indirect, were carefully collected, it would be more possible than it is at present to trace the history of western Aramaic speech and its real relations to the Greek. It seems on the face of it highly improbable that there should be a great breach of continuity in this history. It would be very strange if at the beginning of the period parts of the Scriptures themselves should have been written in Aramaic, and at the end of the period the Aramaic paraphrases of Scripture, long orally transmitted, were fixed in writing, while in the middle of the same period the Books of the Old Testament were habitually read in another and foreign tongue. It would be especially strange if the interval in which this is said to have been the case was (as we know that it was) a time of passionate national aspirations and excited patriotic feeling. But indeed I suspect that, apart from probabilities, there is considerable evidence, direct or indirect, that this was not the case.[13] The Targum of the Book of Job is known to have been written before the destruction of the Temple. A writer like Credner, examining the quotations from the Old Testament with a care and thoroughness of which it would be well if there were more in some of our English scholars, finds in several of them such marked coincidences with the text of the Targums as prove to his satisfaction the use of a Targum by the Evangelist. Thus in Mt. 12.18 the Evangelist, like the Targum of Isa. 42.1, has θήσω where the LXX has ἔδωκα, and both the Evangelist and the Targum give to the passage a Messianic application. Similarly, in the application of Jer. 31.15, Credner thinks that a Targum has been used. In the quotation of Mic. 5.2 he traces to this source the insertion of οὐδαμῶς (οὐδαμῶς ἐλαχίστη for ὀλιγοστός) and also the insertion of ἡγούμενος—two very marked peculiarities. Credner sums up his researches on this section of quotations thus: 'In several places the materials still at our command are sufficient to prove the intervention of a Targum, so that we are justified in coming to the conclusion that, wherever a connection with the Hebrew appears, this has not been caused by a direct recourse to the original, but has been

---

13　Let me commend to Dr Roberts more especially E. Deutsch's *Literary Remains of the late Emanuel Deutsch: With a Brief Memoir* (London: J. Murray, 1874), p. 328, from which it appears that the Mishnah, which itself dates from about AD 200, contains repeated references not only to oral but to written Targums and these, it is known, came into use very gradually.

brought about through the medium of a Targum'.[14] I merely quote this as the opinion of a scholar unsurpassed in this particular department, and not because I am in a position to check it myself. The coincidences, however, are striking.

But though, as I believe, the more accurate determination of the relation of Greek to Aramaic belongs specially to the Hebraist, the erroneousness of Dr Roberts's theory must, I think, be clear even to the ordinary scholar. There are two passages of Josephus with which it comes into direct and immediate collision. The first seems to have escaped most of the Germans who have dealt with the subject, but did not escape the learned Harmonist Greswell. Speaking of the facilities which he had enjoyed for obtaining a true account of the Jewish war, Josephus says:

> Vespasian also, and Titus, had me kept under a guard, and forced me to attend them continually. At the first I was put into bonds, but was set at liberty afterwards, and sent to accompany Titus, when he came from Alexandria to the siege of Jerusalem; during which time there was nothing done which escaped my knowledge, for what happened in the Roman camp I saw and wrote down carefully, and the reports brought by deserters *I alone understood* (μόνος αὐτὸς συνίην).[15]

I imagine that there can be no real doubt as to the meaning of συνίην. The deserters who were brought in to headquarters spoke Aramaic, hence no one there understood them but Josephus, and we may infer that he was employed to interpret their reports to Titus and his council. No doubt there may be some exaggeration in this. Josephus was not the man to diminish his own self-importance, and Dr Roberts is probably right in saying that there were in the Roman camp many besides himself who understood Aramaic. He seems to mean, however, not so much in the Roman camp as in the immediate *entourage* of Titus. Titus would be glad to make use of him (Josephus), because he combined with a knowledge of the language both general intelligence and a special knowledge of his countrymen. But even if the exaggeration were greater than it is, it is surely a very hasty logic to argue, as Dr Roberts does,[16] that because the statement proves too much, it really proves nothing at all. The inference seems to me absolutely unavoidable that the Jewish

---

14. See K. A. Credner, *Beiträge zur Einleitung in die biblischen Schriften* (2 vols.; Halle: Buchhandlung des Waisenhauses, 1832–38), II, pp. 144-55.

15. *Apion* 1.9.

16. Roberts, *Discussions on the Gospels*, p. 291.

deserters did as a rule speak Aramaic, and not Greek, just as he himself spoke Aramaic and not Greek when he addressed his besieged countrymen.

The other passage is the very well-known one at the end of the *Antiquities*, which should be given entire, in order that the full force of it may be appreciated.

> I am so bold as to say, now that I have completed the task set before me, that no other person either Jew or Greek, with whatever good intentions, would have been able to set forth this history to the Greeks as accurately as I have done. For I am acknowledged by my countrymen to excel them far in our national learning. I also did my best to obtain a knowledge of Greek by practising myself in the grammar, though native habit prevented me from attaining accuracy in its use.[17] For it is not our custom to honour those who learn the languages of many nations, and adorn their discourse with smoothly-turned phrases; because this is considered a common accomplishment, not only to any ordinary free man (ἐλευθέρων τοῖς τυχοῦσι), but also to such servants as care to acquire it; while those only are accounted wise who are well versed in our law, and are skilled in interpreting the meaning of our sacred books. It has thus happened that though many have taken pains to obtain this learning, only two or three have succeeded, and they were not long in being rewarded for their trouble.[18]

The statements of this passage are remarkably definite. A knowledge of Greek was common enough among the middle and lower classes (i.e., the classes that would naturally be engaged in traffic, either with Hellenistic Jews or with foreigners): among the upper classes (except, we should probably have to say, the Herodian court and party) it was rare, and few spoke it correctly; but the idea that Greek was the current language of the country, is contradicted in every line.

I should be quite content to rest the case on these two passages. They are both direct, precise, clear, and positive. And they seem to me to tally

---

17. τὴν δὲ περὶ τὴν προφορὰν ἀκρίβειαν πάτριος ἐκώλυσε συνήθεια. 'Use' seems to be the nearest English word for προφορά, though it is not a very satisfactory rendering. The word covers both oral and written 'production', in the one case 'pronunciation', in the other case 'style'. πάτριος συνήθεια is referred by Dr Roberts (*Discussions on the Gospels*, p. 288, etc.) to the habit of speaking *Greek*, and not Hebrew. It is, however, hardly necessary to point out that Josephus is apologizing for the incorrectness of his Greek, on the ground that the Jews did not encourage the study of *foreign* tongues, of which Greek is obviously the one more especially in his mind.

18. Josephus, *Ant.* 20.11.2.

exactly with the view put forward in these pages, while they alone would be sufficient to overthrow the paradox maintained by Dr Roberts. I have selected these two passages as a simple, plain, and compact way of stating the case, and I think I might safely challenge Dr Roberts to produce anything at all comparable to them on the other side. At the same time I believe the conclusion to which they lead to be in the strictest accordance with the rest of the evidence both literary and historical. So far as I can see at present, Dr Roberts appears to have been misled by a few obvious difficulties to which the history of the time affords an easy solution.

Chapter 8

DID CHRIST SPEAK GREEK?—A REJOINDER[*]

I am sorry that Dr Roberts should think the difference between us greater than I had supposed it to be. It is true that I wished to make as little of it as I could. At the same time I thought the reader would see precisely in what respect the difference seemed capable of being minimized, viz., so far as it related to the purely critical and historical question to what extent and in what proportion Greek and Aramaic respectively were spoken in Palestine at the time of our Lord.

I purposely excluded other considerations, from the fear that they might prevent the question from being decided upon its own merits, and excite a prejudice which it ought to be our object rather to allay. The question is one of fact and evidence, not of feeling; and if feeling is introduced, it is only too apt to make 'the wish father to the thought'.

And yet even here I think Dr Roberts is inclined to overstate his case. Even supposing that the discourses in the Gospels were all originally delivered in Greek, there would still be the most serious difficulties in the way of supposing that we had received an exact transcript of them. But even if we could put these difficulties on one side, it might still be asked whether to insist upon such syllabic exactness was not to attach too much importance to the 'letter'. It is one of the singular excellences of the Gospels that they lose so little by translation. Many most devout and learned men have lived and died quite content with the belief that they were reading a Greek version of words spoken in Aramaic. Nor is the beauty of our own Version destroyed—it is hardly even diminished—by the knowledge that it is not the original. There is more than one passage—such as, 'Consider the lilies, how they grow', and parts of 1 Corinthians 13 and 15—where the English seems even to surpass the

[*]   This chapter originally appeared as W. Sanday, 'Did Christ Speak Greek?—A Rejoinder', *The Expositor* 7 (1878), pp. 368-88. Sanday wrote in response to A. Roberts, 'That Christ Spoke Greek—A Reply', *The Expositor* 7 (1878), pp. 278-95.

Greek. And if the theory which I have upheld be true, there is nothing irreverent in allowing ourselves to think so.

I am obliged to confess that both Dr Roberts's original articles and his reply do not make upon me the impression of a strictly impartial and unprejudiced judgment. Perhaps it was not to be expected that one who has made a particular subject his specialty for years should sit down to consider quite calmly the arguments brought against his own view of it. In such a state of mind any sort of weapon seems good enough that first comes to hand. The main point appears to be that it should deal a ponderous and resounding blow. The real justice and validity of the argument is little considered. A very slender argument goes a long way when it makes for his thesis. A considerable argument is thrust aside, or met by some irrelevant appeal, when it tells against it. And the deficiencies of the argument are made up by peremptory challenges and rhetorical declamation. A hasty reader might easily be misled by these. Confident and emphatic statement, however insecure the foundation on which it rests, is apt to carry with it conviction. Few have the time and patience really to test an argument when it is put before them. And yet, in order to get at the truth, some trouble, I am afraid, will be necessary. I shall be obliged to ask those who take sufficient interest in the question to follow carefully the whole course of it, to place statement and answer side by side, rigorously to sift out all irrelevant matter, and to take the arguments on either side strictly for what they are worth.

I propose to take Dr Roberts's points one by one, not knowingly omitting any, though some are really of very slight importance, and then briefly to review the position of the question. As Dr Roberts, I believe, followed the order of my paper, I shall follow the order of his. At the end perhaps it may be possible to arrange the different items of the evidence a little more according to the weight that ought to attach to them.

1. The first point that Dr. Roberts mentions is one that has a quite insignificant bearing upon the main issue. I observe in a note that Dr Roberts is too ready to infer from the use of the words, Ἕλλην, Ἑλληνίς, that any other language than Greek is excluded. He calls this a 'pretty strong assertion', and adds, 'that people styled "Greeks", and that cities styled "Greek cities", made use of the Greek language, is surely the dictate of common sense'. This is just the kind of argument to draw down cheers from the gallery, but I did not expect it from a scholar like Dr Roberts. Indeed, I think I can safely leave him to answer

himself; for in the sentence immediately preceding that in which he speaks of the 'pretty strong assertion', he states that, 'as every one knows, Greek and Gentile are in the New Testament convertible terms'. 'Greek' is in fact often simply equivalent to Gentile, or non-Jewish. It cannot, therefore, be concluded with certainty that the term necessarily implies the use of the Greek language.[1] The probability is that many of the inhabitants of the cities described by Josephus as Greek were Syrians, who spoke Aramaic themselves, and would not have to 'learn' it at all.

2. I maintain, then, that there is no sufficient proof that the people from Decapolis who were present among the audience of the Sermon on the Mount understood no language but Greek. It makes very little difference if they did understand no other, but even as to this preliminary step no unambiguous evidence is forthcoming. Dr Roberts is very confident as to this portion of his argument. He speaks of the 'linguistic conditions of the cities of Decapolis as really decisive as to the language of the Sermon on the Mount, and therefore decisive as to the whole question at issue'. But this is evidently running on very fast. Dr Roberts himself will hardly deny that if the Decapolitans understood only Greek, some of the Galilean villagers understood only Aramaic. But if so, as I asked in my first paper, why should these be sacrificed to the Decapolitans, any more than the Decapolitans sacrificed to them? Really the premises are quite insufficient to bear out the conclusion. It would be just as easy to argue that the proceedings of an Eisteddfod must be conducted in English, because Englishmen were to be found amongst the audience.

1.   Dr Roberts hardly seems to be aware when the *onus probandi* is on his side and when it is on mine. For instance, he accuses me of 'begging the question' on the point before us. But I was not endeavouring to show (what, indeed, it was not incumbent on me to show) that all the inhabitants of Decapolis actually spoke Aramaic. All I said was that the arguments adduced by Dr Roberts do not suffice to prove that they spoke nothing but Greek. When I maintain a conclusion myself, I shall be quite prepared to prove it positively. In regard to the arguments put forward by Dr Roberts, it is enough for me to disprove them negatively; i.e., to show that the premises do not bear out the conclusion. If I can show on other grounds that the Jews of Palestine spoke in the main Aramaic, it is for Dr Roberts to show that the particular inhabitants of Decapolis who were present at the Sermon on the Mount *cannot* have understood that language. The mere statement of the case within its proper logical form is enough to show how very insufficient Dr Roberts's reasoning is.

3. The same remarks apply to the argument from the presence at the same Sermon of a contingent (we are not told how large) from Tyre and Sidon. Here again Dr Roberts insists, with equal confidence and vigour, first, that the inhabitants of Tyre and Sidon spoke no other language but Greek; and then, as a necessary consequence, that the whole discourse must have been delivered in the Greek language. Neither point can in the least be made good. The inhabitants of Phoenicia doubtless spoke Greek to some extent, but there is no proof that they spoke no other language as well. The old Phoenician language, which was a dialect nearly akin to Hebrew, 'with large elements of Chaldee' (Deutsch), i.e., Aramaic, did not become extinct until the third century AD.[2] Besides, a narrow strip of territory like Phoenicia, with a people much engaged in commercial pursuits, would be sure to be penetrated by the language of its neighbours, whatever that language was. But even were it clear that the particular Phoenicians who joined the crowd that gathered round our Lord spoke nothing but Greek, still many possibilities would intervene before we came to the inference that the Sermon on the Mount itself was delivered in no other tongue.

4. I am next charged with the 'sweeping assertion' that the 'mass of the nation hated all that was Greek'. I had hoped that I had guarded myself sufficiently against sweeping assertions. I fully admitted, not only that Greek was used in Palestine, but that it was largely used. I tried to define amongst what classes this was the case, and to what causes it was due. I was therefore prepared for statements which went to show a considerable prevalence of Greek; but inasmuch as the great rebellion against the Romans was practically a rising against Hellenism in all its forms, I thought myself justified in saying that the 'mass of the nation was hostile to everything Hellenic'.

Dr Roberts admits this in regard to the Greek religion or philosophy: he denies it in regard to the Greek language. But no such distinction can really be drawn. There is direct evidence to the contrary. I quoted an emphatic statement to this effect from Rabbi Akhiba. Dr Roberts himself says that 'the study and employment of the Greek language were formally prohibited during the course of the wars conducted by Vespasian and Titus'. What could more entirely bear out my statement?

---

2. J.J. Kneucker, in D. Schenkel's *Bibel-Lexikon Realwörterbuch zum Handgebrauch fur Geistliche und Gemeindeglieder* (5 vols.; Leipzig: Brockhaus, 1869–75), IV, p. 579 [citing E. Deutsch, *Literary Remains of the late Emanuel Deutsch: With a Brief Memoir* (London: J. Murray, 1874)].

For the war against Vespasian and Titus was only the furious outbreak of passions that had long been gathering. And yet in the very next sentence after making this admission, Dr Roberts reads me a schoolboy's lesson on *the Fallacia a dicto secundum quid ad dictum simpliciter*. I can assure him that it was not needed. Besides the evidence above given, there are the express statements of Josephus in a passage to which we shall have to return presently, and also of Origen, οὐ πάνυ μὲν οὖν Ἰουδαῖοι τὰ Ἑλλήνων φιλολογοῦσι, 'The Jews are not at all given to the study of Greek.'[3]

5. Ewald, it is true, speaks of 'an irruption of Greek culture and art', and again of 'an intrusion of the Greek element by no means limited to Alexandria or other Greek cities, but that spread also speedily and powerfully to Jerusalem, and especially to Samaria'. This is exactly for what I contend. A very considerable 'irruption' or 'intrusion' I not only admitted, but described. But the very words signify that it was not so universal as Dr Roberts would have us believe. We speak of an 'irruption' or 'intrusion' of that which *partially* displaces something else, but not of its *complete* displacement. In like manner we might speak of an 'irruption' or 'intrusion' of French at the Norman conquest, but that did not make French the language of England. Dr Roberts cannot claim the authority of Ewald for his main proposition, that our Lord spoke Greek. But if so, an isolated sentence should not be quoted in support of a conclusion that its author was very far from holding.

6. What was said in regard to the Epistle to the Hebrews I have no hesitation in repeating. Dr Roberts has added nothing to his previous argument, and hardly seems to be aware of its logical weakness. In order for it to hold good, it would be necessary, first, that it should be certain or in a high degree probable that the epistle was written to Palestinian Jews; and, secondly, that it should follow from this that it would not have been written in Greek unless Greek had been the dominant language in Palestine. The two propositions depend upon each other, so that any uncertainty in the first doubly tends to weaken the second. But really both propositions are most uncertain. The ordinary reader naturally supposes that the title 'to the Hebrews' must mean to the Jews of Palestine. The instructed reader knows far differently. Without going into the argument as to the address of the epistle, a brief and simple

---

3   *Contra Celsum* 2.34. Dr Roberts is welcome to amend the translation as he pleases. It is not easy to give the exact force of φιλολογοῦσι and at the same time to leave τὰ Ἑλλήνων as open as it is in the original.

proof that no stress can be laid on it for Dr Roberts's purpose is to be seen in the list of critics who assign to it another destination than Judaea. The following suppose that it was intended for the Jews of Alexandria: Schmidt, Ullmann, Schleiermacher, Schneckenburger, Köstlin, Credner, Ritschl, Reuss, Volkmar, Hilgenfeld, Bunsen, and Wieseler, who has argued the point in much detail. Nicolas de Lyra held that it was addressed to Spain; Bengel, Schmid, and Cramer, to Pontus, Galatia, Cappadocia, Bithynia, and Asia; Wall and Wolf to Asia Minor, Macedonia, and Greece; Semler and Nösselt to Thessalonica; Storr and Mynster to Galatia; Baumgarten-Crusius and Röth to Ephesus; Stein to Laodicea; Böhme to Antioch; Michael Weber, Mack, and Tobler to Corinth; Credner (at an earlier date) to Lycaonia; Ewald to Italy; Wettstein, Alford, and recently Holtzmann to Rome. Such discordance of opinion is proof enough in itself that the address of the epistle to the Jews of Jerusalem cannot be taken for granted. Nor, if it could, as I think I have shown, would it really prove anything in favour of the thesis Dr Roberts is maintaining. The author of the epistle may just as well have written to the Jews in Greek, though their 'proper tongue' (Acts 1.19) was Aramaic, as the Apostle Paul writes in Greek to the Church at Rome.

7. I have no wish to deny that Peter occasionally, and perhaps even frequently, spoke Greek, though the narrative of the betrayal seems to prove that his native and natural dialect was the Galilean Aramaic. My chief object in pointing to his connection with Mark was to show how many possibilities intervene between the premises and conclusion of Dr Roberts. Nor is the suggestion that Mark (or someone else) may have had a share in the composition of his epistle a hypothesis so 'totally gratuitous' as Dr Roberts seems to suppose. I stated my reasons for making it, and I do not think that Dr Roberts should have applied to it such an epithet without attempting to answer those reasons. They were, first, the frequency of the practice of using amanuenses; and, secondly, the express statement of Papias, Irenaeus, and Tertullian, that Mark acted as the interpreter of Peter. I may add to this the apparent necessity of some such assumption if both the epistles attributed to Peter are to be considered genuine. Nor is it any argument at all against this that in the Epistle to the Romans the amanuensis, Tertius, sends a greeting to the church in his own name. The First Epistle to the Corinthians, Galatians, and the Second to Thessalonians, were certainly written by amanuenses, and yet in none of these is there any distinct greeting. But the point has

really the very slightest bearing on the subject before us. I should not have mentioned it if Dr Roberts had not done so.

8. It is otherwise with the next paragraph of Dr Roberts's reply. Here we are taken up to what is really the main question at issue. Nor have I so much to object to in the first half at least of Dr Roberts's statement. It only illustrates what I said, that the difference between us as to the extent to which Greek and Aramaic were spoken in Palestine is not really so very great. Dr Roberts admits that Aramaic was the vernacular tongue. He says: 'Aramaic might still be said, though with difficulty, and amid many exceptions, to maintain its position as the mother tongue of the inhabitants of the country'. I should only be inclined to strike out here the words 'with difficulty'. Considering that forty years later every inhabitant of Palestine was, by Dr Roberts's own showing, expected to speak it, and that the rival language Greek was entirely prohibited, I do not think we can say that it maintained itself 'with difficulty'. The encroachments of Greek upon it did not amount to so much as this. At the same time I am quite ready to allow that there were 'many'—or at least not a few—exceptions.

The strangest thing appears to be that Dr Roberts should think it possible to make this admission and yet to maintain that our Lord habitually spoke Greek. We know that he addressed his teaching especially to the poor. Our own version tells us that 'the common people heard him gladly', and though this is a paraphrase rather than a translation of ὁ πολὺς ὄχλος, 'the great multitude', it does not really misrepresent its meaning. Dr Roberts, I suppose, would not question this. But if so, it is to me quite incredible—and I ask if it is not to every one else—that our Lord should have preached the gospel to the people in any other language than their own vernacular. If he had done so, can we believe that it would have had the effect it had? Let us transfer ourselves to modern times. Suppose some great evangelist were to arise in Wales: is it not absolutely certain that he would preach in Welsh? Dr Roberts quoted the case of the Scotch Highlands. He says: 'Celtic may be said to be the vernacular tongue of many Scottish Highlanders, who yet scarcely ever hear it on public occasions. Gaelic may be said to be their mother-tongue, but the language which they read in books, and what they listen to in public, is English.' I do not know how this may be. Dr Roberts ought to be a better authority on the subject than I am. Yet my own experience has not been quite what he describes. I once spent a Sunday at Balmacarra, opposite the coast of Skye. We went to the nearest Scottish kirk, and I distinctly remember that though there was a service in English it was preceded by one in Gaelic, and, as we might naturally expect, the Gaelic service was evidently the more popular. One is more familiar with the condition of things in Wales, and I put it with confidence to my readers whether a preacher who sought to obtain a real hold upon the people could possibly address them in anything but Welsh? Has not this been notoriously the cause of the want of success of the clergy of the Established Church? English is, it is true, the language of notice-boards, of the hustings, the language even of books, but it fails to touch the finer chords of religious feeling.

9. Dr Roberts proceeds in a somewhat peremptory manner to demand some reason for the occurrence of Aramaic expressions in the Gospels. It is superfluous to give him this, because even he cannot maintain, after what has been said in the last paragraph, that the few fragmentary phrases embedded in the Gospels are all that our Lord really spoke in Aramaic; and if that is the case it is as much for him to say why there are so few as for me to say why there are no more. It is always a precarious matter assigning motives to persons far removed from ourselves in time and circumstance, but I suppose the reasons would be somewhat similar to those which might lead to the insertion of a few French phrases here and there in an English story the scene of which was laid in France. (a) Some of the phrases, like *Ephphatha*, *Talitha cumi*, are single short emphatic sayings, which produced an instantaneous miraculous effect, and they are therefore retained for the sake of graphic realistic presentation. It is to be observed that both these phrases occur in the graphic Evangelist, Mark. (b) Words like *Rabboni* (in Mk 10.51, Jn 20.16, which is insisted upon by Dr Roberts) are introduced for the sake of the touch of reverential and tender regard which was not conveyed by the cold διδάσκαλε of the Greek. The word is not translated, and the Evangelist says (in effect) that he does not translate it because it is untranslatable.

10. I do not care to lay very much stress on the next point, the statement that *Aceldama* in Acts 1.19 belongs to the 'proper tongue' of Jerusalem, though Dr Roberts's treatment of it is entirely beside the mark. The argument from authority is out of place where as many or more authorities can be quoted on the other side. Besides, it is hardly ingenuous to leave it to be inferred that I am going against authority when the 'majority' of commentators are really on my side. I do not rest my case on authority, but I used certain definite arguments to which

Dr Roberts has given no answer. The main point, however, I suppose I may take for granted, that the 'proper dialect' of Jerusalem was Aramaic. At the same time I admit that the passage is not decisive, because it tells us nothing about the proportions in which the two languages were spoken.

11. I postpone for a moment what I have to say on the subject of Talmud and Targum, and come to Josephus. Dr Roberts thinks it unfair in me to attach so much weight as I do to this writer, 'since we have in the New Testament itself no fewer than eight different authors of the period, who ought all to have a voice in determining the matter'. I need hardly say that I was not measuring the evidence by quantity. My only reason for attaching importance to Josephus was that his evidence is direct and definite, while that which is gathered by inference from the New Testament is not. The point of the *relative* extent of Greek and Aramaic is a nice one, and more difficult to prove with any precision than Dr Roberts seems to think. My belief is not in the least degree shaken that Josephus affords the best, and indeed conclusive, evidence upon the subject.

Dr Roberts quotes as a set-off against the two passages adduced by me, a third, which I venture to think tells so far as it goes in the same direction. Josephus tells us that he wrote his *History of the Jewish War* originally in 'his native tongue', and afterwards translated it into Greek. The Aramaic version he sent to the 'barbarians of the interior', i.e., probably in the first instance to the Jews of Babylonia and the East. The Greek version, he says, was destined for 'those who lived under the government of the Romans'. There is nothing to show that he meant by this the remnant that still remained in devastated Judaea. The last persons who would need the history would be those who had been the foremost actors in it. He meant rather the whole body of Hellenistic Jews, of whom there were a million in Alexandria alone. Besides these, he had in view, as he himself says,[4] the Roman court and the educated Roman world generally. No argument at all can be drawn from the address of the work; but, on the other hand, there is some slight weight in the expression which Josephus uses to describe the Aramaic in which he wrote. He calls it distinctly 'his native tongue' (πάτριος γλῶσσα), and though I do not suppose that Dr Roberts would question the epithet, it falls in well with the description in the next passage that I am going to touch upon.

4.   *Life* 65.

It is quite true that I laid stress on the concluding chapter of the *Antiquities*. I thought it, and I think it still, the clearest piece of evidence that can be produced. Dr Roberts seeks to turn the edge of it by confronting with the conclusions which I draw from it two statements by Grinfield and by Renan. I infer that 'a knowledge of Greek was common enough among the middle and lower classes'. Grinfield would confine it 'chiefly to the upper orders', and Renan uses similar language. I was simply paraphrasing the language of Josephus: διὰ τὸ κοινὸν εἶναι νομίζειν τὸ ἐπιτήδευμα τοῦτο οὐ μόνον ἐλευθέρων τοῖς τυχοῦσιν ἀλλὰ καὶ τῶν οἰκετῶν τοῖς θέλουσι. It is for the reader to say whether the paraphrase is a just one. But in any case, the fact that Grinfield and Renan seem to have overlooked this passage does not affect my argument in the least. To reconcile their statements with the language of Josephus is their concern. But to introduce such conflicting statements in an answer to me is something more than irrelevant: it is an *argumentum ad invidiam*, which ought to be excluded from a controversy conducted on the terms that I hope this is.

The point of what I allege is that Josephus speaks of Greek throughout as a foreign and 'intrusive' tongue, which might be easily acquired, and was acquired to a considerable extent among the classes that I named; but nothing can be more opposed to his views than the supposition that it was habitually in use, as superseding the language of the country. Such a supposition is, as I said, 'contradicted in every line', and Dr Roberts has brought nothing to show that it is not.

The same applies to the next passage adduced by me. The answer—if it is intended for an answer—that Dr Roberts gives to this flies wide of the mark altogether. Josephus says that he alone understood the Aramaic of the deserters who came into the Roman camp. I explain this by saying that Josephus means himself alone of the immediate *entourage* of Titus, and that there may be in it some little exaggeration. On that explanation there would be no contradiction of importance to any other portions of the narrative.[5] But however gross the exaggeration may be, it is still an exaggeration of the statement that he (Josephus) alone

5.   Of the two passages which Dr Roberts quotes in proof that others in the Roman army besides Josephus understood the speech of the Jews—in one (*War* 4.1.5) it is expressly stated that the party which overheard a conversation in a Jewish house understood what was said '*because they were Syrians*' (i.e., because they spoke Aramaic themselves); in the second, a single Jew addresses Titus—very possibly in Greek.

understood the reports of the deserters. This must have been because
they were in Aramaic. Greek every one would have understood.
Aramaic would only be understood by a few Syrians. Dr Roberts does
not meet this inference in the least. He says: 'Either another meaning
than "understood" must be given to συνίην, or the passage must be
regarded as one of many in which Josephus seeks, at the expense of
perfect truthfulness, to magnify his own importance'. The suggestion
that another meaning should be given to συνίην may, I think, be left to
itself, as the meaning of the word is perfectly plain. The rest of the
sentence leads nowhere. Suppose we grant all that is asked for, that
Josephus does 'seek to magnify his own importance': what then? Unless
his statement is absolutely and glaringly false, whether he alone
understood the deserters, or some few, or even many understood them
besides, still they must have spoken Aramaic, and not Greek.

Such are the answers that Dr Roberts has given to arguments that he
describes as 'flimsy'. I leave it for the reader to decide whether they are
'flimsy' or not, but I must also ask the reader to decide as to the way in
which they have been met.

12. The last point upon which I shall touch is the evidence of the
Talmud and Targums. I did not enter into this before for reasons which I
gave. At the same time I expressed my opinion that it was precisely in
this direction that a really full and scientific treatment of the subject
ought to be sought. I quoted from Credner some minute but very sound
and accurate reasoning in favour of the use of a Targum by the first
Evangelist, which Dr Roberts meets with his own subjective opinion,
that when our Lord said 'Search the scriptures', he cannot have referred
to an Aramaic translation.[6] He adds further, that of these Aramaic
translations, or Targums, 'we hear nothing in Jewish or patristic
antiquity'; and again he speaks of 'those Aramaic Targums which have
so often, without the least ground of evidence, been conjured into
existence'.

I do not know how to characterize a statement like this with due
regard to the moderation which I have wished to observe. It certainly
seems to reckon upon an amount of ignorance which I should hope is
not to be found amongst the readers of *The Expositor*. We have only to
take up the first standard authority on the subject. I gave a reference in

---

6.   I doubt if the reference in these words is to a translation at all. They would be
directed, in the first instance, to the scribes and lawyers, the authorized exponents of
the Law, whose duty it was to study it in the original.

my previous paper to Deutsch's *Literary Remains*. As this has passed unnoticed, I now write it out in full. After giving an account of the gradual substitution of Aramaic for the ancient Hebrew after the Captivity, Mr Deutsch proceeds to trace the origin and growth of Targums.

If the common people thus gradually had lost all knowledge of the tongue in which were written the books to be read to them, it naturally followed (in order 'that they might understand them') that recourse must be had to a translation into the idiom with which they were familiar—the Aramaic. That further, since a bare translation could not in all cases suffice, it was necessary to add to the translation an explanation, more particularly of the more difficult and obscure passages. Both translation and explanation were designated by the term *Targum*. In the course of time there sprang up a guild, whose special office it was to act as *interpreters* in both senses (*Meturgeman*), while formerly the learned alone volunteered their services. These interpreters were subjected to certain bonds and regulations, as to the form and substance of their rendering. Thus (comp. Mishnah Meg. *passim*; Mass. Sofer. xi.1; Maimon. Hilch. Tephill. xii. § 11ff.; Orach Chaj. 145, 1, 2), 'neither the reader nor the interpreter are to raise their voices one above the other';... 'the Meturgeman is not to lean against a pillar or a beam, but to stand with fear and with reverence'; '*he is not to use a written Targum*, but is to deliver his translation *vivâ voce*', lest it might appear that he was reading out of the Torah itself, and thus the Scriptures be held responsible for what are his own dicta; 'no more than one verse in the Pentateuch and three in the Prophets shall be read and translated at a time'. Again (Mishnah Meg. and Tosifta *ad loc.*), certain passages liable to give offence to the multitude are specified which may be read in the synagogue and translated; others, which may be read, but not translated; others, again, which may neither be read nor translated... The same cause which in the course of time led to the writing down—after many centuries of oral transmission—of the whole body of the traditional Law,... engendered also, and about the same period as it would appear, written Targums, for certain portions of the Bible at least. The fear of the adulterations and mutilations which the Divine Word—amid the troubles within and without the commonwealth—must undergo at the hands of incompetent or impious exponents, broke through the rule that the Targums should only be oral, lest it might acquire undue authority (comp. Mishnah Meg. iv. 5, 10; Tosifta, *ib.* 3; Jer. Meg. 4, 1; Bab. Meg. 24 *a*; Sota 39 *b*). Thus a Targum of Job is mentioned (Sab. 115 a; Tr. Soferim, 5, 15; Tosifta Sab. c. 14; Jer. Sab. 16, 1) as having been highly disapproved by Gamaliel the Elder (middle of first century AD), and he caused it to be hidden and buried out of sight. We find, on the other hand, at the end of the second century, the practice of reading the Targum generally commended, and somewhat later Jehoshua Ben Levi enjoins it as a special duty upon his sons. The Mishnah even contains regulations about the manner (Jad. iv. 5) in which the Targum is to be written.[7]

The vague and indiscriminating censures which Dr Roberts passes upon the Talmud in his larger work[8] are not the slightest answer to definite and coherent statements such as these. Granting that some of the evidence made use of by Mr Deutsch is comparatively late, much of it is drawn from the Mishnah itself, which dates from about 200 AD, and was then only the codifying of a much older oral tradition. If Dr Roberts wishes to continue this controversy, it would be instructive to know what are his views on this matter. And I would ask that the discussion of it might be really to the point, and not consist in a few selected quotations which were written without any reference to the question at issue.

I have thus taken up in all twelve different points: (1) The linguistic inference from the use of the word 'Greek'; (2) the argument from the presence of people from Decapolis at the Sermon on the Mount; (3) the like argument from the presence of people from Tyre and Sidon; (4) the relation of the Jews to the Greek language; (5) the special statement of Ewald as to the 'intrusion' of Greek into Palestine; (6) the Epistle to the Hebrews; (7) the Apostle Peter; (8) the Galilean dialect; (9) Aramaic expressions in the Gospels; (10) Aceldama; (11) Josephus; (12) Talmud and Targums.

Of these, I do not care to press 10, though, as far as it goes, it is in my favour. Neither is much to be gathered either way from 7 and 9. On 1 and 2 (which should be taken together), 3 and 6, Dr Roberts's premises are doubtful, and, if they were certain, the conclusion would not follow from them. 5, which is quoted against, tells really for the view which I have maintained. On 4 and 12 the existence of evidence is denied where clear and definite evidence has been produced. On 8 a conclusion follows from Dr Roberts's own admissions which is fatal to his theory and which he has done nothing to remove. It remains as decisive against him as it was, the answer given being quite irrelevant.

Apart from the positive evidence which has been adduced in support of the opposite conclusion, Dr Roberts himself has made admissions

---

7.   Deutsch, *Literary Remains*, pp. 324-28.

8.   A. Roberts, *Discussions on the Gospels: In Two Parts: Part I: On the Language Employed by Our Lord and Disciples: Part II: On the Original Language of St Matthew's Gospel, and on the Origin and Authenticity of the Gospels* (Cambridge: Macmillan, 2nd edn, 1864), p. 297.

which are enough to prove that his own position is untenable. He admits that Aramaic was the 'vernacular language' of Palestine. He admits that in the wars of Vespasian and Titus 'the study and employment of the Greek language were formally prohibited'. From the first admission it follows that our Lord must have taught, for the most part, in Aramaic. From the second admission it follows that Greek cannot have been, in the generation before the Jewish wars, the dominant tongue.

I have been much disappointed with Dr Roberts's reply. I expected at least to have the subject treated in a scholarly and critical manner, and I have seldom read anything less critical. By 'critical' I mean exact in definition, cautious in statement, strictly relevant and logical in reasoning. I have met with many rough-and-ready arguments that are such as an advocate might urge before a popular jury; I have hardly met with one that would carry weight with a scholar who took the trouble to give it a few moments' consideration. Anything like a judicious and impartial weighing of objections is very far to seek. I do not know what the readers of *The Expositor* may think, but Dr Roberts has lost at least one convert who might easily have been made if the case would have admitted it. I am now more convinced than I was before that he is spending his powers on a quite untenable cause.

Chapter 9

GREEK INFLUENCE ON CHRISTIANITY[*]

The world knows what it has lost in Dr Hatch. It is needless now to lay stress on his wide learning, his breadth of view, the freshness and independence which he brought to bear on every subject which he took up, his thorough scientific method, and his remarkable powers of clear and forcible exposition. If any one of the many German specialists were asked who were our foremost writers on early Ecclesiastical History, he would probably name Dr Hatch, Mr Gwatkin, and Bishop Lightfoot; and, regarding Bishop Lightfoot rather as a masterly editor of patristic texts than as a historian strictly so-called, he would be pretty sure to give the first place to Dr Hatch. I do not say that the list would be exhaustive; we should ourselves have some important additions to make to it; still, we may take it as representing a standard in some respects more objective than our own.

Dr Hatch died in the full height of his powers. A life spent in the laborious amassing of evidence under circumstances of great struggle and difficulty was just reaching its maturity. For about a decade he was allowed to draw from the stores of his knowledge, and he was still far from having come to the end. As Dr Fairbairn truly says in his preface to the present volume: 'Those of us who knew him know how little a book like this expresses his whole mind, or represents all that in this field he had it in him to do'. It could not be otherwise with a writer whose studies had been so thorough: a single book could not contain all that he had to say. Place the Hibbert by the side of the Bampton Lectures, and the small extent to which they touch each other, although covering

 *   This review and appreciation of E. Hatch, *The Influence of Greek Ideas and Usages upon the Christian Church* (Hibbert Lectures, 1888; ed. A.M. Fairbairn; London: Williams & Norgate, 1890), who was Reader in Ecclesiastical History in the University of Oxford, originally appeared as W. Sanday, 'Greek Influence on Christianity', *The Contemporary Review* 59 (1891), pp. 678-90.

much the same period, will give some indication of the author's range. It cannot be said that the later book shows any falling off. Published as it is at great disadvantage, posthumously, and, as the preface will explain, in part from very rough and imperfect notes, it will yet stand out as one of the leading books, not only of its *lustrum* but of its century. It has missed the revising hand of its author, but, thanks to the faithful labours of Dr Fairbairn and his helper, Mr Vernon Bartlet, the rough edges and the gaps are far less noticeable than might have been expected. We owe them a debt of gratitude that the book appears at all.

It is not then from any want of characteristic excellence if the 'Hibbert Lectures' fail, as in some quarters, at least, I fear they may, to meet with due recognition. There is an inherent fault in English criticism and in the opinion which that criticism helps to form. It is one of our strong points that we have in this country a great amount of curiosity in matters theological, but it is a curiosity which is easily satisfied. The public interested in religious conceptions is large, but it has not the time or the necessary qualifications to examine into them closely for itself. It is anxious to appropriate results rather than processes, and therefore it is apt to inquire concerning any book which is set before it, what are its *tendencies*, without caring so much to know what it *is*.

The student whose object is knowledge goes the reverse way to work. His opinions are his own; he cannot take them from any one; what he needs is accurate and well assorted data on which to build his conclusions. Tendencies count for little with him. The balance of an argument is easily altered. He will have some principle that he has won for himself, to which new facts will be assimilated. His first care is to digest these new facts and work them into the substance of his mind.

It will make a considerable difference from which of these two sides the Hibbert Lectures are approached. The book is one which, if it is approached controversially, may easily lend itself to controversy. In the days which now seem to be happily fast dying out, its opening page would have been enough to excite prejudice against it. We are coming on all hands to a more reasonable temper; still, the prejudice needs to be guarded against; resolute justice must be done.

For the better doing of such justice, I purpose to keep well apart the two sets of questions which the book raises. I purpose to ask first, What does the book contribute to theological knowledge? before I touch upon the further question, In what direction does it tend? Not because I think that there is any reason to evade the question of tendency, but because I wish to put in its proper place, and present in its proper order, the material of great and solid value which the book contains.

Dr Hatch starts, as I have said, with a statement of his problem which may well put some of his readers on the defensive. He points to the wide difference between the Sermon on the Mount and the Nicene Creed— the one laying stress upon conduct, the other on belief; the one dealing with questions of ethics, the other of metaphysics; the one a sermon, the other a creed. He asks how this difference came about; and he observes that it coincides with a change of soil—the transference of the centre of gravity of the Christian faith from Palestine to Greece.

It may be objected, and I think rightly objected, that this is too absolute a way of putting it; that it makes the antithesis greater than it really is. Even the Sermon on the Mount implies a theology; but the Sermon on the Mount is not the whole of primitive Christianity; it belongs to an early stage of Christ's teaching; it touches only incidentally on those questions which could not help arising as to the nature and person of Christ himself. These questions, when once put, required an answer, and could not be simply ignored.

It seems to me, therefore, that the Sermon on the Mount and the Nicene Creed are not, strictly speaking, alternatives to each other; and they can only be presented as such by leaving out of sight the links by which they are connected. At the same time, Dr Hatch's way of stating the case has the merit, which is indeed conspicuous at every step in his argument, of propounding the thesis which he seeks to prove with the utmost possible clearness.

He seeks to trace the process by which Greek ideas and Greek usages gradually effected a lodgment in Christianity; and he chooses for his inquiry the most critical period in that process—the period which extends from the first century to the fourth, with the Sermon on the Mount at the beginning, and the Nicene Creed at the end.

The first thing to be done is to lay down the method of the inquiry. And we may note, in passing, how congenial discussions of method always seem to be to Dr Hatch's mind. He marshals his forces like a commander-in-chief, with something of the pomp and pageantry of the parade-ground.

The peculiarity of the evidence is that 'it is ample in regard to the causes, and ample also in regard to the effects, but scanty in regard to the process of change'. The characteristics of Greek thought may be collected readily enough from writers like Dio Chrysostom, Epictetus,

Plutarch, Maximus of Tyre, Marcus Aurelius, Lucian, Sextus Empiricus, Philostratus; and to this list Dr Hatch adds Philo of Alexandria, with a remark which the historian may be glad to note, that 'several of the works which are gathered together under his name seem to belong to a generation subsequent to his own, and to be the only survivors of the Judaeo-Greek schools which lasted on in the great cities of the empire until the verge of Christian times'. The immediate tendency of research, thanks especially to the labours of the French scholar, Massebieau, is rather in a direction opposite to this, to vindicate for Philo himself treatises which had been adjudged away from him. This, however, is one of the problems which the criticism of the near future will have to settle.

The *terminus ad quem* of Christian doctrine is equally well-marked by the Fathers of the fourth century. It is the intermediate process for which the evidence is most defective. In the outline that is given of this there are again two *obiter dicta* which are worth recording. One is an illustration of the chances by which portions of this early literature have come down to us: that whereas Tertullian (*adv. Valentin.* 5) speaks of four writers of the previous generation as standing on an equal footing, Justin, Miltiades, Irenaeus, and Proculus, 'of these Proculus has entirely perished; of Miltiades only a few fragments remain; Justin survives in only a single MS, and the greater part of Irenaeus remains only in a Latin translation'. The other is, the opinion that Asia, for which we have but the scanty fragments of Melito and Gregory of Neo-Caesarea, 'seems to have been the chief crucible in the alchemy of transmutation'. At first sight this appears to be a questionable proposition in view of the wide-reaching influence of Origen, the practical importance for Church organisation of Cyprian, and the germs which began to show themselves in the third century of the school of Antioch. It is, however, perhaps justified by the central and epoch-making significance of Irenaeus, and by the prominent part played by Asia Minor in raising Marcion, and in first raising and then putting down Montanism. The extant evidence, scattered as it is, shows us the churches of Asia Minor as a focus of great activity in the last quarter of the second century; and nowhere did Christianity make such rapid progress.

Foremost among the influences which Dr Hatch discusses is that of education. He reminds us that the Roman world into which Christianity entered was a highly educated world. The system of this education is described with admirable conciseness and lucidity. The description was the easier, because the Graeco-Roman education was the direct and lineal ancestor of our own. Even more exclusively than ours it was concerned with language. The forms which it took were grammar, rhetoric, and philosophy. Grammar was, in a larger sense than that in which we use the word, the study of literature. It aimed at correctness of diction. It dealt with the subject-matter, the antiquities, and criticism of ancient authors. Rhetoric was an extension of grammar. The professor of rhetoric read extracts from classical writers, with comments upon their style. He delivered model compositions of his own, or corrected those of his pupils. His method largely consisted of the 'lecture'. The 'lecture', too, was employed in the teaching of philosophy. Reasoning was taught; dialectics were practised; the writings of the philosophers were analysed, interpreted, criticised. Philosophy had come to be taken very much at second-hand. This led, no doubt, to a certain reaction. The higher minds, like Epictetus, saw and insisted upon the necessity of combining philosophy with practice.

Still more like our own was the machinery of this elaborate system. Almost every town had its 'grammar-school'. Not only Rome and Athens and Alexandria, but many other provincial centres, had what might be called their 'universities', which even in the fourth century were still the training grounds of Christian teachers—Basil, Gregory Nazianzen, Jerome, Augustine.

The endowment of the teachers of rhetoric dates back from Vespasian. Many were freely subsidised by Hadrian and Antoninus Pius. Marcus Aurelius founded regular chairs at Athens. It was formally enacted by Antoninus Pius that smaller cities might place upon their free list (free that is from the municipal burdens which weighed so heavily upon the wealthier classes) five physicians, three teachers of rhetoric, and three of literature, and so in an ascending scale up to ten physicians, and five teachers each of rhetoric and literature. Teaching thus became a recognised profession, and not only so, but a highly-fashionable profession, the descriptions of which often read like those of the 'chaplains' of the last century.

The inevitable consequence followed. Rhetoric and philosophy alike became artificial; and this artificial character they communicated to Christianity. If we compare the 'prophesying' of the first century with the 'preaching' of the fourth, it is the sophistical element in it which strikes us. Greek rhetoric created the Christian sermon. The applause of the congregation was like the applause of the lecture-room; and even more mercenary motives had their weight. One Syrian bishop,

Antiochus of Ptolemais, goes to Constantinople, and makes money by preaching, and another, Severianus of Gabala is incited to follow his example.

In a deeper way the methods current in the Greek schools affected Christian teaching. The philosophy of the day was characterised by the use of allegory. This arose in the process of adapting the thought of one age to the purposes and standard of another. The great text-book of Greek education was Homer; but as the old mythologies began to be criticised, and as a more comprehensive view began to be taken of the universe, the Homeric stories could no longer be taken literally as they stood. Recourse was had to allegory, which was largely employed, especially by the Stoics. From the Stoics it passed over to the Alexandrian Jews and pre-eminently to Philo, who found the method as useful for removing the difficulties of the Pentateuch as the Greeks had found it for modernising Homer. It became the established method for dealing with the Old Testament. The Gnostics and the great Alexandrian teachers went further, and applied it to the New. Yet the use of allegory was not admitted without a protest from more quarters than one. The Christian apologists saw in it only a gloss over the immoralities of the old mythology. The pagan philosophers, Porphyry and Celsus, questioned it in its application to Christianity. A firm stand was made against it in some Christian circles. Even at Alexandria it had an opponent in Nepos of Arsinoe, and the rejection of allegory was at first the central feature in the rival school of Antioch.

Allegory was one of the most important links through which Christianity was brought into contact with Greek philosophy. The fact of this ever-growing contact is the great phenomenon of the first two centuries of Christian history. It is in delineating the course and effects of this gradual approximation that Dr Hatch puts forth all his strength. His mind had a natural bent for the handling of ideas; and the combined firmness and precision with which the outlines of his picture are drawn will, we may be sure, rank high among the specimens of philosophical writing.

Just one deduction must, I think, be made. In such an intricate field, it is exceedingly difficult to have the eye everywhere at once; and I seem to myself to see in these chapters, admirable as they are, a certain preponderance of the abstract over the historical. To do perfect justice to both at once would have been indeed a feat; and it is little to say that it has not been accomplished. But if I mistake not, Dr Hatch is at his best in treating of ideas and their logical co-ordination rather than in tracing the subtler play of their embodiment in historic persons: he seems more sure of his ground in describing the essential affinities of ideas in themselves than in either fixing the order of their chronological succession or in defining the channels through which they were transmitted.

I may be wrong, but this is the impression made upon me by the opening chapter, Lecture 5, which takes a survey of the general relations of Christianity and Greek Philosophy. This, too, is ably written. The fact that the one exercised so large an influence upon the other is referred, I have no doubt, to the right cause—a real kinship and mutual attraction between them. The nature of the compromise which resulted is also, I think, well described. The features in which the Greek mind left its impress upon the subsequent history of Christianity are seen in the tendency to define, the tendency to speculate—'to draw inferences from definitions, to weave the inferences into systems, and to test assertions by their logical consistency or inconsistency with these systems'—and lastly, in the importance attached to these intellectual processes, which were elevated into conditions of Christian union.

There is nothing here to question; but the points which are left for the future philosophic historian seem to me to be (1) the exact extent of the inherent kinship between Christianity and Greek Philosophy—how far the Hellenic or Hellenistic element entered into the substance of New Testament teaching, and received the sanction of Christ and the apostles; and (2) by what steps and in what proportions Greek Philosophy on its side met Christianity in the persons of the Christian teachers of the second century. Fully to work out all this no doubt lay beyond the scope of a course of twelve lectures.

The mutual attraction of Greek and Christian thought and endeavour is next traced (Lecture 6) in the sphere of ethics. Here again there were converging lines. The old idea of the absolute decadence and depravity of the first and second centuries is naturally discarded. Dr Hatch, after Friedländer—not perhaps without a certain swing of the pendulum in the opposite direction to that which used ordinarily to be taken—lays stress on the exaggeration to which the evidence for this supposed extreme depravity is subject, and on the counter-evidence of a gradually increasing effort after reformation of life and manners in pagan society put forth chiefly by the Stoics, and culminating in the teaching of Epictetus and Marcus Aurelius. Dr Hatch had made a special study of

Epictetus; and his own reading enabled him to draw a very noble picture of the Stoicism which he represented. The effort after reformation came to be more and more directed towards conduct; the necessity of self-discipline was more and more insisted upon, and more and more systematically undertaken; and in the hands of men like Epictetus philosophy had more and more the tendency to rise into religion.

A movement such as this met Christianity half way, and no doubt contributed to its early successes. Yet there was difference as well as agreement between Christianity and Stoicism—the great difference being that what with Stoicism was failure, with Christianity was sin. At first the Christian communities had for their most marked characteristic the strenuous endeavour after purity of life. This was sought to be attained by rigorous discipline, but as the societies enlarged the discipline broke down. The Puritan party fought hard to retain it, but the result was their own expulsion. Twice again they returned to the charge—first in the form of Novatianism, afterwards in that of Donatism. But the main body of the Church acquiesced in the change. Nor were they content to take this lower ground in practice. The mixed composition of the Church was elevated into a theory: it was the net which gathered alike of bad and good.

Meanwhile, the ascetic spirit found an outlet in another direction. It concentrated itself upon the rise of Monasticism. The monastic system tended to form a Church within the Church. There was one code of morals for the Monk and another for the ordinary Christian. Thus the raising of the moral ideal for one part of the Church was compensated by its lowering for another. The conception of a layman's duty fell back to the level of Stoicism. Ambrose took his ideas of lay morality from Cicero; and the book in which he did this became the basis of the moral philosophy of the Middle Ages. At the same time, the Stoical lawyers drew up a system of personal rights which also reacted strongly upon moral conceptions; so that the foundation on which modern society rests might be said to be Stoical rather than Christian.

The three chapters which follow (Lectures 7–9) are, I am inclined to think, the most valuable in the whole book. I describe them thus because of the difficulty of the subject-matter with which they deal, and the conspicuous success with which that difficulty is grappled with. There is no part of the ground on which we are more glad to have the help of one who, both by natural gifts and preliminary studies, was so well able to furnish it.

The chapters deal with the highest conceptions of Christian theology, under the three heads: (1) God as Creator; (2) God as the Moral Governor; (3) God as the Supreme Being. It would have been hardly possible to indicate their contents but for the circumstance that so many of the threads of Greek and Christian thought which are here unravelled are found to draw together and unite in a single conception, the doctrine of the Logos or Divine Word. I doubt if so masterly an analysis of this doctrine, both as to its antecedents in the Pagan schools and as to all but its earliest stages in the Christian conception has ever been given. No more striking example exists of the way in which Pagan and Christian thought converged upon the same point. It might well seem a special providence which put into the band of the Christian thinker so effective a key for the solution of his hardest problems; and we cannot be surprised at the promptitude with which he availed himself of it, or at the tenacity with which he clung to it as the axis of his whole system. Two main questions were exercising the thoughts of men in the early Christian century: one cosmological, How could God come in contact with matter? The other metaphysical, How can a transcendent God know and be known? The course of development by which these questions came to be so pressing is traced by Dr Hatch with great skill; but in this we have not space to follow him. Suffice it to say summarily that just as the syncretistic philosophy of the day was coming to seek the solution of both in the idea of a Divine Logos (sometimes by the Stoics distributed in a plurality of *logoi*), the Christian, too, found himself supplied with an answer identical in form, and not widely removed in substance, which had the further and immense advantage of accounting theologically for that Divine manifestation, or 'economy' as it was called, from which he took his name. For this solution he had not far to go; it was put into his hands by the Fourth Gospel.[1] The difference between the two conceptions was that the Logos of the Stoics was impersonal, the Christian Logos personal. But that was no insuperable barrier, especially where the Christian presented Christ along with it. No wonder, then, that Christianity gained the philosophers, and that the two streams of thought coalesced and flowed together.

In considering the character of God as Moral Governor there was perhaps a deeper cleft between the Greek and Christian conceptions at

---

1.   For the supplying of this link I am responsible. Dr Hatch only once refers to the influence of the Gospel, and that quite incidentally; but it was in any case earlier than the Christian writings with which he deals.

starting—the one dominated by the idea of the πόλις, the other deriving its metaphors rather from the Eastern sheikh or king; and yet they ran a course analogous to that of which we have just been speaking, and also ending in approximation. There was the same perplexity on both sides in reconciling the goodness and justice of God, and in accounting for the presence of moral evil. On both sides (though in somewhat different ways) the compatibility of goodness with justice was asserted—the Christian Church rejecting the ditheistic solution proposed by Marcion; and on both sides, along with this, there went the assertion of free-will. Dr Hatch gives in full the system of Origen, 'in which Stoicism and the Neo-Platonism are blended into a complete theodicy', and he pronounces, not without reason, that 'a more logical superstructure has never been reared on the basis of philosophical theism'. But the most characteristic features in this theory—the pre-existence of souls in other worlds, and their ultimate purgation—did not obtain further acceptance.

Lecture 10 is devoted to the Greek mysteries, which are first described and then have their influence estimated upon that branch of Christian usage which stands in the closest relation to them—the two Sacraments. The notes to this and the succeeding lecture are mainly supplied by the editor, and represent an amount of research which deserves a word of special mention, for it is one thing for an author to annotate his own text as he goes on, and quite another for one who has made no special study of a subject to collect illustrations of it afterwards. Dr Hatch lays stress upon the large extent to which the phraseology of the mysteries was borrowed by Christian tradition. He points out that 'it was inevitable when a new group of associations came to exist side by side with a large existing body of associations, from which it was continually detaching members, introducing them into its own midst with the practices of their original societies impressed upon their minds, that this new group should tend to assimilate, with the assimilation of their members, some of the elements of these existing groups' (p. 292). Among these elements, Dr Hatch would see the tendency to greater secrecy, the extension of the time of preparation for baptism, along with the elaborate character of that preparation, the use of a password, or σύμβολον—the name which came into general use for the baptismal formula or creed, the exclusion of the uninitiated from the highest part of the Christian worship, the conception of it as a 'mystery', and of the holy table as an 'altar', with a number of other detailed coincidences, and with the general tendency to heighten the dramatic effect of the

Christian ceremonies. It is needless to say that all this is stated with Dr Hatch's usual incisive clearness, a clearness which, in this, as in some other cases, seems to be not altogether free from exaggeration. The Christian Sacraments are contemplated too exclusively in the light of the influences to which they were exposed from without, and too little account is taken of the inherent germs of development which they contained within themselves. For instance, it may be quite true that the ideas of 'enlightenment' (φωτισμός, φωτίζεσθαι) and 'seal' (σφραγίς), which are among the commonest of early designations applied to baptism, have their analogies in the mysteries; but both ideas have the way already paved for them in such passages as Heb. 6.4; 2 Cor. 4.4-6; Rom. 4.11 (where the idea of the 'seal' is derived not from the mysteries, but from circumcision), and a number of other expressions, which no doubt are taken ultimately from the mysteries belonged to the common stock of Christian metaphor from the very first.[2]

The two remaining lectures (11, 12) are taken up with a tracing of the process by which 'faith' which was at first essentially 'faith in a Person' came to be transferred by degrees to a body of doctrine, and that body of doctrine assumed a shape which was more and more metaphysical; the system of metaphysics thus erected becoming also, after a time, the basis of union between churches, and being modified at the pleasure of a fluctuating majority in the church assemblies. In the course of this are discussed briefly, as the occasion required, the development of creeds, the growth of the canon, the struggles of those parties within the Church which fought for the retention of that stricter moral standard with which it had started. It cannot be said that the text of these chapters is all that the author would have made it, but there is great cause for thankfulness that so much of his work has been preserved.

This completes the sketch, which it was incumbent on me to give, of the contents of this volume of Hibbert Lectures; and, slight as it has been, I cannot help hoping that it will send not a few of its readers to the book itself. Looking back over it, I doubt whether so important a contribution has been made to the real understanding of the first three centuries within our memory. It is indeed unique amongst English books dealing with this period, because it aims at the *philosophical* understanding of the data, the disentangling of the great strands of contemporary thought, the relation of the new faith to its environment both in respect to thought and life, to ideas and usage. The value of such

2.   Compare (e.g.) a passage like 1 Cor. 2.6-10.

a book by no means depends upon its being entirely right. Merely to have raised many of the questions which Dr Hatch has raised, and with the clearness which he has imparted to them, is to take a stride in advance towards the solution of a group of most important historical problems.

I should much have liked to pause here, and in endeavouring to estimate the tendency and effect of this whole inquiry, I should have been glad first to attempt—for it would have been only an attempt—to put it in its place in the history of recent thought both in this country and on the Continent. We are naturally reminded of the way in which that clear-sighted critic, Matthew Arnold, used to emphasise the antithesis between Hebraism and Hellenism. This inquiry bears to his the relation of a deliberate and searching study by a trained historian and theologian to the *apercus* of a brilliant man of letters. Of more importance would it be to determine the relation in which Dr Hatch's work stands to the parallel movement initiated by Albrecht Ritschl in Germany. I believe it to have been, both in its inception and in its execution, wholly independent of this movement; and yet there can be little doubt that the two present fundamental points of contact. More exactly to define these, however, would be not only beyond the scope of a paragraph in a review like the present, it would also involve a more comprehensive study of the German movement than I have as yet been able to make. The subject must needs attract the attention of any one who desires to weigh and appreciate the leading forces of modern theology.

Ritschl, like Hatch, aims a blow at metaphysics, though he seems to have been more inclined to lay stress on the Church as a corporate body. Here we are concerned with the metaphysics. But I am free to confess that Dr Hatch's argument on this head impresses me less than his treatment of the historical problem. This is, perhaps, in part a consequence of his method. He approaches his subject from the circumference rather than from the centre. He takes sections of Greek thought and Greek usage, and places them in juxtaposition with analogous sections of Christian doctrine and practice. It would have been another matter if he had begun with the New Testament, and had first defined the elements which he found there, and then traced them as they successively came in contact with different phases of Pagan culture. If the analysis had taken its start from Paul and John, instead of Philo and Epictetus on the one hand, and Basil and Gregory Nazianzen on the

other, I believe that the result would have been different. It seems to me
that in proportion as he approaches the centre of the position, Dr
Hatch's utterances become more uncertain. His final summing-up
presents the reader with two alternative theories:

> It is possible to urge, on the one hand, that Christianity, which began
> without them—which grew on a soil whereon metaphysics never throve—
> which won its first victories over the world by the simple moral force of
> the Sermon on the Mount, and by the sublime influence of the life and
> death of Jesus Christ, may throw off Hellenism, and be none the worse,
> but rather stand out again before the world in the uncoloured majesty of
> the Gospel. It is possible to urge that what was absent from the early form
> cannot be essential, and that the Sermon on the Mount is not an outlying
> part of the Gospel, but its source. It is possible to urge on the other hand,
> that the tree of life, which was planted by the hand of God Himself in the
> soil of human society, was intended from the first to grow by assimilating
> to itself whatever elements it found there. It is possible to maintain that
> Christianity was intended to be a development, and that its successive
> growths are for the time at which they exist integral and essential. It is
> possible to urge that it is the duty of each succeeding age at once to accept
> the developments of the past, and to do its part in bringing on the
> developments of the future. Between these two main views it does not
> seem possible to find a logical basis for a third. The one or the other must
> be accepted, with the consequences which it involves. But whether we
> accept the one or the other, it seems clear that much of the Greek element
> may be abandoned. On the former hypothesis it is not essential; on the
> latter it is an incomplete development, and has no claim to permanence
> (pp. 351-52).

I quite agree as to the importance of both these sets of propositions;
but they seemed to me to be too important, and to have too direct and
fundamental a bearing upon the whole subject of the book to be left
merely as an open question at the end. Neither can I regard them as so
mutually exclusive as they appear to be represented as being. To judge
from several passages which might be quoted from the first page of the
book onwards, Dr Hatch is himself disposed to accept the first
alternative. And it seems to me to contain this great truth, that
Christianity all proceeds ultimately from a Person, and that all its parts
and members are vital in proportion to their proximity to that Person.
From this point of view I should fully endorse Dr. Hatch's regret at the
shifting of meaning in the word 'faith' from the sense which it bears in
the New Testament to its sense in relation to ecclesiastical dogmas. But,
at the same time, there is surely no less an element of truth in the second

alternative. Christianity is an assimilative force; it has a development of its own; it does draw in to itself material from this side and from that.

Three things, it appears to me, may be said in qualification of the indictment which Dr Hatch brings against what he calls Greek metaphysics.

In the first place, they were inevitable. The historical conditions being what they were, a metaphysical creed could not have been avoided. The Greeks were the leaders of European thought, and it was through conquering them that Christianity conquered Europe. It happened that the Greeks were a metaphysic-loving people, and, therefore, theology with them took a metaphysical form. But we are all metaphysicians, consciously or unconsciously. Human life has a metaphysical background, whether it comes to sight or not. The Old Testament has its latent metaphysics as well as the New. Dr Hatch himself repeatedly implies this. The unity of God, the problem of evil, are at bottom metaphysical questions. And the questions raised by the New Testament are still more complex and still more difficult. Yet they are real questions; and once raised, they naturally pressed for an answer. The world can get on with latent metaphysics; but when the course of events brings them out of the latent stage and men's minds are really alive to them, then there is nothing to be done but to use the best methods which contemporary thought has available.

This brings me to the second qualification, which is that there was a real affinity between the New Testament itself and a great part of the superstructure that was built upon it. Take the Logos doctrine, for instance. Dr Hatch says nothing in this connection of the Epistle to the Colossians, or the Epistle to the Hebrews, or the Fourth Gospel; but they have surely an essential bearing upon the question. And the same holds good of much besides. Here, again, is another point of which Dr Hatch appears to be partly conscious. His book will give some future scholar most valuable materials for comparison with New Testament teaching; but that comparison must be made more closely before we can afford to throw over the legacy of the early Christian centuries.

Lastly, in regard to the decisions of the Church resting upon the verdict of a mere majority, that too seems to me a matter which cannot be dismissed quite so lightly. None of the great decisions were obtained by a snatched or stolen majority. They were all the result of long and hard fighting. If ever intellectual questions were thrashed out by argument these were. The side which ultimately won the day often had the greatest difficulties to contend against. Court favour, statecraft, the power of armies, the vigour of youthful nations were often all in the opposite scale. Surely we may say, at least of the earliest and clearest decisions, *vietrir causa Deo placait*. Relatively to their own age, at least it is difficult to think that these decisions were not right, and it still remains to be proved that they are not right for ours. That this early development was incomplete I grant most willingly. That something is left for our own age to do, I also grant. But it is not a healthy or sound development which discards and ignores all that has gone before.

One considerable concession may however be made. The taste and capacity of different races for metaphysics vary. There are some, as I have said, which can get on very well with latent metaphysics. For most of us it is not in metaphysics that the real centre of gravity lies. Ethics, too, seems to me an inadequate name for what we seek. There is yet a middle term between metaphysics and ethics, which alone describes what we find so pre-eminently in the Bible, and what the Bible far more than Fathers and Councils can give us. That term is Religion.[3]

---

3.   The present writer may perhaps be allowed to refer to a little book of his own—*The Oracles of God: Nine Lectures on the Nature and Extent of Biblical Inspiration and on the Special Significance of the Old Testament Scriptures at the Present Time* (London: Longmans, Green, 1891), pp. 85ff., 118ff.—where more is said about this distinction.

PART III EXEGESIS

Chapter 10

THE PARABLE OF THE LABOURERS IN THE VINEYARD:
MATTHEW 20.1-16[*]

The parable of the Labourers in the Vineyard is peculiar to Matthew, and is placed by him in a context which is evidently in direct relation to it. A rich young 'ruler' (i.e. as we may suppose, like Jairus, the ruler or director of a synagogue), seizing the spirit of Jewish legalism, and thinking that from the new Rabbi he should obtain some new formula with which he was hitherto unacquainted, came to Jesus, and asked him eagerly 'what he should do to inherit eternal life'. He was told in reply that if he would be perfect—if he would come up to the highest standard—he must distribute all his wealth among the poor and cast in his lot unreservedly with the band of wandering Galilean peasants and fishermen whom he saw before him. For some reason, which we must not stay now to inquire into, our Lord put before this young man a lofty and severe ideal of duty, to which, for the present at least, he was not equal. Whether at any future time he accepted the terms that were offered him does not appear; but, at any rate, he could not make up his mind to them at once, and he went away disappointed and crestfallen.

After his departure the conversation turned upon the hindrance that riches oppose to any true discipleship of Christ. And Peter, contrasting, not without some self-satisfaction, the sacrifices that he and his fellow-disciples had made with the unwillingness to part with his wealth displayed by the young ruler, asked what reward he and they were to have. The answer to such a question must evidently cut both ways. On the one hand it must assert the truth that any seeming loss which the disciple undergoes is not really such, but rather a gain. God does not require of his servants any surrender which will not be amply, and far more than amply, made up to them. And, on the other hand, the

*   This paper originally appeared as W. Sanday, 'The Parable of the Labourers in the Vineyard: St Matthew xx. 1–16', *The Expositor* 3 (1876), pp. 81-101.

ambition and self-assertion of Peter must needs receive correction. The first of these two objects is met in the last verses of Matthew 19, and the second in the parable which forms the opening section of Matthew 20. The one is linked on to the other by means of the clause of reservation added to the promise of reward. The reward indeed shall be in highly augmented ratio. It shall be nothing less than the gift of eternal life. But, 'many who are last shall be first, and the first last'.

The eye naturally passes from these words to those which conclude the parable that follows, Mt. 20.16. Here they are almost exactly repeated, and with a less qualified exactness than would appear from our Authorized Version. In this there is an addition that must in all probability be set aside as not part of the original Gospel. The clause, 'Many are called, but few chosen', though undoubtedly genuine in the second place where it occurs, Mt. 22.14, is wanting in the two oldest manuscripts, the Vatican and Sinaitic, with two other important uncials,[1] and also in the two Egyptian versions, a group which is shown by accumulated evidence to represent the best type of text. The corrupt addition, like so many more, seems to have been early made and soon to have spread, especially over the Syrian and Latin Churches. It is important that this excrescence should be cleared away, as some commentators have been perplexed,[2] and others (e.g., notably Stier) have been entirely misled by it in their interpretation of the parable. The

---

1. Z, the Dublin Palimpsest, which contains only 290 verses of the First Gospel, but is of the highest value, indeed second only to ℵ and B, for any passage on which its testimony is extant; and L, the Codex Regius, at Paris, which marks a transition text, sometimes siding with the oldest authorities and sometimes heading the array of later witnesses. The clause was bracketed by Tregelles (before the discovery of the Codex Sinaiticus) (S.P. Tregelles, *An Account of the Printed Text of the Greek New Testament* [London: Samuel Bagster & Sons, 1854]) and is omitted by Tischendorf (8th edn, not 7th) (C. Tischendorf, *Novum Testamentum Graece* [Leipzig: Giesecke & Devrient, 8th edn, 1869; Leipzig: A. Winter, 7th edn, 1859]), Westcott and Hort (B.F. Westcott and F.J.A. Hort, *The New Testament in the Original Greek* [2 vols.; Cambridge: Macmillan, 1881]) and McClellan (J.B. McClellan, *The New Testament: A New Translation on the Basis of the Authorized Version, from a Critically Revised Greek Text* [London: n.p., 1875]).

2. Archbishop Trench among the number: 'There is more difficulty in the closing words, "For many be called, but few chosen". They are not hard in themselves, but only in the position which they occupy', etc.—*Notes on the Parables of Our Lord* (London: John W. Parker, 1850), p. 189. This was written before quite so much attention had been paid to text criticism as it has received since, otherwise the difficulty would have found an easy solution.

genuine text ends with the words, 'So the last shall be first and the first last'. In these we are to look for the summing up, or moral, of the parable, which we shall come to consider in due course.

There are three points in the parable that it may be well for us to take separately: (1) the hiring of the labourers, (2) the times of the hiring, (3) the payment which they receive.

(1) *The Hiring*. The late Dean Alford begins his comment upon the parable by laying down as its *punctum saliens* that 'the kingdom of God is of grace, not of debt'. I do not wish to imply that this is not true; but, strange to say, the very opposite might almost be deduced from it. If we take the first set of labourers only, their relations throughout are strictly those of debt. They are hired for certain work, at a certain price. They are to do a day's work at the ordinary rate of a denarius—which, without very much straining, we may paraphrase, with Mr McClellan, as a 'shilling'. They go into the vineyard; they fulfil their part of the contract; they earn the promised wages, and they receive them. It is a plain commercial transaction, in which both parties duly perform their share.

It may seem to be somewhat otherwise with the labourers who are sent into the vineyard last. They also receive a shilling, though they have worked but a single hour. We can well understand that this would seem to them to be due to the bounty of their employer. They would hardly expect to receive as much. And yet when we look back at the terms of the contract, here, too, the same element of justice appears. 'Whatsoever is right (δίκαιον) I will give you'; 'Whatsoever is right, that shall ye receive'. The second of these clauses, indeed, like the latter part of v. 16, seems to be not strictly genuine.[3] It is wanting not only in the group of manuscripts mentioned already, but also in the Old Latin translation. It is a later Alexandrine and Syrian reading, which thence passed into the current Constantinopolitan text. The sense, however, is the same. There can be little doubt that the condition, 'whatever is right I will give you', which is expressly stated at the hiring of the second party of labourers, is to be extended to those who were sent into the vineyard later. They, too, were to receive what was *just*. Their pay is a μισθός—wages for work done.

Some of the commentators on the Protestant side have tried hard to evade this conclusion. Starting from the Reformation doctrine of

---

3.   The best critical editors are agreed in its excision. Mr McClellan, again, appears on the side to which he is, in some important instances, opposed.

justification by faith only, and seeming to see a contradiction of this in an exegesis which would represent the gift of God as in any way earned by the works of man, they have sought to explain away the nature of the gift and to restrict it to merely temporal goods. They have made it out to be the 'houses, and brethren, and children, and lands' of 19.29, but not the 'everlasting life' that is coupled with these earthly possessions. It is sufficiently clear, however, that no such limitation is really possible. The eventide is the Parousia—the second coming of the Son of Man, when all who have served him will be summoned into his presence, to receive according to that they have done.

Our language is apt to fall into metaphors taken from this very act, the payment of wages. Necessarily and naturally. It is the language of Scripture: 'The Son of man shall come in the glory of his Father, with his angels; and then shall he reward every man according to his works'; 'God shall render to every man according to his deeds'; 'Every man shall receive his own reward according to his labour'; 'We must all appear before the judgment-seat of Christ; that every one may receive the things done in the body according to that he hath done, whether it be good or bad'; 'The Father, without respect of persons, judgeth according to every man's work'; 'I will give unto every one of you according to his works'; 'Behold, I come quickly; and my reward is with me, to give every man as his work shall be'.[4]

We can afford to let these passages have their full weight all the more as we are less inclined to give a one-sided prominence to the opposite doctrine. For an opposite (or, shall we say rather, complementary?) doctrine there is, which is equally true: 'By grace ye are saved'; 'We are justified freely by his grace through the redemption that is in Christ Jesus; Now to him that worketh is the reward not reckoned of grace, but of debt. But to him that worketh not, but believeth on him that justifieth the ungodly, his faith is counted for righteousness'; 'Therefore it is of faith, that it might be by grace; to the end the promise might be sure to all the seed'.[5] Both sets of passages are equally explicit. On the one hand the future reward is represented as determined by what a man does to deserve it. On the other hand it is represented, not as owed or earned, but as given out of the manifold mercy and bounty of God, through the reconciliation wrought by his Son.

---

4. Mt. 16.27; Rom. 2.6; 1 Cor. 3.8; 2 Cor. 5.10; 1 Pet. 1.17; Rev. 2.23; 22.12.
5. Eph. 2.5; Rom. 3.24; 4.4, 16.

These two different points of view seem to be naturally reached according as we follow different lines of thought. If we contemplate immediately and in itself the relation of the work done to the reward received, at once it is seen to be out of all proportion. There is no merit in anything we can do to account for the bountifulness of the promises that God has vouchsafed to us. There is a taint, if not actually on, yet very near to, the best we do. That the stumbling, heartless, inconstant service of earth should meet with such an infinitely glorious return can only be of grace—a free gift, not bought, but bestowed. Yet, on the other hand, if we ask upon whom is that gift to be bestowed? for whom is this grace to be exercised? in what comparative proportions shall it be exercised? then we inevitably fall back upon the question what the man is in himself. If man is a free agent at all (and that he is so is the first postulate of all morals and religion), then it follows that his place must ultimately be determined by the way in which he has used his power of willing.

The contradiction, indeed (so far as there is one), runs through from the very beginning. Man is a creature of circumstances: yet he is free. He is bidden to work in God's vineyard: yet at best his labour will be unprofitable. He will be judged according to his works: and yet by grace he is saved. It is not that works have a merit, directly and immediately, in themselves. But works are the test of what a man *is*—they are the test, the outward visible sign of faith itself. And by what he is he will be classed at the day of judgment. But if a man were judged simply by what he is—if a severe balance were struck between his good and his evil deeds—no reward would be possible to him at all. That he should receive a reward and such a reward as he will receive is an act of grace. Relatively to his fellow-men, to that division and classification on which any system of judgment must be based, salvation is of works. Absolutely, and in regard to the relation between the soul and its God, salvation is of grace.

Perhaps this comes out somewhat more clearly in another parable, which may be used to illustrate this of the Labourers in the Vineyard—the parable of the Talents. There one servant receives five talents, and by putting them out to trade he gains five talents more. Another, who receives two talents, gains two. But how is the reward proportioned to the merit? Is it at all on the same scale? The contrary is brought out expressly and vividly. 'Thou hast been faithful over a few things, I will make thee ruler over many things.' Or, as it appears in a still more precise and definite form in the Third Gospel, he who has gained the ten pounds is made to have rule over ten cities, he who has gained five pounds over five. That which is measured on the one hand in terms of retail trade, is measured on the other in terms of regal authority and power. 'Not as the offence', nor yet as the service, 'so is the free gift'.

> God doth not need
> Either man's work or his own gifts.

And the limit of man's power to work for him is not the limit of his grace.

(2) *The Times of Hiring.* The question is frequently raised as to the presence of secondary meanings or applications in Scripture. No doubt they exist, and, in our Lord's words especially, to a very large extent indeed. But the account of them seems to be, not so much that the sacred writer or speaker has in his mind, at one and the same time, two or more different sets of events, but that he penetrates to the single law which binds those events together. The laws of the Divine action are uniform. They are made so in order that we may have the power of forecasting their operation and of acting upon them. God deals upon the same principles with individuals separately and with nations and bodies of men collectively. Hence it is not strange if the parables, which express such deep spiritual truths, should be found to have applications on many sides. There is hardly an end to the possible applications of them.

Thus we are not really compelled to choose, as some commentators have felt bound to do, between different ways of applying the parable before us. A true interpretation will embrace them all. The master of the vineyard is represented as going out in the early morning, i.e., soon after sunrise, when work began, or, according to our modern reckoning, approximately, at six o'clock, at nine, at noon, at three, and at five. And on each occasion he sends labourers into his vineyard, at the later hours not without reproach to them for standing idle so long.

Those called early, say some, were the Jews; those called later are the Gentiles. Origen maintained that the different hours were rather epochs in the history of the world, such as the Flood, the Call of Abraham, the Mission of Moses. Bengel would take them as periods in the ministry of our Lord Himself, from the first calling of the Apostles to the Ascension and Day of Pentecost; Meyer, periods in the whole Messianic dispensation, from the coming of the Messiah to the Parousia. Others, with Chrysostom and Jerome, say that they refer to periods in the lifetime of individuals. The labourers who are hired in the early morning are those who, 'like Samuel, Jeremiah, and John the Baptist, can say with the Psalmist, "Thou art my God, even from my mother's womb"'. To go into the vineyard at the third hour is to enter the service of God in youth. Noon represents manhood; the ninth hour declining years; the eleventh, old age, when some have even yet heard and obeyed the heavenly call.

There is no need to pick and choose. The summons of God is made at sundry times and in divers manners, both to nations, to bodies of men, and to individuals. The same rule holds good for one as for the other. It is this rule that our Lord expresses in so lively a manner in the parable, not any of the particular cases that come under it. It may be applied to them, but they do not exhaust it. It has been, is being, and will be, fulfilled. It belongs equally to past, present, and future.

(3) *The Payment of the Labourers.* In these ways, then, the parable is instructive. They do not, however, touch its main point. That is reserved for the end. And here the more serious difficulties of the parable begin.

The labourers are called in to receive their day's wage; and all of them alike, both those who had worked the whole twelve hours and those who had worked only one, receive the sum stipulated for with the first body—the denarius, or shilling. The order, too, in which they are paid is an inverted one. The late comers are called up first, and so on backwards.

Now this much is clear. The evening, when work ceases and the paying-time comes, is the Great Audit. The master of the house is he in whose name that Audit is to be held, and the ἐπίτροπος, or steward, is Christ. We reject as erroneous all interpretations which explain the payment in any other way. It is the gift of eternal life.

There are, however, some points that this parable leaves open. It is not intended to convey any decision as to the relation between the hour of death and the hour of judgment. Both are represented as taking place at the same time, or as immediately following each other. The labourers leave the vineyard, and they are at once summoned into the counting-house to receive their due. The interval, such as we believe there will be, is foreshortened. The parable is silent as to specific information on this head.

Neither is any inference to be drawn from the quality of the sum paid. All the labourers receive the shilling; but it does not therefore follow that future rewards will be equal. The direct contrary is stated in other parables. The servant who trades with the money his lord committed to him and makes ten pounds becomes governor over ten cities: he who has been less successful, but yet successful, has rule over five. The Twelve Apostles are to 'sit on thrones'. There are 'least and greatest' in the kingdom of heaven. Many are called, but few are raised to any elect or special dignity. These are direct statements made with reference to the particular point of the ranks or gradations in the Messianic kingdom. But here, in the parable of the Labourers in the Vineyard, there is a different purpose. It deals indeed with the question of rank and gradation, but only in a relative sense, as between different individuals or bodies of men. For the purposes of the parable it comes to the same thing, whether equal labour (or what seems to be equal labour) receives reward upon a graduated scale, or seemingly different amounts of labour are paid on the same scale. The point of the parable does not turn upon this, 'Whatsoever is right, that shall ye receive'.

The real question and the real difficulty lies in the comparative treatment of the different parties of labourers—in the fact that the first are made last and the last first. It is round this sentence that the whole parable hinges. It is not to be denied that there is a difficulty, which cannot be explained as merely accidental. It is part of the intention of the parable, and is just what makes it so instructive.

When it comes to be the turn of the first set of labourers to be paid, they too receive the shilling for which they had bargained. At this they grumble and complain, and they make bold to remonstrate with the master of the house. 'These last have spent [or "made", literally, but idiomatically, as our own workmen sometimes say] but one hour, and thou hast made them equal to us, who have borne the burden and heat of the day.' The reply that they receive is quiet and courteous, but absolutely decisive and uncompromising: 'Friend, I do thee no wrong; didst thou not agree with me for a shilling? Take up thine own, and go thy way. It is my pleasure to give unto this last even as unto thee. Is it not lawful for me to do what I please with mine own? Or is thine eye evil because I am good? Art thou envious because I am liberal?' There can be no rejoinder to this. The grounds alleged are beyond dispute: first, the bargain—a shilling they were to receive and a shilling they got; and, secondly, the will and pleasure of the master of the house; his money was his own, and if he chose to give to one and not to another, his right none could question.

We, too, must needs acquiesce in this reasoning. And yet is there not a faintly-heard murmur in our own consciences? Have we not at heart a lurking sympathy with the disappointed workmen? If such a case were to happen in real life, if any one of us were to treat his workmen in this way, we should indeed admit, as we needs must, the justice of the reply; and yet there would be an undertone of remonstrance and doubt as to whether, after all, the men who met with such rigorous measure had not some right on their side, and did not do well to be aggrieved. What shall we say to this? It is not wrong to ask such questions. It is best not to blink difficulties, because by turning back upon and seeking to penetrate deeper into them, we often reach a truer meaning.

Is not this an instance of that wonderful phenomenon which we may, perhaps, venture to call the *irony* of Jesus? This is not the only time or occasion that he, the Holy One, spoke in a way that may seem for the moment to a superficial eye to contradict the tenor of his own mission. He disclaimed for himself the title of 'Good'. He likened the Christian elsewhere to a fraudulent steward. He drew one of his parables from an unjust and selfish judge, who is wearied, by sheer persistence on the part of the petitioner, into granting what his own sense of right is insufficient to move him to grant; another from the conduct of a man who will do to save himself annoyance more than ever he will do for the sake of friendship. A criticism, shallow with all its ability and learning, has stumbled at these sayings and cast a doubt upon their genuineness.[6] But which of the disciples possessed that finely-tempered and gracious audacity which could invent them? It is not the sinner who speaks, but the deep and thrilling humanity of him who was 'in all points tempted like as we are, yet without sin'.

In the answer of the master of the house something is spoken and something is withheld. The reply is adapted to the nature of the remonstrance. If that had been made in a different manner and spirit we may believe that perhaps less reserve and more confidence would have been shown. As it is, the answer that is given is absolutely valid and true. It is one side of the truth, and the side that will always be turned against murmurers. It reminds us of the words of Paul: 'Nay, but, O man, who art thou that repliest against God? Shall the thing formed say to him that formed it, "Why hast thou made me thus?" Hath not the potter power over the clay of the same lump to make one vessel unto honour and

---

6.   See T. Keim, *Geschichte Jesu von Nazara in ihrer Verkettung mit dem Gesammtleben seines Volkes, frei untersucht und ausführlich erzählt* (3 vols.; Zürich: Orell, Fussli, 1867–72), I, p. 74, n. 2.

another unto dishonour?'[7] A view of destiny stern and severe, but true, though clearly not an exhaustive account either of Divine Justice or Divine Mercy. So here in the parable we have to do only with the apparent aspect of things. The time at which the labourers had been at work is disregarded in the wages which they receive. But time is, as all experience shows, a very imperfect test of the value of labour.[8] It is only said that the later-called labourers worked for a shorter time, not that their work was essentially of less value than that of those who were called first. The reverse of this is implied: 'Whatsoever is right, I will give you'. The promise is put upon the ground of justice. It was really, we may be sure, justice, and not partial or capricious generosity, that regulated the reward. This is the unwavering language of Scripture: God will

> render to every man according to his deeds;...unto them that are contentious, and do not obey the truth,...indignation and wrath, tribulation and anguish, upon every soul of man that doeth evil, of the Jew first, and also of the Gentile; but glory, honour, and peace, to every man that worketh good, to the Jew first, and also to the Gentile: for *there is no respect of persons with God.*[9]

Apply the parable, in each of its different senses, and all becomes clear. The Jew was first called. God had made with him a solemn covenant. His were 'the adoption, and the glory, and the covenants, and the giving of the law, and the service of God, and the promises'. His were 'the fathers of whom, as concerning the flesh, Christ came'. There was a time when all the rest of the world was standing idle in the market-place, when it could be said, 'You only have I known of all the families of the earth'.[10] And yet the Gentile kingdoms, even those who were last admitted, would not therefore be at a disadvantage if they were faithful to their calling. Even then the first might be last and the last first.

Or, still more strikingly, within the circle of the Apostles: Peter himself, it was true, had been among the first to receive the summons, and yet he was outdone by one who spoke of himself as 'born out of

7.   Rom. 9.20-21.

8.   'Finis parabolae est mercedem vitae aeternae non tempori quo quis aboravit, sed labori et operi quod fecit respondere'—Maldonatus, quoted by Trench. Dr Trench criticises this view unfavourably, and no doubt it is mistaken in assigning as the main object of the parable what is really, as it were, only a kind of hidden background to it.

9.   Rom. 2.6, 8-11.

10.   Amos 3.2.

due time, the least of the apostles, and not meet to be called an apostle', who had not only stood idle, but had actually persecuted the Church of God. This relation between Peter and Paul may be said to be prophetically anticipated in the parable. In it a warning was conveyed to the elder Apostle that, though he had left all to follow Christ, still no primacy was assured to him; and he was at the same time admonished not to look forward in that spirit of jealousy and self-assertion (in his case, perhaps, thoughtless rather than deliberate) which prompted his question, 'What shall we have therefore?'.

This is the main purport of the parable. In calling attention to the fact that the mention of the time at which the labourers had been at work tells us nothing as to the nature and value (i.e., relative or comparative value) of that work, it is not intended that this is more than an incidental feature. We insist upon it only because it is here that the difficulty of the parable and the explanation of the difficulty seem to lie. The judgments of God are not arbitrary, though they might seem so, if looked at through the glasses of human jealousy and ignorance. The first may be last and the last first, and yet justice, infinite and perfect justice, governs the divine awards. Those who make so bold as to murmur at the lot apportioned to them will be answered as they deserve. The severer side of God's Providence will be turned upon them. They will have the mysteries of Omnipotence unfolded to them rather than the mysteries of Grace. In a truly humble, and gentle, and reverent mind such questions will never arise at all.

And yet, on the other hand, we must not take too exaggerated a view of the character of those who found themselves so unexpectedly levelled and degraded. They, too, receive each the wages that were agreed upon. We must take our stand upon this and not suffer ourselves to be led away by any comments that, through a narrow conception both of human nature and Divine grace, construe the rebuke into a sentence of complete and final reprobation. All that is meant is the often-taught lesson, that those who are greatest in their own estimation and in that of the world shall be least in the kingdom of heaven. A place in that kingdom, though a much humbler one than they supposed, will not be denied them.

The class of minds indicated in the parable is very similar to that which is exemplified by the older brother in the parable of the Prodigal Son. There, again, it is a mistake to suppose that, though offending on that one point, the murmurer is unreservedly and utterly condemned.

We might almost go so far as to say that in neither case is the murmuring quite of the essence of the parable. The state of things that gives rise to the murmur is the real point. The murmur itself is accessory rather than principal. It serves to 'justify the ways of God to men', by introducing a proposition that helps to explain them. At the same time, incidentally, it throws in a touch of true psychology. It is not intended that at the Last Day there will be even the possibility of querulous appeal. But there are some minds the unspoken thought of which would be such an appeal. There are querulous and thankless spirits who do indeed that which is required of them, but in a cheerless, unimpassioned, dull, precise, and mechanical way. Like most formalists they have a good opinion of themselves and of their own place in the sight of God. They are apt to count up their good deeds: 'We have borne the burden and heat of the day'; 'Lo, these many years have I served thee, neither transgressed I at any time thy commandment'. Their religion does not begin in self-abasement. They have never known that peculiarly crushed and helpless feeling that is implied in the word 'contrition'. They have something of the Pharisaic leaven about them, though they are not quite Pharisees. They are hard and unsympathetic in their judgments, and though they confess in words their own unworthiness, still at heart they barely escape congratulating themselves that they are not as other men.

Still there is a truth in their plea. They *have* borne the burden and heat. They *have* laboured and suffered. They have *not* been caught in open transgression. They *have* lived decent and respectable lives. And, therefore, we are not led to the paradox of supposing that they will be ultimately excluded from the kingdom of heaven. They are not sent away empty. Nay, they may even receive some consolatory explanation of what seems to them an injustice—'Son, thou art ever with me, and all that I have is thine'.

The parable of the Prodigal is, in this respect, a still further development of this of the Labourers in the Vineyard. It tracks out still more tenderly and delicately the human aspects and relations of these two different modes of service. In the eyes of him by whom it was spoken nothing was common or unclean. He could raise and dismiss the weeping penitent, but he did not therefore repel the colder Pharisee. He admitted Nicodemus among his disciples. He made his grave in Joseph's tomb.

We fall into opposite errors in reading Scripture and in real life. In the one we allow no kind of merit, no redeeming qualities at all, to that very class of persons who in the other almost monopolize our respect. The truth lies between both extremes. There is room even for the Pharisee in the kingdom of heaven, though from the first he will become last, and from the greatest least. His early call, his life-long service, his regular religious habits, his punctilious payment of his dues, will not prevent him from being forestalled by many whom, living, he had despised. They will be bidden to go up higher, and he will take the lower place with shame. Still he may not murmur at his lot, for he can be no fair judge in his own cause. Rather let him be resigned and prepared for it beforehand, and thankful that he should fare no worse. What he has is sure to be far more than he deserves, and the less mercenary the spirit in which he labours the better it will be for him.

In the highest Christian temper the mercenary element will be entirely wanting. It will be reward enough for him who has it that he should be permitted to work in God's vineyard at all. He will not be casting his eyes this way and that, to see how others are working or when their service begins. He will know that the Lord of the vineyard is no mere contractor who will deal with him after the letter of his bond, but an infinitely kind and loving Father to all who prove themselves his children. God is to us really what we ourselves make him to be. If we are formalists and legalists we shall be judged by the letter, but to those who love much, much shall be both given and forgiven.

Thus, so far from there being anything partial or unequal in the Divine judgments, they are really the necessary, and, we might almost say, automatic consequences of our own conduct. There may be parts in them that we cannot understand, just as there are parts of our own conduct that we cannot, or at least do not, sufficiently analyse. But these two things are correlative. The seeming anomalies in the moral government of the world proceed from our ignorance, and not from any failure of Divine justice. That, we may be sure, is absolute and perfect; and if we are wise we shall acquiesce gratefully in its decisions, whether the reasons for them are discovered or concealed.

Chapter 11

A NEW WORK ON THE PARABLES[*]

Professor Adolf Jülicher of Marburg is a writer of some note among younger German Professors. He is conspicuously able in the narrower sense of the word, i.e., he has a strong grasp of his own position, and he writes forcibly and logically. Judging by a German rather than an English standard, he might be described as belonging to the Left Centre or more Conservative Left. His robust judgment is intolerant of absurdity and exaggeration on either side; and he is not a slave to the tradition of any particular school. He exercises to the full German freedom in criticism, but he takes his own impressions freshly from the facts with much independence and honesty of purpose.

Jülicher is best known for his elaborate work on the parables, of which the first volume appeared eleven years ago, and the second—quickly followed by a new edition (largely rewritten) of the first—in 1899. But he has also brought out an *Introduction to the New Testament* which holds a good place in the series of compact handbooks (*Grundrisse*) published by Mohr of Freiburg and Leipzig. It may help to define his standpoint to say that, while rejecting the Pastoral Epistles, he goes further than up to that time (1894) Liberal theologians generally had gone, in accepting not only Colossians, but even the more strongly opposed Ephesians as possibly (he will not say more) a genuine work of Paul. In this he marked a tendency which has since been still more clearly pronounced. He also accepts 2 Thessalonians. And it is characteristic that he is a more uncompromising critic of the Fourth Gospel than e.g. either Schürer or Harnack.

The following may perhaps throw some light on the mental physiognomy which finds its natural expression in these views. I do not

[*]   This review of Adolf Jülicher, *Die Gleichnisreden Jesu* (2 vols., with vol. 1 in the 2nd edn; Freiburg: Mohr Siebeck, 1899), originally appeared as W. Sanday, 'A New Work on the Parables', *Journal of Theological Studies* 1 (1900), pp. 161-80.

know any of the younger Germans who reminds me so much of the 'vigour and rigour' which Matthew Arnold found in the Tübingen criticism. By no means all the Tübingen critics had really what we should call the attribute of 'vigour'. Jülicher has this in a higher degree than most of them; and if in his case the 'rigour' is not that of the school, or of any pre-conceived philosophy, it is, I believe, all the more an inborn quality of man. Half measures, subtle distinctions, the finer shades of delineation do not come to him so naturally as clear, definite, trenchant statement which does not admit of exceptions.

In dealing with the parables, Jülicher's great object is to get rid of allegory at all costs. He holds that to represent the parables as elaborate compositions, in which a number of points on the one side correspond to a number of points on the other, is to import into them something to which they were originally foreign. He believes that in their origin they were quite simple. Their object being to illustrate and enforce, he regards it as a contradiction that they should themselves need lengthy interpretations. He will not allow any one parable to carry with it more than a single lesson or moral. And that lesson or moral is not to result from any single feature, but from the parable as a whole. There may be a *tertium comparationis*, but not *tertia* (I, p. 70).

It will be obvious that these principles are not compatible either with the form in which the parables have come down to us, or with what we are told about them in the Gospels. To a certain extent—not perhaps a very great, but yet an appreciable extent—they have to be rewritten. Where details are introduced which tend to complicate the issue, these are usually discarded as later interpolations. Perhaps this is done on the whole less often than might be expected.

But besides these minor changes there are two main points on which Jülicher deliberately throws over the tradition of the Gospels. These are: (1) all the cases in which by the side of the parable there is also given what purports to be its explanation; and (2) the account that is given of the object which our Lord had in speaking in parables.

The two instances in which our Lord is described as himself explaining a parable after it has been told, both occur in the great collection of parables in Matthew 13. They are, of course, the Sower, and the Wheat and the Tares. The explanation of the Parable of the Sower is found in all three Gospels. The Wheat and the Tares, with its explanation, is peculiar to Matthew. Besides this, there is the express statement in Mark that 'privately to his disciples' our Lord expounded all his parabolic sayings (Mk 4.34). All these statements are necessarily rejected. They are set down to the Evangelists rather than to Jesus, as the product of a mistaken idea which had grown up that the parables were difficult and enigmatical, 'mysteries of the kingdom' which needed a solution, dark sayings that could not be understood without the key.

It will also be remembered that in all three Gospels our Lord is represented as giving his own reason for the use of these dark sayings by applying to his hearers the words of the prophet Isaiah, 'This people's heart is waxed gross, and their ears are dull of hearing, and their eyes they have closed,' etc.; as though it were his deliberate intention to conceal his meaning from the great majority of his hearers, and to reveal it only to the select few. According to Jülicher there was no intention to conceal at all, and nothing to conceal if there had been. The parables were meant to be a help only and not a stumbling block; and, rightly regarded, they were so clear that he who ran might read.

In Jülicher's view the paragraph on the object of teaching by parables was not an authentic record of words spoken by our Lord, but embodied the conclusions of the later Church drawn from the rejection of Christ by the Jews. The Jewish people had shown themselves blind and deaf. And this blindness and deafness had seemed to the disciples as in part penally inflicted. The nature of the teaching offered them was such as to leave them as they were. They *would* not hear, and therefore they *should* not hear. The Evangelists saw in that the sum of the whole matter. But the verdict was theirs and not their Master's.

This therefore is Jülicher's general conclusion: the sections containing interpretations of parables and all allusions to such interpretations go; the section which purports to give the object of this particular method of teaching goes; and all those side-touches which, if they were allowed to stand, would convert parable into allegory, also go. As Jülicher does not accept the Fourth Gospel as apostolic, the confessed allegories in that Gospel do not trouble him.

With these deductions the rest of the parables, very much as they stand, are genuine words of Jesus. And Jülicher devotes a chapter, or practically two chapters, of his introductory volume (Chapters 1: 'Die Echtheit der Gleichnisreden Jesu', and 5: 'Die Aufzeichnung der Gleichnisreden Jesu') to the proof of their genuineness.

It will be seen that there is a logical unity and completeness about the whole theory; and it is put forward as the one theory that is scientifically tenable. Jülicher writes throughout with the force of conviction, and is perhaps rather dogmatic in tone. He certainly shows neither fear nor favour in his treatment of other writers on the subject, but he is generous in the recognition of what seems to him merit, from whatever quarter it may come.

All this is calculated to impress opinion; and I should not be at all surprised if the theory found a more or less general acceptance with those who claim to treat the New Testament on strictly scientific principles.

And yet I shall not hesitate to express my dissent from it. Logic is one thing, science is another. A science of which the subject-matter is life cannot always be logical. To call it logical often means that it pursues some one train of thought too much to the exclusion of others. The play and subtlety of living thought is apt to escape in the process. So it seems to me to be with Jülicher. He rides his one idea too hard. He is not really a pedantic writer, because he comes to his subject with great deal of freshness, and sets down honestly what he sees. But I believe that the way in which he has worked out his idea is what might be called, not unfairly, pedantic. It is too *a priori*, and excludes more than it ought to exclude. Much of this exclusion seems to me to rest upon insufficient grounds.

I shall try to make good this position presently. But before attempting to argue the case, it will be more just and more satisfactory if I first give a few concrete examples of Jülicher's treatment of the parables. Perhaps we shall learn something by whatever objections we may have to details—and there is one rather sweeping objection that I may mention before I have done—however all this may be, the book as a whole has many good qualities. It is the most considerable work on the parables since Trench[1]—not forgetting A.B. Bruce—and in penetrative grasp and strength I believe that it surpasses both our English works.

I ought to say that Jülicher divides the parables into four classes: (1) Similitudes (*Gleichnisse*) or Undeveloped Parables, in which one thing is simply compared with another; (2) Fables (called in volume 2 *Parabeln*)

---

1.   The English reader may be interested in Jülicher's estimate of our own leading writer. To his method, of course, he objects. In detail the work contains much that is excellent, in the way of grammatical and antiquarian notes, but too little sharp definition of ideas, too many dogmatical and edifying effusions, and no application of criticism (I, p. 300, referring to R.C. Trench, *Notes on the Parables of Our Lord* [London: Macmillan, 1870]; cf. A.B. Bruce, *The Parabolic Teaching of Christ* [London: Hodder & Stoughton, 1882]).

or Narrative Parables, in which the comparison is worked out in the form of a story; (3) Typical Stories (*Beispielerzählungen*), illustrating some principle or other by means of a concrete example; (4) Pure Allegories, which, as confined to the Fourth Gospel, are not further treated.

The number of the Parables may be very differently estimated, according as the dividing line is drawn between Parable and Similitude or Metaphor on the one hand and Allegory on the other. Steinmeyer put the number at 23 or 24, Göbel at 26 or 27, Trench at 30, Bruce at 33, with 8 'parable germs'; van Koetsveld, the Dutch pastor (*ob.* 1893), to whom Jülicher assigns the place of honour as a commentator on the parables, would make the number 80 (or, more strictly, 79), though in his abridged *Hausbuch für die christliche Familie* this number is reduced to 35. One writer, von Wessenberg, rises to as many as 101 (Jülicher, I, p. 28). Jülicher himself fluctuates slightly in his estimate as well as in his classification; in his second volume he has treated in all 53, arranged thus:

A. Similitudes (Gleichnisse)

1. The Fig-Tree as Harbinger
   Mt. 24.32-33; Mk 13.28-29; Lk. 21.29-31
2. The Slave Bound to Labour
   Lk. 17.7-10
3. The Children at Play
   Mt. 11.16-19; Lk. 7.31-35
4. The Son's Request
   Mt. 7.9-11; Lk. 11.11-13
5. Disciple and Master
   Mt. 10.24-25; Lk 6.40
6. The Blind Leading the Blind
   Mt. 15.14; Lk. 6.39
7. Real Defilement
   Mk 7.14-23; Mt. 15.10-20
8. Salt
   Mt. 5.13; Mk 9.49-50; Lk. 14.34-35
9. The Lamp on the Stand
   Mk 4.21; Mt. 5.14a, 15-16; Lk. 8.16, 11.33

10. The City Set on a Hill
    Mt. 5.14b
11. Revealing what is Hidden
    Mk 4.22; Mt. 10.26-26; Lk. 8.17, 12.2-3
12. The Eye as the Light of the Body
    Mt. 6.22-23; Lk. 11.34-36
13. Divided Service
    Mt. 6.24; Lk. 16.13
14. The Tree and its Fruits
    Mt. 7.16-20; 12.33-37; Lk. 6.43-46
15. The Instructed Scribe
    Mt. 13.52
16. The Eagles and the Carcass
    Mt. 24.28; Lk. 17.37
17. The Thief
    Mt. 24.43-44; Lk. 12.39-40
18. The Faithful and the Unfaithful Steward
    Mt. 24.45-51; Lk. 12.42-48
19. The Master's Delayed Return
    Lk. 12.35-38; Mk 13.33-37
20. 'Physician, Heal Thyself'
    Lk. 4.23
21. The Physician and the Sick
    Mk 2.17; Mt. 9.12-13; Lk 5.31-32
22. The Bridegroom
    Mk 2.18-20; Mt. 9.14-15; Lk 5.33-35
23. The Old Garment, the Old Bottles, the Old Wine
    Mk 2.21-22; Mt. 9.16-17; Lk. 5.36-39
24. Tower-Building and War-Waging
    Lk. 14.28(25)-33
25. The Beelzebub Similitudes
    Mk 3.22-27; Mt. 12.22-30, 43-45; Lk. 11.14-26
26. On the Way to Judgment
    Mt. 5.25-26; Lk. 12.57-59
27. Precedence at Feasts, and the Right Kind of Guests
    Lk. 14.7-11, 12-14
28. Children and Dogs
    Mk 7.27-28; Mt 15.26-27

B. Parables (or Fables)

29. Building on the Rock and on the Sand
    Mt. 7.24-27; Lk. 6.47-49
30. The Importunate Friend
    Lk. 11.5-8
31. The Widow and the Unjust Judge
    Lk. 18.1-8
32. The Creditor and the Two Debtors
    Lk. 7.36-50
33. The Unmerciful Servant
    Mt. 18.21-35
34. The Lost Sheep and the Lost Piece of Silver
    Mt. 18.10-14; Lk. 15.1-10
35. The Lost Son
    Lk. 15.11-32
36. The Two Brothers
    Mt. 21.28-32; (Lk. 7.29-30)
37. The Wicked Husbandmen
    Mk 12.1-12; Mt. 21.33-46; Lk. 20.9-19
38. The Unwilling Guests
    Mt. 22.1-14; Lk. 14.15-24
39. The Barren Fig-Tree
    Lk. 13.6-9
40. The Ten Virgins
    Mt. 25.1-13; (Lk. 13.23-30)
41. Like Pay for Different Work
    Mt. 20.1-16
42. The Lent Money
    Mt. 25.14-30; Lk. 19.11-27
43. The Unrighteous Steward
    Lk. 16.1-12
44. The Four Kinds of Soil
    Mk 4.3-9, 14-20; Mt. 13.3-9, 18-23; Lk. 8.5-8, 11-15
45. The Seed Growing of Itself
    Mk 4.26-29
46. The Tares among the Wheat
    Mt. 13.24-30, 36-43
47. The Draw-Net
    Mt. 13.47-50

48. The Mustard-Seed and the Leaven
    Mk 4.30-32; Mt. 13.31-33; Lk. 13.18-21
49. The Treasure and the Pearl
    Mt. 13.44-46

C. *Typical Stories (Beispielerzählungen)*

50. The Good Samaritan
    Lk. 10.29-37
51. The Pharisee and the Publican
    Lk. 18.9-14
52. The Rich Fool
    Lk. 12.16-21
53. Dives and Lazarus
    Lk. 16.19-31

The first question that we naturally ask of one who gives up the interpretations in the Gospels is what he will say of the Parable of the Sower. This is Jülicher's account of it:

> The Parable of the Sower was certainly meant by a concrete case from rural life to illustrate the law, that no labour and no expenditure of strength or means can everywhere count on the same success, the same blessing, the same acceptance; that while much is always done in vain, there is also much that has its fruit and its reward. This law also holds good for the Kingdom of Heaven: the Gospel need take no shame to itself that it constantly falls on deaf ears, and meets with but partial assent, uncertain love; enough if one way or another by the side of this some hearts surrender themselves to it for full fruition, for fulness of faith. Unreasonable pessimism and unreasonable optimism among the evangelists, the missionaries of the Kingdom, was what the Lord desired to check by the very telling effect of this story... [As in the case of Jotham's parable] so also in this of the Sower, not too much is said about the Sower's failures: as they—as all failures, especially those of the missionaries of the Kingdom—are to be explained by very different causes, Jesus was obliged to seek some striking expression of this difference; and it is for that purpose, and not for the sake of poetic adornment, that He speaks of the three kinds of soil in which the seed will not grow, although He will not have supposed Himself to enumerate exactly in this way the various classes of human hearts that do not attain to fruit-bearing; these are indeed many more than three (I, pp. 110-11).

We will reserve our criticisms and proceed to give a few more specimens of Jülicher's method.

The other parable with an interpretation is that of the Wheat and the Tares. This, as we have it, stands alone in the series. It is pure allegory. Only as such does it become intelligible, which as an incident it would not be. Not until we see that the householder is Christ, the servants his disciples, the enemy the Devil, and the reapers angels, the treatment of the wheat and the tares that of the righteous and the wicked at the Last Judgement, does the story assume coherence and plausibility. These features are added by the Evangelist himself, who shows by the elaboration of his picture the pride that he took in his own composition. For the rest we cannot tell what was the form of the original parable, except so far as we can guess at this by comparing the Parable of the Draw-Net, which in the document used at this point probably formed a pair with it, like the Mustard-Seed and the Leaven, the Treasure and the Pearl. The Draw-Net is thrown to the end for the sake of the impressive warning with which it concludes. As in that parable, so also in the genuine version of the Wheat and the Tares, there would be no place for an 'enemy'; it would be just a simple story of the two growths appearing side by side, the one at harvest-time collected for burning, the other gathered into the barn.

We are glad that Jülicher does not think it necessary to interfere with the figure of the elder brother in the Parable of the Lost Son. Here it is only a question of the stress that is laid on the salient point of the parable. This, as in the case of the other two parables in the same chapter, is really the rejoicing over the return of the penitent.

> So the Father does not dispute any of the contentions of his Elder Son, nor yet does he complain of misrepresentation or of his self-praise, or of his ungrateful suppression of kindnesses received; he does not even blame him expressly for feeling no joy at his brother's return. Only himself, his own seemingly paradoxical and unfair behaviour, will he defend; and that by the telling juxtaposition of vv. 31 and 32: 'While thou hast never been dead and lost to me, hast caused me no break in the even tenor of our domestic life, thy brother, by the surprise at his return to life and at his recovery after his clouded past, has indeed given me cause for unwonted joy; and so it is, the loudest jubilations are called forth, not by the happiness of uninterrupted possession, but by the restoration of that which has been lost'.

> So the story ends: whether the Elder Son followed his Father into the banquet-hall, we are not told, any more than whether or for how long the

friends and neighbours of vv. 6 and 9 complied with the invitation to join in
the rejoicing (compare also 13.9). The interest of the parable does not turn
upon deciding how the Elder Son ended by behaving to the Younger, or
whether the Younger was finally cured of his evil courses (II, p. 358).

That seems to me to be fine and true criticism, which singles out a
right note, and sustains it as it ought to be sustained.

It would be another thing to say that the figure of the elder brother
was introduced only in order to give an opening for the father's
explanation. Jülicher does not in so many words give this as his opinion,
but I imagine that he would imply it. I shall return to this point.

Another parable that is, on the whole, well treated is that of the
Labourers in the Vineyard. The name that is given to this parable shows
at once what is considered to be its main significance. It is headed 'Like
Pay for Different Works'. Jülicher here, as we might perhaps expect,
cuts away the parable from the connexion which it has in the Gospel of
Matthew, as an example of the 'last' becoming 'first', and the 'first'
'last'.

The equal payment is the one reward of the Christian—his final
admission to the kingdom of heaven. It does not exclude the existence of
different ranks and degrees in that kingdom, which is elsewhere taught
quite clearly. What it does insist upon is the fact that in this reward there
is an element of grace, something that has not been earned. As an act of
grace it rests wholly with the goodwill of him by whom it is given. The
questions to which it might give rise are sufficiently answered by calling
attention to this: 'Is thine eye evil because I am good?' On the one hand
there is grace and goodness, but on the other hand there is also strict
performance of what is promised. As Jülicher well puts it:

The God who has but one common salvation for all the children of men,
for chief priests and elders as well as for publicans and harlots, ought not
to be blamed, as only a pitiful jealousy would dare to blame Him, but rather
deserves thankful recognition, whether it be for the righteousness with
which He keeps His promises to those who have kept His commandments,
or for the goodness with which He rewards, far beyond merit or desert,
those in whom the idleness of hours, of years, even of a whole life, called
for censure or for punishment (II, p. 467).

It is true that the text gives no hint as to any compensating difference
in the quality of the work that is spread over a longer or a shorter
time—either in the spirit in which it is done, or in the positive result
attained. It is true also that we are intended to keep such considerations
steadily out of sight. The main point of the parable in no way turns upon

them. But I think that Jülicher goes a step too far when he lays down that the same common average of value is to be assumed throughout (pp. 461-62). I should prefer to put it that the question of value is not raised, that it does not enter into the parable. If the question were raised, then I think we may be sure that the difference of value would really come in. The teaching of the Gospels elsewhere certainly recognizes such compensating differences of value. The time that a man has been at work is only one part, and it may be a small part, of that which determines the estimate of his labour—

> In small proportions we just beauties see;
> And in short measures life may perfect be.

And over and above the amount done, and its quality when laid in the scales, there must always be the spirit in which it is done. The woman who was a sinner received a warmer meed of praise than the self-satisfied Pharisee, and her love and gratitude were warmer. She who loved much was also greatly forgiven; but in the case of the Pharisee there was neither much love nor much forgiveness. There is a whole cycle of teaching to this effect to which this parable might also have been attached, if that had been its object.

I have said that Jülicher treats this parable without regard to the context in which it is found in the First Gospel. There it is placed between two repetitions of the saying that 'the last shall be first and the first shall be last', and the parable is clearly intended to illustrate that saying. And there is indeed an inversion of order in the way in which the labourers are called up to receive their pay. That however is, as Jülicher says, a very subordinate point in the parable. It is necessary to the parable because the murmurers who receive no more than their due must have had the opportunity of seeing the generous measure accorded to their predecessors. But the order of payment is a minor detail; and it might be thought, as Jülicher thinks, that it would be more likely to suggest the place assigned to the parable by the Evangelist than to establish an integral connexion with the saying about 'the first and the last'.

And yet, if we do not limit ourselves as Jülicher does, but take in the whole significance of the parable, including the reference, which is really after all not very remote, to the Pharisees as representing the first called, and the outcasts as representing those who are called last, then we shall allow that there is at least a more substantial reason for associating the parable with the saying.

A rather similar point arises in regard to another parable—that of the Unrighteous Steward. There, in the text as we have it, two lessons are drawn from the parable. One is the commendation of the steward 'because he had done wisely: for the sons of this world are for their own generation wiser than the sons of light'. The other is, 'Make to yourselves friends by means of the mammon of unrighteousness; that, when it shall fail, they may receive you into the eternal tabernacles'. Jülicher accepts the first of these, but rejects the second. He would make the lesson of the parable, to take betimes the appropriate means for attaining the end; he sees in it the case of one 'who rescues himself from a position to all appearance desperate by taking thought and acting while both thought and action can still be of use, while he has the means still in his hands' (II, pp. 510-11). For Jülicher the emphasis falls 'not on the right application of wealth, but on the resolute utilizing of the present as the condition of a happy future'.

On his principles a choice between the two lessons is necessary; and it is natural, and no doubt right, that he should choose the one that covers best the parable as a whole. But if we suppose that the parables did admit more than a single lesson, and if we believe that our Lord did from time to time explain his own figurative language to his disciples, then it cannot be denied that the other lesson—to make such a use of wealth as to win for ourselves friends who will welcome us into the world to come—is in itself perfectly good and legitimate, a lesson which has a very distinct point, and is worth teaching.

Why should we be precluded from accepting it on grounds that seem to be so *a priori* as Professor Jülicher's? The gist of the whole matter lies in a single sentence:

> To understand a parable [we are told] we must not look for points of resemblance in the single constituent ideas of the parable, but we must note the resemblance between the *relation of the ideas* on the one side and that of those on the other. As the similitude is meant to illustrate a single word, *so is the parable meant to illustrate a single thought by a means of an* ὅμοιον, *so that here too we can speak only of a* tertium comparationis, *not of several* tertia (II, p. 70).

Indeed a strange restriction! May we never group ideas, and compare not only the whole of a conception but the parts that make up the whole? Why should we not do this, if the parts really invite comparison? Why should we so cramp the free play of the mind? Jülicher does not really observe his own rule. He says that the Parable of the Sower is meant to teach that no labour always succeeds, and that much of it is sure to be expended in vain, and yet he calls the parable *Vom viererlei Acker*, 'The Four Kinds of Soil'. What difference does it make that these four kinds do not exhaust all the possible kinds of soil? It would be sheer pedantry to expect that they should. Here, as elsewhere, we may well be content to have put before us a few striking and picturesque examples as specimens of the rest.

It would be a curious mind which permitted itself no side-glances. And such side-glances as we find in the parables come in so easily, so simply, and so naturally, that it is doubly wrong to ignore them.

Again, to go back for a moment to the elder brother. The character and attitude of this brother corresponds exactly to a permanent type, often hinted at in the Gospels and specially common at the time to which they belong. Are we to suppose that there is no allusion whatever to this type, and that he is only introduced as a lay figure to which to attach the Father's apology for his conduct?

I praised Jülicher's treatment of this incident, but I cannot be debarred from reading into it more significance than he does. The incident may help us to form our estimate of Jülicher's book as a whole. It brings out at once its strong and its weak side. I believe that in the whole its effect will be salutary. It is so important that the central, and that the other subordinate ideas should be duly graduated in relation to them, that it is well, even at some cost, to have this side of the matter emphasized. But Jülicher, I feel sure, goes further than he need. He lays down a rule which is too rigid, and which violates the many-sidedness and varied interest of life.

Let us try to throw ourselves into the position of those Galilean peasants and fisherman, with a sprinkling of the more educated classes, who formed the audience of Jesus. Is it so incredible that the parables needed explanation to them? It is hard for us to judge now that they have been so many centuries before the world, and we ourselves have been brought up from childhood upon them. We assume the Gospel of Jesus as a known quantity. We are familiar with the thoughts which he wished to elicit, the type of character which he wished to create. Strike away these conditions; suppose them non-existent; and put in their place the mental equipment of an ordinary Galilean crowd of the time. Where would the intelligence come in? What would it find to take hold of? The disciples themselves, even the chosen Twelve, are represented in the Gospels as very dull. But at least this representation seemed to have verisimilitude at the time. It was passed on from document to document, and became practically the accepted view of the second generation of Christians.

I am unable to see any adequate reason for doubting the tradition that has come down to us on any one of the three connected points to which Jülicher takes exception: that the hearers of Jesus did need some explanation of the teaching set before them, that as a matter of fact Jesus gave such explanation, and that the explanations were, generally speaking, of the kind of which specimens are given in the case of the Parables of the Sower, and of the Wheat and the Tares. The second of these two specimens is not quite so well attested as the first, and is perhaps open to a little more question; but if we accept the first, and accept also the statement of Mk 4.34, there can be no objection to it in principle.

And if we see our way to sustain the tradition as far as this, I believe that we shall also be prepared to sustain it further—to sustain it at least in the same general sense without absolutely pledging ourselves in detail. Jülicher, as we have seen, sets down to the account of the Evangelists the whole of the paragraph which professes to give the reason assigned by our Lord for speaking in parables. I have already referred to the fact, and it is important to remember, that this paragraph belongs to the fundamental document; so that in no case does the responsibility for it rest with the authors of our present Gospels. They simply copied what they found in the place where they found it. We will not say that the words were necessarily spoken on the occasion of the delivery of the first parable. Neither will I undertake to say that our Lord used exactly the form of words ascribed to him and no other. Two out of the three Gospels make it the express object of the teaching by the parables to confirm the hearers in their obstinacy and to hide the mysteries of the kingdom from them (ἵνα βλέποντες βλέπωσιν καὶ μὴ ἴδωσιν κ.τ.λ. Mk 4.12; ἵνα βλέποντες βλέπωσιν κ.τ.λ. Lk. 8.10); Matthew puts this rather differently (διὰ τοῦτο ἐν παραβολαῖς αὐτοῖς λαλῶ, ὅτι βλέποντες οὐ βλέπουσιν [13.13]). It would seem as though ἵνα βλέπωσιν had been the form in the original document; it would not follow with stringency, that it was the form in which the words were actually spoken by Jesus. I should not like to say that they were not so spoken merely in order to ease the historical or dogmatic inference; but I also should not like to build too confidently upon the assumption that they were. All that I should have some confidence in extracting from the passage would be that our Lord probably did, at some time in the course of his ministry, apply or adapt in reference to his own teaching, the words that were given as a special revelation describing the effect of his teaching to the prophet Isaiah.

Nor does there seem to be sufficient ground to reject the application to teaching by parables, though it is possible that the original reference may have been to the teaching of our Lord, or even to his ministry, as a whole. But the main point is that there is solid foundation for ascribing the words, or something like them, to our Lord. The Synoptical passage, Mk 4.10-12 and parallels, does not stand alone. In the Fourth Gospel where the ministry of our Lord is drawing to a close, and the Evangelist is looking back over its course, he too applies the prophecy of Isaiah as fulfilled in the unbelief of the Jews: 'For this cause they could not believe, for that Isaiah said again, He hath blinded their eyes, and He hardened their heart, etc. These things said Isaiah, because he saw His glory; and he spake of Him' (Jn 12.39-41).

Then again when Paul arrives at Rome and receives a deputation from the Jewish colony there, he is represented as closing the debate by an appeal to the same prophecy: 'Well spake the Holy Ghost by Isaiah the prophet unto your fathers, saying, Go thou unto this people, and say, By hearing ye shall hear, and shall not understand', etc. (Acts 28.25-27).

These indications go to show that the passage was one of the standing quotations current in the apostolic age as a summary verdict upon the refusal of the Jews to listen to the Gospel. We cannot of course infer for certain that its use was suggested by a similar use of the passage by our Lord himself, but the probabilities seem to point that way. The facts would hang together very naturally and intelligibly if the first impulse came from him.

And there is yet another observation that seems to me to point in the same direction. I refer to the places more particularly in John's Gospel, where our Lord speaks of his own preaching as of itself, by a sort of automatic process, dividing between believers and unbelievers, 'If any man hear My sayings and keep them not... the word that I spake, the same shall judge him in the last day' (Jn 12.47, 48), and again, 'For judgment came I into this world, that they which see not may see, and that they which see may become blind' (Jn 9.39). It was but a working out of the prophecy of Simeon, 'Behold, this Child is set for the falling and rising up of many in Israel' (Lk. 2.34). The whole ministry of Jesus had this effect; but we might regard it as culminating in the parables.

This simple and yet profound teaching left men either better or worse, according as it was apprehended and taken to heart. If it was not so taken at all, it did leave them worse—and that in proportion to the opportunities they had of really understanding it. That it should do so was not an act of special severity on the part of the Teacher. It was simply due to a law of Divine providence, which applies to all men and to all times, but to that generation in supreme degree, because its opportunities were the greatest.

This effect of his teaching our Lord foresaw, and I believe that it was in view of it that he appropriated words originally spoken of the life-work of a prophet in some degree like himself.

My readers must judge how far Jülicher is justified in his final antithesis:

> One thing or the other (*Entweder-Oder*): *either* the aim to produce hardening levelled at the masses—that and nothing else—and with it the trustworthiness of the Synoptics in this matter too, *or* an erroneous inference on their part due to error in their premises and the same object that, as every one feels, parables elsewhere serve, including those of our Lord. This 'one thing or the other' goes deep: *either* the Evangelists *or* Jesus (I, p. 148).

Perhaps it will now be understood what I meant when I began by taking Jülicher as a rather specially apt example of 'vigour and rigour'. The sentences just quoted are a good specimen of his style. The phrase *Entweder-Oder* is one that has attractions for him: he elsewhere speaks of Jesus Himself as 'the Man of the *Entweder-Oder*' (II, p. 456). For that there may be some ground: but, at least in the passage just quoted, it seems to me that the antithesis presented is too sharp, and the method too peremptory.

The most important aspect of Jülicher's book is no doubt his general view of the parables, and of the principles of interpretation to be applied to them. But the book offers much more than this: the second volume is nothing less than a close critical and exegetical study of so much of the text of the Synoptic Gospels as comes under the head of the parable.

The author himself is aware that there may be two opinions as to the policy of this elaborate treatment. I do not doubt that the book would be more effective if it had been not more than a third of the length—just a broad summarizing treatment of each parable, with salient points brought into relief, but otherwise not going into detail. This is the kind of book which an English writer would have aimed at; and I believe that

Herr Jülicher might do well to consider whether he would not even now find it worthwhile to sit down and rewrite the whole on this much condensed scale. Being a German, he is not likely to be weary of his self-imposed task; and after his laborious study of the details of his subject, he would now have it so thoroughly in hand that the book would be sure to come out a far more rounded and artistic whole. An artistic whole it cannot be called at present; and some self-repression would be needed to make it one. But in rewriting from the full mind the process of sifting, grouping, and shaping would come naturally of itself.

It is not only that by taking this course I believe that the author would be doing the best for his own reputation in years to come—he might produce a classic in its way for which a long life was assured—but besides this he would, I imagine, reap a far more substantial harvest than the present two volumes are likely to bring him. A good translation of such a work as I have suggested would, I believe, have a large and steady sale in Great Britain and America.

It is an instance of German thoroughness that the author has made his book what it is; and it would be ungracious not to acknowledge the abundant material that he has laid before us. The mere fact of collecting and setting down all this material must needs be of great value to the author; and for the student and scholar no abridgment can supersede it. It is one commentary the more on a large section of that part of the New Testament which at the present moment most needs commentaries, the Synoptic Gospels.

What exactly are we to say as to the objective value of this commentary as it stands? Herr Jülicher is, as I have said more than once, an undoubtedly able man; and a commentary by such a man, which represents many years of study, cannot fail to deserve attention. But I have my doubts as to whether it is quite the work of a heaven-sent exegete.

Here again I should take exception to the form. As compared with the old-fashioned *Scholia*, a sort of running commentary is at present time far more fashionable. But I much suspect that the fashion is a mistake. It is rare indeed for the running commentary to be really readable; and if it is not readable, what is gained? It is apt to be far more prolix than the *Scholium*, and it is far more difficult to find one's way about in it. Terseness and clear printing, with the reference figures well thrown out, are essential to the *Scholium*. And the pressure that is thus put upon writer and printer is all to their own advantage. Bengel's *Gnomon* still remains the best model of style.[2]

In Jülicher's commentary, as in all commentaries, there is much with which one agrees, and much from which one dissents; and he would be a conceited critic who took the measure of his own agreement or dissent as a sufficient index of value. But I have expressed my doubts as to the extent to which Herr Jülicher will carry his readers irresistibly with him. As to one whole class of annotations these doubts rise to a considerable degree of scepticism. I refer especially to the treatment of the text.

It may seem strange to say it of one who (in his *Einleitung*) has written in such a generally competent manner about the text, and who has applied to that part of his subject so much thought as Professor Jülicher; but I cannot dismiss from my mind the impression that in spite of these qualifications he handles questions of text like an *amateur*. I mean by this that he takes each reading as if it stood alone, and needed little for its determination besides the relation which the reading bears to the context. Jülicher speaks of 'better MSS' and 'inferior MSS', and of this or that family of witnesses, but these distinctions appear to have a *minimum* of significance for him. He is prepared to throw them over without compunction at the bidding of internal inclinations, and especially in deference to what he thinks is required by the context. He seems to forget how very double-edged such indications constantly are. The decisive considerations for Herr Jülicher are often just what we might conceive to have been at work in the mind of the scribe who had the best attested reading before him, but felt bound to alter and 'improve' it. Herr Jülicher's, I imagine, is often just an 'emended text'— a text emended, not as usually happens by an ancient scribe, but by a modern editor.

I therefore, upon the whole, do not regard Herr Jülicher's commentary as by any means ideal. Still it is, as I once more repeat, an able piece of work, and one that the exegete cannot afford to neglect. Even when it does not command his assent, it will constantly suggest interesting points of view.

---

2.   Blass on the Acts is also a good recent example (*Acta Apostolorum sive Lucae ad Theophilum liber alter* [Göttingen: Vandenhoeck & Ruprecht, 1895]); and the Cambridge commentaries (Lightfoot, Hort, Westcott, Swete) are essentially of the same type; they are still 'notes' though very full 'notes'.

Chapter 12

ON THE TITLE, 'SON OF MAN'[*]

A little work has recently appeared, *The First Three Gospels, their Origin and Relations*, by the Rev. J. Estlin Carpenter, the modest and unpretending form of which hardly does justice to the character of its contents. This is indeed the one thing that I should most regret about it. The book is addressed, in my opinion, to an inappropriate public. It is published in a series of 'Biblical Manuals', under the auspices of the Sunday School Association (Unitarian). It may therefore be inferred that it is intended for the young. And for the highest class of young pupils it is in many respects excellently fitted. It is written with a clearness of development and a flowing ease of style which draw on the reader and prevent his interest from flagging. There is just the right degree of warmth about it. It is elevated in tone, without being stilted or rhetorical. Even one who does not sympathize with the author's point of view, and who cannot profess to be indifferent to his conclusions, will find them presented with as little unnecessary friction and aggressiveness as possible.

These are considerable merits, and the author is fully entitled to the credit of them. The drawbacks are: First, as I have said, that the book is addressed to the wrong public. Books for the young are not the proper field for critical experiment. They should be confined to ascertained and acknowledged fact. Theories which depend upon critical premises should first be threshed out in the schools before they are taken down into the highways and hedges. They should first be propounded in a form in which they can be adequately discussed and tested. The writer should have before his eyes the wholesome knowledge that he is writing for scholars who will not allow his statements and theories to pass

[*] This chapter originally appeared as W. Sanday, 'On the Title "Son of Man"', *The Expositor*, Fourth Series, 3 (1891), pp. 18-32, responding to J.E. Carpenter, *The First Three Gospels: Their Origin and Relations* (Biblical Manuals; London: Sunday School Association, 2nd edn, 1890).

unquestioned. It seems to me that Mr Carpenter's book has distinctly suffered from the fact that this has not been the case. Much of it is not really suited to the young, and if it had been submitted in the first instance to those for whom it is suited, it would, I think, have been written differently.

This is the second qualification that I should have to make in regard to it, that it looks at first sight critical in a higher sense than it really is. I do not refer merely to certain unguarded expressions, such as on p. 115, where it is assumed without a hint of doubt that the last words of Mk 1.1, 'The beginning of the Gospel of Jesus Christ [the Son of God]', are an interpolation, although they are wanting only in a single uncial manuscript (ℵ), and although their omission (supposing them to be genuine) might be due to one of the commonest accidents. I do not say that the omission has nothing to be said for it; but the right verdict is undoubtedly that of Drs Westcott and Hort, that 'neither reading can be safely rejected'. It is a more serious matter when we find a sentence like this on the fourth Gospel: 'The rich background of nature and society, the variety of occupations, the manifold touches which reveal the teacher's close and loving observation of his countrymen, are merged in a few great and universal ideas, *in whose glow all local colour has been blanched away*'. The first orthodox commentary on the Gospel that is taken up—Dr Westcott's or Dr Plummer's—will show that this is the very reverse of the fact.[1] The fourth Gospel is really full of local colour, and to deny this is to give a wholly misleading aspect to the evidence on one of the most fundamental questions.

The Synoptic Gospels are less dangerous ground, and Mr Carpenter gives a critical analysis of these to which little exception can be taken. His last three chapters are indeed a welcome sign of the progress which is being made towards agreement on this head. The Gospel of Mark is placed about the year 70 AD, and that of Luke some ten tears later, both very probable dates. And if there is a tendency to bring too far down the latest touches in the Gospel which bears the name of Matthew, it is acknowledged that the mass of the materials of which it is composed are the older. The whole of this part of the case is stated with moderation, and I should myself feel that it would not be difficult to arrive at an

---

1.   B.F. Westcott, *The Gospel According to St John* (Speaker's Commentary; London: John Murray, 1882), pp. 5ff.; A. Plummer, *The Gospel According to St John: With Maps, Notes and Introduction* (Cambridge Greek Testament; Cambridge: Cambridge University Press, 1882), pp. 27ff.

understanding about it. It is however rather strange, and perhaps not without significance, that the chapters dealing with this side of the subject are the last in the book. They come in rather as an ornamental appendage to the reconstruction of the history than as the foundation on which it is based. And accordingly we find that the critical determination of the sources has had less to do with the main body of the book than might have been expected. It needs, in fact, little reading between the lines to see that certain dominant ideas are present to the mind of the author throughout, and that his decision on particular points is far more affected by them than by any strictly objective documentary standard. There looms before him a dim ideal of what he conceives that the Christ ought to be; and if the Gospels do not of themselves yield exactly that ideal, they must be corrected into accordance with it.

This is to me another disappointing feature in the book. It claims to be critical, and it uses a critical language; but when it comes to being looked into, the criticism will be found to be far more subjective than objective. And, as a consequence, it will satisfy the author himself, and those of his own way of thinking, more than others who differ from him. An example may be seen in the appendix dealing with the title 'Son of Man', which contains the central and distinctive idea towards which a great part of the volume may be said to be working. The treatment of this title is, to the best of my belief, new and original; and although I cannot regard it as at all tenable, it may yet seem to deserve some closer examination.

Mr Carpenter's idea is, briefly stated, this: He thinks that our Lord did not really use the title in the sense attributed to it in the Gospels. He would link on the actual use to the context in which it originally occurs in the book of Daniel. It will be remembered that the first instance in which the phrase occurs in any exceptional sense is in connexion with the vision of the four great monarchies: the first represented by a lion; the second, by a bear; the third, by a leopard; the fourth, by a monster with iron teeth and ten horns. The Ancient of days takes his seat upon the throne of judgment; the last of the beasts is destroyed, and the others deposed; and there comes with the clouds one 'like unto a son of man', who is brought before the Ancient of days, and receives a dominion which is universal and eternal.[2] There is some little divergence in the interpretation, especially of the second of these symbolical creatures; still there is no doubt that they stand for a succession of monarchies,

2.   Dan. 7.1-14.

according to the most common view, the Babylonian, Median, Persian, and Macedonian, or the empire of Alexander and his successors. In contrast with these, the Form 'like a son of man' represents, no doubt, in its primary significance, and in the horizon of the prophet, the idealized, regenerated, purified Israel. From a Christian point of view it is not wrongly transferred to him who embodied and fulfilled the ideal vocation of Israel.

Mr Carpenter however—quite reasonably from his standpoint—adheres to the primary application to a regenerated Israel. He thinks that the use in the Gospels grew directly out of this. The 'Coming of the Son of Man' he takes to be a synonym for the triumph of 'the kingdom', that great social change and renovation to which there can be no doubt that Jesus looked forward. In more than one passage the equation is found in the Gospels, 'Coming of the Son of Man' = 'coming of the kingdom' (e.g. in Mk 9.1 = Lk. 9.27 = Mt. 16.28). These passages Mr Carpenter takes as a key to the explanation of the rest; and he skilfully works out the view that, wherever personality is ascribed to the Son of Man, this is due to a misunderstanding of the real teaching of Jesus. What he said impersonally the Church, at a very early date, understood personally. Starting from the belief that Jesus was the Messiah, his disciples soon came to refer what was meant for the Messianic people to the Messiah himself. Hence the existence of a number of passages in the Gospels in which Jesus is made to speak of himself when in point of fact he did not do so; hence in particular the appropriation of a large group of sayings in which mention is made of the 'Coming of the Son of Man', from the inauguration of an age of righteousness, or coming of a righteous people, to the personal coming, or Second Coming, as we are in the habit of calling it, of the Messiah.

I have said that this hypothesis is skilfully worked out, but I do not for a moment believe that it is true. It involves, as will be seen at once, a wholesale rewriting of the Gospels. It is no doubt the case that there is one important group of passages in which the title 'Son of Man' is specially connected with this future or Second Coming. There is no great difficulty in re-interpreting these in the sense desired. But there is also a number of other passages which are broken up entirely by the attempt to force any such meaning upon them. These have to be got rid of by less legitimate methods.

No very great straining is indeed involved in the explanation of the question in Mt. 16.13 ('Who do men say that the Son of Man is?') as a simple periphrasis for 'that I am' which is found in the other two Gospels. Nor is it in itself difficult to account by this expedient for the occurrence of the phrase in the predictions of the passion, although the persistent way in which it is repeated on all the four occasions where these predictions are uttered (Mk 8.31; 9.9, 12, 31; 10.33) cannot fail to arrest attention and arouse some misgiving.

Mr Carpenter does not allow that these predictions were so precise as they are made to be. He thinks that Jesus knew the risks he was running, and that he deliberately faced them; but the definite predictions he would explain rather as 'the Church's apology for Messiah's death. The stumbling-block of a crucified Christ was removed if it could be shown that he had himself predicted his end in conformity with ancient prophecy.'[3] But then he goes on to attribute a delicate tact to those who first gave shape to the traditions, which makes a larger demand upon our opinion of them.

> But why should Messiah be here designated 'Son of Man'? Because in the formation of the tradition the language assigned to Jesus accommodated itself to his historic utterances. Now the synoptic Gospels never represent him his designating himself as the Messiah. He does not repudiate the title when it is offered him, but he carefully refrains from assuming it; the official designation is never on his lips. It was impossible then that the Church should exhibit Jesus as habitually employing a name which he carefully avoided; and the Messianic feeling therefore had to embody itself in some other term which could find a sanction in his own practice. Such a term was ready in the name 'Son of Man', which had been employed by Jesus to describe the immediate advent of the 'kingdom' in which God's will should be done on earth as is it was in heaven.[4]

I leave it to the reader to say how far a procedure of this kind—at once so bold in its recasting of one set of facts and so sensitive and scrupulous in its regard for another—was probable in the circles in which the Christian tradition was formed in the middle of the first century.

But however this may be, there are other cases which are more intractable. One such comes early in the Synoptic narrative, and is deeply seated in the triple tradition. In the healing of the paralytic at Capernaum our Lord pronounces an absolution over the sick man and then heals him, claiming the right to forgive sins as the 'Son of Man'.

3. Carpenter, *The First Three Gospels*, p. 374.
4. Carpenter, *The First Three Gospels*, p. 374.

Mr Carpenter objects to this in that it 'involves the conception of a causal connexion between the sin and the disease which it is difficult to believe that Jesus really entertained', and that it is contrary to the view implied in his question about the eighteen on whom the tower of Siloam fell.[5] But is there no connexion between sin and disease? Is there any reason why there should not have been such a connexion in this particular case? The catastrophe at Siloam is not parallel. A further objection is, that the part about the forgiveness of sins comes in as a parenthesis. It is a parenthesis (in Mark) of some six verses, and is found, as we have seen, with remarkable closeness of language in the other Synoptics. It therefore goes back as far as the documents can take us, and clearly belonged to their common original. Incidents like this are needed to sustain the charge of blasphemy; and the mere fact that one part of a narrative is separable from the rest by no means proves that it ought to be separated.

Another example follows soon after this. Our Lord supports the act of his disciples in plucking the ears of corn, not only by the precedent of Abiathar, but also by laying down the principle that 'the Sabbath was made for man, and not man for the Sabbath', to which, according to Mark, he adds the further corollary, 'so that the Son of Man is Lord even of the Sabbath'. A natural and appropriate climax, say we, to whom the title 'Son of Man' presents no difficulties: 'exceedingly unsatisfactory' is Mr Carpenter's verdict; but the difficulty in his eyes is clearly not critical, but dogmatic.

It is not surprising that the passages against which a criticism of this kind is directed are many of them those which Christendom specially values.

> Whosoever would become great among you, shall be your servant: and whosoever would be first among you, shall be servant of all. For verily the Son of Man came not to be ministered unto, but to minister, and to give His life a ransom for many (Mk 10.43-45).

It is observed upon this that, while Matthew is in almost complete verbal agreement with Mark, he introduces

> the saying about the Son of Man with 'even as' instead of 'for'. But the very fact that the phrase receives this introduction[6] awakes the suspicion

---

5.   Carpenter, *The First Three Gospels*, p. 378.

6.   The ancients were less careful than we are in preserving causal connexions. For instance, in the Latin versions *enim* and *autem* are frequently treated as almost interchangeable.

that we are presented rather with a comment or reflection of the narrator than with a word from Jesus; and it contains a reference to the mystic efficacy of his death which shows at once what is the significance of the name 'Son of Man', and appears to be due rather to the interpretation of the Church than to the word of the teacher. The equivalent in the third Gospel, Lk. 22.27, 'I am among you as he that serveth [ministereth]', is much more direct.

According to the critical analysis, the presence of a phrase in two out of the three authorities decides its claim to acceptance as representing the common original of all three. Mr Carpenter himself appears to recognise this principle;[7] but he ignores it altogether when it comes into collision with what he considers *a priori* probability, i.e. with anything that favours the thesis which he aims at proving.

No better foundation seems to underlie the rejection of Lk. 19.10, the commendation of Zacchaeus: 'Today is salvation come to this house, forasmuch as he also is a son of Abraham. For the Son of Man came to seek and to save that which was lost.'

It is admitted that it cannot be proved, but at the same time suggested as 'not improbable, that some original utterance of Jesus has been cast by the Church into this form, and that the phrase has grown out of the effort to portray Messiah as the world's redeeming power, the Saviour even of the lowest of mankind'. We cannot help asking, Whence came that effort? It certainly was not prompted by the current Jewish conception of the Messiah; and it can hardly have been derived from any other source than the teaching of Jesus himself.

There is more that is attractive in the acute observation that the mention of blasphemy 'against the Son of Man' in Lk. 12.10 (= Mt. 12.32) may possibly have arisen from misreading of an original which had the 'sons of men' ('all their sins shall be forgiven unto the sons of men'), as in the parallel context of Mark. But here we have again the agreement of two of the synoptic columns against the third; so that we should have to believe that the same misreading lay behind each. And if there is a questionable element in the passage about the sign of Jonah (Mt. 12.40 = Lk. 11.30), that element is contained, not in the allusion to the Son of Man ('so shall the Son of Man be [a sign to this generation]'), which is common to both accounts, but rather in the expansion of this which is found in Matthew.

7. Carpenter, *The First Three Gospels*, pp. 264, 266.

It will have been seen that too many of the examples quoted above are not only not suggested by the critical analysis, but directly opposed to it. The temptation has been too strong to choose, not that form of a saying which approves itself as most original, but that which lends the most support to the hypothesis which is being advocated. Mr Carpenter, I cannot but think, has been progressing too fast. He has formed his theories too soon, and allowed them to mix themselves with his statement of the facts. I can only see in the result a confirmation of what I have long held, that in order to get at any sound conclusion about the Synoptic Gospels we need to execute a 'self-denying ordinance', and for some sufficient period of time exclude all theories of this higher sort involving the supernatural, whether in the way of affirmation or of denial; and that we should confine ourselves strictly to the critical problem of ascertaining what is the absolutely earliest form of the tradition, and by what steps and gradations other later forms are built up round it. We have Mr Rushbrooke's *Synopticon*,[8] but we have not yet that series of close and minute studies for which it ought to furnish the text. And pending the prosecution of those studies, I would respectfully invite the authors of 'biblical manuals' such as that of which I am speaking to think twice before they engage in what may be a spreading broadcast of error.

It must not however be supposed that my sole objection to the particular theory before us is that it involves the rewriting—and the premature rewriting—of the Gospels. Another group of reasons, historical rather than critical, tells in the same direction. There is one marked omission in Mr Carpenter's argument. He says nothing (in this connexion) of the *Book of Enoch*. Probably the simplest interpretation of this silence is that he sets down the passages implicated as of Christian origin. The view is that of a minority of critics: still it is held by Dr Drummond in his *Jewish Messiah*; and I can quite understand his colleague sharing the opinion. The point is however important, not to say vital, in its bearing upon the whole question. Perhaps this is another instance in which the exigencies of a school manual have interfered with the proper scientific discussion of a problem which demands science. If the so called 'parables' in the *Book of Enoch* are pre-Christian, then the whole conditions of the problem are different. In that case it cannot be questioned that the title 'Son of Man' was already applied, before Jesus

---

8.   W.G. Rushbrooke, *Synopticon: An Exposition of the Common Matter of the Synoptic Gospels* (London: Macmillan, 1880).

used it, to the personal Messiah. Here for instance is a passage which excludes all doubt upon the subject:

> There I saw One who had a head of days [i.e. was old], and His head was white like wool; and with Him was a Second, whose countenance was like the appearance of a man, and His countenance was full of grace, like one of the holy angels. And I asked one of the angels who were with me, and who showed me all the secrets, concerning this Son of Man who He was and whence He was, and why He goes with the Head of days. And he answered and said to me: This is the Son of Man who has justice, and justice dwells with Him; and all the treasuries of secrecy He reveals, because the Lord of the spirits has chosen Him, and His portion overcomes all things before the Lord of the spirits in rectitude to eternity. And this Son of Man whom thou hast seen, will arouse the kings and mighty from their couches, and the strong from their thrones, and will loosen the bands of the strong, and will break the teeth of the sinners... (*1 Enoch* 46.1ff.).[9]

There are several other passages equally explicit, and all much to the same effect. Schürer places the chapters in which they are found about the time of Herod the Great. He argues that there is nothing in them which is not entirely explicable on Jewish premises; that they are either wholly Jewish or wholly Christian, the hypothesis of interpolation being inadmissible; but that if they are Christian, the wonder is that they are not more Christian, as they speak of the Messiah only as coming in glory and for judgment, and do not give a hint of any other coming in a state of suffering and humiliation.[10] This seems to me, I confess, sound reasoning. There is nothing to identify this Judge of quick and dead with the historical person of Jesus of Nazareth.[11] We may observe further that judgment is threatened mainly against heathen potentates and tyrants and not upon individuals. This is exactly in accordance with the temper of the Jews, who consoled themselves for the oppression from which

---

9. I have followed the translation from the Ethiopic by G.H. Schodde (*The Book of Enoch: Translated from the Ethiopic, with Introduction and Notes* [Andover: W.F. Draper, 1882]), except for one slight verbal alteration.

10. E. Schürer, *Lehrbuch der neutestamentlichen Zeitgeschichte* (2 vols.; Leipzig: J.C. Hinrichs, 1874), II, p. 626.

11. Dr James Drummond admits that this is 'a formidable difficulty' (*The Jewish Messiah: A Critical History of the Messianic Idea among the Jews from the Rise of the Maccabees to the Closing of the Talmud* [London: Longman, Green, 1877], p. 61), and therefore does not assert that the 'parables' as a whole are post-Christian, but has recourse to the hypothesis of extensive interpolation. Allowance should in fairness be made for the possibility of this.

they suffered by the prospect of seeing their cause avenged; but it is far less in accordance with the spirit of primitive Christianity.

I think therefore that the balance of probability is decidedly in favour of the pre-Christian origin of the passages in question. But I incline to this view still more because of what appears to be the excellent historical sequence if we assume that to be the case. If we suppose that the title 'Son of Man' was already attached to the personal Messiah before the coming of Christ, then it seems to me that all the facts fall beautifully into their places. Mr Carpenter takes up the very paradoxical position that Jesus accepted undoubtedly Messianic titles when they were applied to him by others, and also (if I understand rightly) that he was himself conscious of a Messianic calling; but that he never spoke of himself directly as the Messiah unless it were in the one character as 'Servant of Jehovah'.[12] In other words, he will not allow the name 'Son of Man', which our Lord is made to give to himself in all the Gospels, and he will allow the name 'Servant of Jehovah', which he does not explicitly give to himself in any of the Gospels, although it was undoubtedly given to him by primitive tradition.[13] Let us make the contrary assumption, and see with what a delicate felicity and appropriateness the standing title in the Gospels is chosen. I take it that among the Jews at the Christian era, at least among such as shared the lively expectations which were then abroad of the great deliverance which was approaching, it was distinctly understood that the 'Son of Man' meant 'the Messiah'. At the same time it was not a common title, because the ordinary usage of the phrase 'son of man' in the Old Testament pointed to that side of human weakness and frailty which the zealots of the day least cared to dwell upon in the King for whom they were looking. But the very reason which led them to avoid the title induced our Lord to take it. It expressed his Messiahship definitely enough for his purpose; but it expressed it in that veiled and suggestive way which characterized the whole of his teaching on his own person. At the same time, it conveyed to those who had ears to hear the whole secret of the incarnation. That which the Jews shrank from and ignored he rather placed in the forefront of his mission. He came as the representative of humanity, not militant and triumphant, but in its weakness and suffering. He was made in all points like as we are, though without sin; so that we might not

12. See *The First Three Gospels*, p.125.
13. Cf. Mt. 12.18; Acts 3.13, 26; 4.27, 30; *1 Clem.* 59.2, 3, 4; *Did.* 9.1; *Mart. Pol.* 14.1, 3.

have a High Priest who cannot be touched with the feeling of our infirmities, but who can bear gently with the ignorant and erring.[14] He entered into human nature, and took it as a whole. That very side of it which men were wont to disparage and to try all they could to escape from he made peculiarly his own. He did so, not only in order to make it the point of contact, the recipient and conductor for his own boundless love and sympathy, but also in order to show that through it lay the true path of salvation; to demonstrate in act as well as in word that he that findeth his life shall lose it, and he that loseth his life shall find it; that the true disciple must take up his cross; and that even an apostle must learn that when he is weak then is he strong.

We note then, running through our Lord's use of this title, two veins of meaning side by side. On the one hand, the Son of Man is he who shall come in the clouds of heaven and judge all nations. On the other hand, it is as Son of Man that he mingles in the innocent festivities of life, as 'eating and drinking', though in the same capacity he 'has not where to lay His head'; it is as the Son of Man that he forgives sins, and comes to seek and to save them that are lost; it is as the Son of Man that he foretells his own passion. Other names bring out his other aspects as the Logos, face to face with God from all eternity; as the Son of God, who alone is admitted to the innermost counsels of the Father; as the Son of David, born of the royal lineage, and claiming his royal prerogative; as the anointed Prophet, as well as King; but there is none like this which so touches the tender place in the hearts of men, or which so explains the paradox of victory through suffering: 'I, if I be lifted up, will draw all men unto Me'.

Lastly, the form and manner in which the phrase is used—the very rhythm, we might say, of the sentences in which it is found—stamp it as original. It was natural enough that the seers in the Book of Daniel and in the *Book of Enoch* should speak as they do of the Son of Man in the third person; but it was by no means so obvious that the Messiah should consistently adopt this objective way of referring to himself. Surely we have here one of those individual and characteristic touches which make the figure of Christ, for all its universality, stand out in the Gospels with such distinctness. It is a touch no less individual than that by which the fourth evangelist at once conceals and reveals his own identity. We may indeed be pardoned for the conjecture that on this point the disciple has not been unaffected by the example of the Master. And it is equally

14. Heb 4.15; 5.2.

striking that as in the Fourth Gospel the term 'Logos', though used by the evangelist, is never put into the lips of the Lord, so throughout the New Testament the term 'Son of Man' is reserved for the Lord himself, with the single exception of the exclamation of Stephen.[15] But it is another matter when we are told that this scrupulously consistent, and beautifully harmonious and significant usage is all due to a misunderstanding, and that it is the work, not of Christ himself, but of the early Church. Many of us will doubt the power of the popular imagination to produce effects so much above its own level. But indeed on all grounds the hypothesis seems to be an untenable one. The texture of the Gospels is too closely knit to allow room for it by any process of critical elimination, and to introduce it is to make the history of the founding of Christianity less coherent and less intelligible.

15. Acts 7.56.

Chapter 13

THE INJUNCTIONS OF SILENCE IN THE GOSPELS[*]

It is now some two years since there appeared one of those elaborate monographs,[1] so characteristic of German theology, presenting an entirely new and original argument, which if it had held good would have had far-reaching consequences. To understand the bearing of this argument it is necessary briefly to glance at a point in the criticism of the Synoptic Gospels which seems to have won very general acceptance.

The great majority of those who have studied the subject are agreed that the Gospel of Mark, or a writing extremely like our present Gospel, if not necessarily the oldest of such writings that have come down to us, is yet the common basis of the three Synoptic Gospels. The other writers, whom we know as Matthew and Luke, made use of this Gospel, and derived from it the large element which is common to all three, and which is the more important because it gave that outline of our Lord's public ministry, beginning with the Baptism and ending with the Crucifixion and Resurrection, with which we are most familiar.

It would be too much to say that the sequence of events as they are given in this Gospel is in all respects strictly chronological. In more than one instance it would seem that the smaller sections of narration are grouped together not in order of time, but because of a certain resemblance in their subject-matter. But taken as a whole, the order of the narratives in Mark's Gospel, which in this may be identified with the common foundation of the three Gospels, is excellent, and presents an evolution of the history which is both harmonious in itself and probably represents in the main the real course of the events.

The narrative, as I have said, begins with the Baptism and ends with the Crucifixion and Resurrection. In the intervening period there is a

---

    * This chapter originally appeared as W. Sanday, 'The Injunctions of Silence in the Gospels', *Journal of Theological Studies* 5 (1904), pp. 321-29.

    1. W. Wrede, *Das Messiasgeheimnis in den Evangelien* (Göttingen: Vandenhoeck & Ruprecht, 1901).

clearly-marked climax at the Transfiguration. Up to that point there is a steady ascent which culminates in the confession of Peter; down from it there is in like manner a descent which finds characteristic expression in the predictions of the approaching Passion, Death, and Resurrection, which begin from the same point, in close connexion with Peter's confession and the Transfiguration.

Another special feature of Mark's Gospel, which has also passed from it to some extent into the other Gospels, is the peculiar air of mystery and secrecy which is thrown over certain aspects of our Lord's career— his marked reserve in putting forward his Messianic claims; the double character of his teaching, and more particularly of his parables, at once so simple in outward form and so baffling to those who sought really to understand them; and a like strangely double character in the miracles, which on the one hand are wrought in rather considerable numbers, and on the other hand, we might say almost frequently are accompanied by an express command that they are not to be made known, or at least not published abroad. And lastly there is a similar injunction of silence in regard to the predictions of suffering, death, and rising again.

It was impossible for a student of the Gospels to avoid noticing these points, which clearly hang together, though the connexion between them might not appear on the surface. Most of those who have made the attempt to write a Life of Christ have been content to take them as they stand, and indeed to accept all this part of the outline which Mark gives of our Lord's public ministry as strictly historical.

And indeed I will venture to say that all these features in the narrative are not only strictly but beautifully historical. Whether we see their full significance or not, there is just that paradoxical touch about them which is the sure guarantee of truth. What writer of fiction, especially of the naïve fiction current in those days, would ever have thought of introducing such features, with just that kind of seeming self-contradiction? I repeat: even if we could not at once understand all that is meant by these subtle oppositions, I think we should not fail to see in them something strikingly lifelike and individual, quite beyond the reach of invention.

That, I cannot but think, will be the feeling of most of us. But what no one (to the best of my belief) has ever done before, that Professor Wrede of Breslau, in the monograph to which I began by referring, has now done. He has called in question the truth of all this delicate portraiture. I will not prejudge the manner in which he has done this; but I will begin with a brief sketch of the argument as he states it.

The main point is this. If Jesus of Nazareth claimed to be the Messiah, he would not have gone about preventing his followers from publishing that claim. If he wrought miracles in support of it, he would not have enjoined secrecy on those upon whom they had been wrought. The two things would neutralize each other. It would be futile to tell some few individuals to keep silence if there were many others who received no such command of silence.

The truth, Wrede maintains, is that Jesus of Nazareth did not during his lifetime put himself forward as the Messiah at all. The whole structure of the narrative which makes him do so is built not on a basis of fact but on the belief of the Early Church. After the Resurrection the disciples came to believe that Christ was God, and they read back this belief into the history of his life. They found themselves confronted with the fact that he had not claimed to be the Messiah while he was alive, and had consequently not given proofs of his Messiahship. To confess the fact would have been fatal to the dogma which they had come to believe; and therefore they tried to conceal it by inventing these injunctions of silence. When they were asked by those who knew what the course of the life of Jesus had really been, why he had not shown himself to be the supernatural being that they claimed, their reply was that he really had shown it in a number of ways, but that he had prevented these proofs from having their full effect by repeatedly commanding both his own more immediate disciples and others to abstain from publishing what he was and much that he had done.

I do not know how it will appear to others, but I confess that to me this theory seems unreal and artificial in the extreme. That any ancient should seek to cover the non-existence of certain presumed facts by asserting that they did exist, but that the persons affected were compelled to keep silence about them, is a hypothesis altogether too far-fetched to be credible.

We observe, by the way, that on this theory an enormous weight is thrown upon the Resurrection. It was the Resurrection which gave rise to that belief in the Divinity of Christ which then coloured the conception of the whole of the preceding history. And yet, on the hypothesis, the Resurrection had nothing to lead up to it. It had never been predicted. Before it occurred the Lord had not given himself out as the Messiah, and still less as the Son of God. Many, at least, of the mighty works attributed to him were pure invention. It is really one incredible thing heaped upon another. The founding of Christianity was in any case a very great and wonderful event; and yet it is thought that it can be explained by reducing the cause of it almost to nothing.

Wrede's book, although no review that I have seen accepts any great part of it, has yet made more impression upon opinion in Germany than I believe that it deserves. My chief reason for referring to it is that it calls attention to an aspect of our Lord's life which does present something of a problem. What account are we to give of these paradoxical injunctions of silence? That they are true I have not the slightest doubt. That they are an important feature in the picture we are to form for ourselves, I have also no doubt. But what are we to think was their reason and purpose?

I am not sure that I am altogether able to say. But in any case I conceive that this feature of our Lord's ministry must be connected with that side of it which was a fulfilment of the prophet's words, 'My Servant shall not strive, nor cry, nor lift up His voice in the streets'. In any case it must be connected with the recasting of the Messianic idea which our Lord certainly carried out, divesting it of its associations with political action and transforming it from a kingdom of this world to a kingdom of God and of the Spirit.

We must try to realize the circumstances; for we may be very sure that the state of things with which we are treating is no embodiment of an abstract idea as Wrede supposes, but intensely concrete, arising out of the collision of different and conflicting motives in the Teacher and the taught.

On the side of our Lord himself we must bear in mind his deliberate purpose to work for the redemption of Israel, but not in the way in which Israel expected to be redeemed. There was to be no flash of swords, no raising of armies, no sudden and furious onset with the Messiah himself in the van. It was beginning to be more and more clear that the end of his ministry was not to be victory in the sense of what was commonly accounted victory. The Messiah saw opening out before him a valley, but it was the valley of the shadow of death, and death itself stood at the end. He was preparing to descend into this valley, not like a warrior, with garments rolled in blood, but like a lamb led to the slaughter, with a supreme effort of resignation, as one who when he was reviled reviled not again.

This is the picture that we have on the Lord's side; and then on the side of those for whom he fought and for whom he worked his miracles we remember that there was a spirit the very opposite of this; eager young men, full of courage and enthusiasm, ready to take the sword, ready at any moment to rise against the Romans, waiting only for a leader. Ever since the dethronement of Archelaus and the annexation of Judaea by Rome in AD 6 there had been this temper of sullen acquiescence biding its time. The memory of the Maccabean rising still lived in men's minds, and of the wonderful feats that had then been wrought against desperate odds. What then might not be done with a prophet at the head—nay, one more than a prophet, who was assured of the alliance and succour of Heaven?

There is a significant story in the Fourth Gospel, a story that bears upon its face the stamp of verisimilitude, much as such marks are overlooked by a criticism that has too much vogue at the present time. After the miracle of the Feeding of the Five Thousand, Jesus, 'perceiving that they were about to come and take Him by force, to make Him King, withdrew again into the mountain Himself alone' (Jn 6.15). He constantly had to avoid this kind of pressure. It was in full keeping with this that he had on several occasions to check the zeal of those who would have hailed him as the Messiah, and to impose silence upon those on whom his miracles had been wrought. Enthusiasm always lay ready to his hand. It could have been fanned into flame with the greatest ease. But it was enthusiasm of the wrong sort; it needed to be enlightened, disciplined, purified; and therefore it was that the Lord refused to give it the encouragement it sought. Hence these seeming cross-purposes, this alternate stimulus and restraint.

Unfortunately we have few details. At the distance of time at which our Gospels were composed, it was hardly possible that we should have them. If we had, much that is now obscure might have been made plain. We might have come to understand the special conditions at work in particular scenes, at one time favouring publicity, at another privacy. We may be sure that our Lord diagnosed with perfect insight the temper of those with whom he had to deal, and adjusted his own attitude to it, like a good physician, adapting his treatment to each case as it arose.

We must recognize that our Gospels speak for the most part in very general terms. Especially the accounts of wholesale miracle-working are subject to deductions for historical perspective. It is remarkable that the Gospels have preserved to the extent they have the instances in which the finger of silence is laid upon the lips of those who were eager to speak.

But I am quite prepared to believe that these instances have a yet deeper meaning than I have as yet suggested for them. I always desire to speak with great reserve of the human consciousness of our Lord. I cannot at all agree with those writers who would treat of this as something that can be entirely known and freely handled; and still less when they eke out the limited data supplied by the Gospels from the Messianic expectations of the time. But where the Gospels themselves clearly emphasize a point, we also shall do right to emphasize it. And it is to be noted that where the Gospels speak of these injunctions of silence their language is constantly emphatic: 'Jesus rebuked (ἐπετίμησεν) the unclean spirit, saying, Hold thy peace, and come out of him' (Mk 1.25); 'And He charged them much (πολλὰ ἐπετίμα αὐτοῖς) that they should not make Him known' (Mk 3.12; cf. 8.39); 'And He charged them much (διεστείλατο αὐτοῖς πολλά) that no man should know this' (Mk 5.43; cf. 7.36, 9.9).

I have given only a few typical passages; there are several others similar. In all of these the language is the same; it is the language of emotion—of strong emotion. How is this? I think perhaps we shall understand it best if we take these passages along with yet another, which naturally goes with them, and in which indeed they may be said to reach a climax. In the Gospel it follows immediately upon Peter's confession. Then we have the first prediction of the Passion and the Crucifixion and the Resurrection. We are told that our Lord 'spake the saying openly. And Peter took Him, and began to rebuke Him. But He, turning about, and seeing His disciples, rebuked Peter, and saith, Get thee behind Me, Satan: for thou mindest not the things of God, but the things of men' (Mk 8.32-33). In Matthew it is stronger still, though the added clause is probably only editorial: 'Get thee behind Me, Satan: thou art an offence [a stumbling-block or scandal] unto Me: for thou mindest not the things of God, but the things of men' (Mt. 16.23).

Words like these come up from the depths. They are not the calm enunciation of a policy, or the didactic imparting of a lesson. Such things are cold, and words like these are not cold. They are spoken—if I may speak as we might speak of one of ourselves—with heat. It is really the reaction against temptation, felt—and keenly felt—as temptation.

Our Lord goes so far as to identify Peter with the very tempter himself. The apostle spoke in the innocence of his heart; thoughtlessly, and with the vehemence of short-sighted affection, but with no evil intent. But in his hasty speech a poisoned dart lay concealed, a dart cunningly aimed at the whole purpose of the Lord's mission.

We are reminded indeed of that of which we commonly speak as 'the Temptation'. There the story is told in a symbolical form, which perhaps gathers up the significance of more than one actual incident in our Lord's life. He is conscious of supernatural power—of power that might have been wielded for other ends than those for which it was really given. When the Son of Man saw, as he might have seen from a lofty mountain, a broad and typical expanse, as it were a sample of the kingdoms of the world and the glory of them, he saw what was entirely within his grasp if he had cared to take it. But to take it would have meant abandoning the whole line of ministry that he had marked out for himself. 'Whether is greater, he that sitteth at meat, or he that serveth? is not he that sitteth at meat? but I am in the midst of you as he that serveth' (Lk. 22.27). It was no common form of service that our Lord had chosen. 'He became obedient unto death, even the death of the Cross.' It was the shadow of the Cross that now fell upon him. And it is very clear that the prospect carried with it a temptation. 'O My Father, if it be possible, let this cup pass away from Me: nevertheless, not as I will, but as Thou wilt' (Mt. 26.39). In that prayer the temptation was finally repelled; but we may be sure that it had been felt before. It was especially felt at the moment when Peter made his unhappy impulsive speech, doing, without knowing it, the devil's work.

We speak of the remodelling of the Messianic idea; and it is absolutely true that our Lord was the Messiah in a very different sense from that in which the name was understood by his contemporaries. But this again was no change worked out, as it were, on paper; it was no product of philosophy, speculative or practical. It was a conflict—if indeed that is the right name, for again I am speaking after the manner of men— fought out deep down, at the lowest depth at which such conflicts are fought, and extending all the way from the first moments after the Baptism to the last bitter cry upon the Cross. Beneath what seemed at times the quiet unruffled surface of that life the conflict was going on, and such scenes as those which we have been passing in rapid review are times when the fires within break forth and are seen.

These scenes were not merely the expression of what we should call an idiosyncrasy of character; they were not merely incidents in a process of education, either of the inner circle of the disciples or of the outer circle of inquirers and sympathizers. They were in some degree, I conceive, both these things; but their origin lay deeper. They were surface indications of the only inward antithesis of which we have any trace in the life of our Lord. He himself described it as an antithesis between 'the things of God' and 'the things of men'. That tender Humanity shrank—as how should it not?—from the terrible end that was so clearly foreseen: an end the terrors of which were enhanced and not diminished by the fact that he who foresaw them was the Son of God. The human mind of Jesus shrank from this; it had doubtless dreams and imaginations of its own, of winning the whole world in other and less dreadful ways. A lifted finger, a breathed wish, and twelve legions of angels would have been at his side. Only one thought hindered—but that a master-thought: How then shall the Scriptures be fulfilled that thus it must be? Behind the Scriptures lay the will of him who gave them, that will in regard to which Father and Son were at one.

We see the antithesis—the conflict, if so it is to be called. But, the Son being what he was, it could have but one issue. It issued in an agony over which we draw a veil. We draw a veil over it, and we turn away; but, as we turn, we say to ourselves 'So much it cost to redeem the race of man'.

Chapter 14

SOME LEADING IDEAS IN THE THEOLOGY OF ST PAUL*

'Faith in Christ' would be allowed by every one to be the central point in the teaching of Paul. But there is reason to fear that these words are often very superficially understood.

The name 'Christ' is so familiar to us that we are apt to think of it almost as a proper name, and to forget its weighty significance and the long chain of associations with which it was bound up. When Paul used the word, he used it as something much more than a proper name. For him it had the most profound and intense meaning. The moment when he became convinced that the title could be rightly applied to him whom by the act of applying it he took for his Lord and Master was the turning-point of his life.

Let us try to place ourselves in thought at the time when Paul left the gates of Jerusalem with a commission from the high priest to apprehend and bring back in chains all the members that he could find of that obscure and persecuted sect which was afterwards to bear the name of Christians. He was a young man, but with none of the usual carelessness and indifference of youth to serious things. On the contrary, he was fired with the most intense religious zeal. He prized to the utmost the privilege that he possessed as one of the Chosen People. He had a sincere reverence for the law in which he had been brought up. He had spent upon it the most diligent study. He had sought the best master that could be obtained. He had sat at the feet of Gamaliel, and had learnt all that the wisest of the rabbis had to teach. Nor did he merely accept the law as his own personal rule of life. He was an ardent patriot, and shared deeply in the hopes of his nation. Like the rest of his countrymen, he felt the galling yoke of Rome, and longed for the time when Israel should rise like one man and hurl back the hated foreigner to the sea. Some vague expectation he may have had that the Great Deliverer foretold by the

*   This chapter originally appeared as W. Sanday, 'Some Leading Ideas in the Theology of St Paul', *The Expositor* 8 (1878), pp. 40-58.

prophets would come in his day, and restore the people to more than their old height of greatness and power. In his youthful enthusiasm he looked forward to the time when Jerusalem should be again the city of the Great King, and all nations should flow unto it.

It was precisely this which horrified him so much in the sect that he was at that moment engaged in persecuting. They too professed to believe in a Messiah. Nay, they asserted that the Messiah had already appeared. But instead of leading his people to victory, instead of expelling the Roman oppressor and restoring the Davidic kingdom, he had perished ignominiously by the death that was usually reserved for malefactors, traitors, and slaves. The mere idea that such an one could possibly be the promised Messiah gave a shock to every principle and every prejudice that birth and education had planted in the young zealot's heart.

Still, it would have been a mistake to think that he was satisfied with his present position. There were some things that caused him serious difficulty. The law held up before him an ideal of righteousness: 'The man that doeth these things shall live by them'. The strict fulfilment of the commandments of the law was the only way to escape the just judgment of God. But was it possible to fulfil the Divine commands? Could any one really keep the law—that law of which it was said that whosoever should keep the whole of it and yet offend in one point, he should be guilty of all? Paul felt that he could not do this. He had tried, and tried in vain. He was conscious that, do the very best he could, he yet should not be able to put in any plea of innocence before God. Much, then, as he was attached to the law, he felt that it was, after all, a hopeless kind of service. It had not brought, and could not bring, him any real peace of mind.

There was also something disquieting in the opinions of the persecuted Christians. They, too, seemed to give men courage and constancy. No fault could be found with the holders of those humiliating tenets except the humiliating tenets themselves. And yet even in these there was one point at least that was strange and doubtful. Every one knew that the Founder of the sect had died. He had died a shameful death. But his disciples asserted a startling fact—that, after he had been laid in the grave, he had risen from it. A stone had been laid at the mouth of the grave, but it had been found rolled away, and he, whom the Jews had left for dead, had afterwards appeared, not once or twice, but many times, to his disciples; and he had promised that as they had seen him go, so also should they see him return.

What if all this should be true? If it were true, then such a strange supernatural intervention must be enough to show that he for whom it was wrought was indeed something more than man. In spite of the manner of his death, his disciples could not be altogether wrong when they claimed that he was the Messiah. Either the fact of the alleged resurrection was not true, or else the whole of his own ideas must undergo a change.

It was while revolving some such thoughts as these that the future Apostle drew near to Damascus. But suddenly his course was arrested. A light flashed across his path; and as he fell terror-stricken from his horse a voice sounded in his ear, 'I am Jesus, whom thou persecutest'.

It *was* true then. Jesus of Nazareth *was* risen. He was, after all, really the Messiah in whom all the hopes of Israel were to centre.

Naturally it was not to be expected that Paul should be able to reconcile to himself this tremendous discovery all at once. He must needs retire, as he himself tells us that he did, into the deserts of Arabia, and there wrestle with the throng of thick-coming thoughts which he was afterwards to weave into a coherent theological system.

The main points in that system were four. First, Jesus was the Messiah. Secondly, the proof of his Messiahship was in the Resurrection. Thirdly, his death upon the cross could not be merely a death of shame, it must have some further and deeper significance as well. Fourthly, faith in Jesus as the Messiah must be the starting-point for the believer.

In the light of these fundamental ideas the Apostle—for now he may be called by that name—found by degrees most of his old difficulties resolved. His misgivings in regard to the law were verified. He became convinced that it was really insufficient to give salvation. It could condemn sin, and, by condemning it, increase its sinfulness; but that was all. It entirely failed to help men to attain that righteousness which its own standard required.

This, then, was the real object and significance of the Messiah's coming. Righteousness had been always recognized as the necessary condition of the Messianic reign. In this the Jewish as well as the Christian literature adhered strictly to the outline drawn in the prophetic books.

The Messiah, therefore, had come to do just what the law had failed in doing—to superinduce upon men a state of righteousness. If man had succeeded in attaining to righteousness by his own unaided efforts and in obedience simply to the law, then this righteousness would have been spontaneous. It would have been the result of his own labour. It would have been human in every sense.

But the righteousness which the Messiah brought was not derived from human efforts. Like the whole of the Messianic scheme, it proceeded directly from God. And therefore the Apostle speaks of it always as a righteousness '*of* God'—a righteousness that is, of which God is *the Author*. The gospel is a revelation of this righteousness to men.

But how is the state of righteousness brought about in them? What was it that the gospel, or message proclaiming the Messianic kingdom, offered which the law could not offer?

There was a twofold answer to this question. The advent of the Messiah had altered both the relation of God to man and the relation of man to God.

It had altered, first, the relation of God to man. Here the Apostle found the profound significance of that act which in his pre-Christian stage had been the great stumbling-block in his way—the death of the Messiah. It had seemed to him impossible that the Messiah should die such a death; but now he came to see that this very death was, not only in accordance with prophecy, but was really the cardinal point in the Messianic scheme of salvation.

Under the old Jewish law the only way in which a condition of righteousness could be obtained, except by the strict literal fulfilment of the legal precepts, was by the offering of sacrifice. Particular offences might be expiated—or at least the forgiveness of God might be sought for them—by particular offerings. As the Jewish history had gone on the doctrine of sacrifice had been deepened. The prophets had taught that the mere act of sacrifice was unavailing without sincere repentance and contrition on the part of the worshipper. Still the offering of sacrifice continued to be enjoined, and the two ideas of sacrifice and of expiation were bound up together.

Was it not possible, then, to regard the death of the Messiah as one great act of sacrifice, and one great expiation? Was there not something permanent—was there not some dimly foreshadowed meaning in this rite of sacrifice, which was not confined to the Chosen People, but diffused, as it were, by some divine instinct over the whole of the ancient world? Yes, we may suppose the Apostle, arguing, there *was* something permanent in it; it *had* a most profound meaning. The death of Christ, the Messiah, was an expiation of sins. He was the Paschal Lamb whose sacrifice made the destroying angel turn away his sword. His death *did* act as a propitiation (ἱλαστήριον), in view of which God became more ready to pardon sin, and admit to the condition of righteousness which the Messianic reign implied.

Let me for a moment ask for a suspense of the judgment and criticism which this statement may seem to provoke, and go on further with our exposition.

The death of Christ operated a change objectively on the relations of God to man. But how was that change to become subjective? How was it to be answered by a change in the relation of man to God? The Messiah had died, but how did this affect the members of the Messiah's kingdom? The means by which it was brought home to them was that act of the mind by which the believer at first claimed and obtained his membership in that kingdom—the act of faith. Faith is the bond of allegiance which unites the Messiah to his people. It is something like the old feudal loyalty transferred into the spiritual sphere. It is the readiness to spend and be spent—an intense, enthusiastic, self-annihilating devotion. It began, of course, in the first disciples, with the intellectual conviction of the true Messiahship of Jesus. But this first intellectual step gave way to an inrush of moral emotion. Every feeling that could possibly be felt by the members of a perfect ideal kingdom for the perfect ideal King did but grow out of this. Love, veneration, implicit trust and firm fidelity, passive obedience and active energetic service, all these had their root in faith.

Faith is thus the key which unlocks the door of the Messianic kingdom, and which therefore admits the believer at once into a sphere of forgiveness and reconciliation with God. The true member of the Messianic kingdom is righteous by the very fact of his membership. He does not need to work out painfully a righteousness of his own, but a righteousness is made for him. It is the gift of God through Christ. As Christ by his death removed the weight of the Divine anger and determined the character of his own kingdom as one upon which God could look propitiously, without any shadow of displeasure, but with the full and free outpouring of his grace and favour, so now the believer by obtaining a share in that kingdom obtains a share in its blessings—no longer stands under sentence of condemnation, but enters upon that state of tranquillity and peace which the favour of God brings with it in its train.

The vain and fruitless efforts which were made under the law thus received their accomplishment, but in another way. By the way of legal obedience it was found impossible to attain to righteousness. But by the way of faith—by the loyal adhesion to Jesus as the Messiah—the believer at once entered into a state of things in which he was accounted righteous before God. His faith *was imputed to him for righteousness*. The standard by which he was judged was no longer the extent of his legal obedience, which must be at the best imperfect, but rather the degree and strength of his devotion to Christ, as in itself the surest guarantee for righteous action of which human nature is capable.

For the righteousness which comes by faith is no merely legal fiction. Faith, or the devotion of the soul to Christ, is not in itself righteousness, but it is the strongest motive and impulse to righteousness that could possibly be found. It is at least a proof, even in its earliest stages, that he who has it is in the right way, that he is not deceived by any blind self-confidence, but that he has allied to himself the strongest moral force that has ever been devised.

And what makes this force still more efficacious, is that it is capable of almost unlimited development. Here is opened out to us another side of the Apostle's teaching. Faith is of the nature of an attachment. Love enters into it very largely, but love includes the desire to become like that which is loved. When mingled, as it must be in the Christian, with reverent admiration, it involves a tender submissive approach, such as that of the woman who said within herself, 'If I may but touch the hem of his garment I shall be whole'. Such is the faith—the loving faith—of the Christian. It draws near, if it may touch the hem of Christ's garment. As time goes on it grows more and more in closeness and intimacy; it becomes such that Paul describes it by a stronger name still: he calls it a union or fellowship with Christ. Strictly speaking, the use of the words, 'union', 'oneness', is a metaphor. The limits of personality are rigidly defined. They are the most fundamental part of consciousness, and no impressions from without, however close and penetrating, can really infringe upon them. Still there is but little of hyperbole in the Apostle's language. It would hardly seem as if any other words could adequately express his meaning, which is that of the closest possible influence that spirit can exercise upon spirit. The Christian and his Lord are one. Even the less advanced Christian is potentially what the advanced and experienced Christian is more or less actually.

This oneness, then, of the Christian with Christ, becomes the base of a new series of ideas. The Christian 'lives and moves and has his being' in Christ. The Spirit of Christ dwells in the Christian, animates his actions, encourages his hopes, ratifies his consciousness of reconciliation with God, joins in his prayers.

The influence of the Spirit of Christ upon the soul becomes a new principle side by side with the human personality. It is the guarantee of all true life—ethical, spiritual, and even physical. For through his relation to Christ the Christian is carried out of the sphere of the perishable, and is made one with that which is immortal and eternal. The seeds of evil and corruption are implanted in the body. It is the impulses of the body which give rise to sin. When, therefore, the Christian has got free from these, as he has through union with Christ, he is separated from that by virtue of which he was a prey to death; he is brought into contact with that which is both itself ever-living and the true source of life. 'If Christ be in you, the body is dead because of sin; but the Spirit is life because of righteousness. But if the Spirit of him that raised up Jesus from the dead dwell in you, he that raised up Jesus from the dead shall also quicken your mortal bodies by his Spirit that dwelleth in you.' The three ideas of moral life—the essence of which is righteousness; of spiritual life—the essence of which is communion with Christ and God; of physical life—the life of the body—which is the result of these other two—are inextricably mixed and blended in the thought of Paul. He treats them all at once, as if each implied the other, and as if they had all one common origin though at the same time he distributes his language somewhat according to its particular appropriateness to the subject of which he happens to be treating. The faith and love of the Christian rise to union with Christ. That union touches every part of the Christian's career, just as it touches every part of the saving work of Christ. The two stand over against and correspond to each other. In the strength of his faith and love for Christ the Christian is gradually enabled to suppress the solicitations of sense, so that they cease to annoy him. That is to die, or be crucified with Christ, to mortify the members that are in the flesh. In the strength of his faith and love for Christ the Christian comes to set his affections on things above; that is, to rise with Christ. And this present resurrection with Christ is the earnest of a future resurrection in which the body also will share.

In this way Paul makes provision for the whole of the Christian's career. The initial part of the process is what is commonly called justification. The continuation and completion of it is what is commonly called sanctification.

The great step in the first is the admission of the Christian into the Messianic kingdom, and his consequent introduction into a state of things the essential character of which is righteousness and peace, instead of guilt and punishment. The great step in the second is the mystical union or communion with Christ, through which the purifying and vivifying influences of the Spirit of Christ himself are communicated to the believer.

The connecting link between the two halves of the process is faith. It is faith by virtue of which the Christian is admitted into the Messianic kingdom, and becomes partaker of its immunities. Faith in the Messiah is the necessary condition of acceptance by the Messiah; and direct acceptance by the Messiah alone can exempt from the dominion and obligation of the law.

But, on the other hand, it is this very same faculty, faith, the ardent and sincere devotion to the Head of the Messianic kingdom, which, by the relation of intimacy that it establishes between the subject and the King, opens out to that subject the fulness of the Messianic blessings. Faith in Christ is the root, of which the life in Christ is the perfected blossom and flower: it is the same feeling and faculty in another and more developed form.

It will be observed, too, that the Christian sacraments have each their place in connection with these two great divisions of the process of salvation. Baptism marks the commencement of the Christian's career, the step by which he is admitted into the kingdom of the Messiah. It is under the New Covenant what circumcision was under the Old, the *seal* of the righteousness which is by faith, the formal act and deed of ratification by which the Messianic or Christian privileges are secured to the believer, by which the state of righteousness is thrown open to him, and the state of sin with its load of past offences, typically and symbolically, washed away.

The Holy Communion bears the same relation to the renewal of the Christian's life through union with Christ. It is itself a typical and symbolical expression of that union; and, like all solemn and serious expression, it helps to strengthen the feelings which it expresses. Union with Christ is a spiritual thing, the closest influence of spirit upon spirit, that has its root in faith, and is itself a development of faith. And the rite by which this union is celebrated is an embodiment in material form of an act which is purely spiritual. It begins and ends in faith. Faith is the one great factor running through it all.

Men, as individuals, come and go; but the kingdom of heaven endures. It has a life beyond that of the individual, and its development is more continuous and unbroken. The establishment of the Messiah's kingdom upon earth is as yet incipient and imperfect. Nature and man alike are progressing towards a far more glorious consummation. At present, the whole creation groaneth and travaileth in pain. The Messiah has come to it, but has been removed from it; and when he comes to it again, the whole inferior creation, animate and inanimate, will join in the glory of his appearing. The members of the Messianic kingdom, who, by virtue of their relation to the Messiah, are in a special sense *sons* of God, will enter upon the full privileges of their adoption. Their very mortal bodies will be transfigured, and the Messiah will be among them as the first-born amongst many brethren. There can be no doubt that Paul expected the second coming of the Lord to take place speedily, in his own generation, if not in his own lifetime. The two parts of the Messiah's coming were to him the necessary complement of each other. The second appearing in glory was only the fitting counterpart and compensation for the first appearing in humiliation. The Jews were not prepared for the humiliating side of the Messiah's appearance. They looked only for the glorious side. And though the Apostle was fully reconciled to the first, he did not lose his hold upon the second. They were only separated in his mind by the teaching of experience. He, like the rest of the apostles, bore out the saying of their Lord, that the true day and hour of his appearing should not be known.

With this eschatology, or doctrine respecting the last things, the circle of the Apostle's teaching is closed. An attempt has been made, as far as possible, to see it with the eyes of the Apostle himself, to follow the train of thought by which it was arrived at, and to see the relation of the different parts of his system to each other in his own mind. The question will perhaps naturally be asked whether too much prominence is not thus given to the particular form of the Jewish Messianic expectations— a form which, though containing in itself a large permanent element, was not itself permanent, but was rather the transitory historical clothing of an idea to which we are accustomed to give a different expression.

However this may be, there can be no doubt that the Messianic idea, as it was current among the Jews, held a large place in the mind of Paul. The ideas that he had imbibed before his conversion remained with him after it, and Jewish became the parent of Christian theology.

But, apart from this, there is reason to think that, if the lineage and relations of the leading terms in this theology had been more considered, it would have saved many mistakes and much superficial and inadequate reasoning.

For instance, does it not tend greatly to deepen our conception of justification by faith and the doctrine of imputed righteousness when we see it in its place in the Apostle's system? Objection has been made to this very doctrine. The idea of imputation has been denounced as immoral. Righteousness, it is said, cannot be imputed. A man is righteous, or he is not righteous. He cannot be considered or accounted righteous unless he is so really.

If such were the stern alternative, what would become of the human race? It is indeed quite true that, when it is stated in a dry scholastic form, the doctrine of imputed righteousness is open to objection. But how far removed is the theology of Paul from a dry and lifeless scholasticism! On the contrary, it is instinct with the most burning enthusiastic life. The faith by virtue of which righteousness is imputed is no hard intellectual abstraction. It is a personal devotion to a personal Messiah, in which all the seeds of the finest and highest Christian morality lie enshrined. It was never intended that such faith should be a substitute for virtuous conduct. Its purpose was much rather to substitute a living and real virtue for one that was merely cold and mechanical—the virtue of the saint for the virtue of the Pharisee. And if when all is done, there is still need for imputed righteousness, what is this but the necessary condition of human frailty? What man among us could hope to stand in his own self guiltless before God? The doctrine that deifies humanity, and that talks much of human perfectibility, is one of the very shallowest that ever was invented. If man is to approach nearer to perfection, it is not by a self-complacent survey of his own achievements, but by seeing and lamenting his sinfulness, and by serious efforts to amend.

Nor can that other step be regarded as unreasonable. If God *is* willing to pardon the offences and shortcoming of men—to treat as righteous those who are not in themselves really righteous—is it not to be expected that this favour should be extended specially to those who have entered with ardour into the service of his Son? That ardour is in itself the surest guarantee that they will do the best that in them lies. And so far from the relation of the believer to his Lord being taken *in lieu of* a holy life, it is treated by Paul as the constant motive to it, the ever present spur and stimulus which will not let the Christian forget who he is and to what he is called.

Thus one of the two main difficulties in the Pauline theology would seem to be sufficiently answered. The other has been hinted at but not as yet discussed, the doctrine of the vicarious atonement. Yet does not this too receive a light from the consideration of its historical antecedents and the ideas to which it is related? There can be little doubt that Paul does regard the death of Christ as sacrificial, and sacrificial in the sense of being expiatory or at least propitiatory. It had not merely the effect of awakening human affection by a transcendent act of love and sufferings voluntarily endured, but it also had a determining influence upon the Divine Will. It did in some way serve to render God propitious towards man. This side of it is not to be ignored or explained away. But two things are to be borne in mind. First, that the sacrifice of Christ upon the cross does not stand alone. It is not an isolated act, but is rather the culminating act in a long series. The idea of sacrifice is almost as old as the human race. It goes back beyond the existence of written records, and is diffused over nations of the most diverse origin. Widespread and deeply-rooted ideas like this are not to be despised. There is something more in them than appears upon the surface. They are part of the vast Divine plan which is unfolded by little and little in the government of the world. One advantage of the theory of evolution as applied to the history of religions is that it brings out this profound unity in the whole God-appointed system of things. It takes perhaps ages to reveal the true final cause or goal of a prolonged series of events; but in the end that goal is revealed, and then at once the antecedent steps that led up to it are illuminated as they had never been before.

Secondly, it must be remembered that we look at these things not from above but from below. We see only the under side of them. We speak, as Paul spoke, of a 'sacrifice propitiatory' to God. But what do we know of the why, or the how, of these tremendous ideas? If there is any field where shallow and flippant curiosity is out of place, it is here. What are we, that we should undertake to define the relations that exist within the incomprehensible sphere of the Godhead? Our language is anthropomorphic. We use human metaphors to express ideas which we feel far transcend them. Such language must be inadequate and mixed to a certain extent with error. There are certain things which are partly before and partly behind the veil. We must take what we see, and leave what is unseen.

The root idea of the redeeming death of Christ is one that must not at any price be let slip. It is one of the great factors in the religious life. The obvious difficulties connected with it have led some amiable and good men to try to explain it away. But this cannot be done without serious detriment to religion. Explain away the redeeming death of Christ, and the work of salvation becomes a subjective process. It is wrought out by the man himself. It begins, and ends, with him. He, and not Christ, is the centre of the Christian scheme. Salvation is a matter of human effort, and no longer the free gift of God. On the other hand, *For us and not by us* is the watchword of Paul. *For us and not by us* is the key to a truly chastened and humble Christian temper.

> Just as I am, without one plea,
> But that thy blood was shed for me.

There is the true motive power of Christianity. History would prove it if theology did not, for the consciousness of it has been strongest in the greatest and most creative religious minds.

It is this which constitutes the strength of the theology of Paul. He has cast the anchor of his faith outside himself. He himself will boast of nothing. He himself can do nothing, but he can do all things through Christ that strengtheneth him. Thus the great paradox is solved. In the moment of his deepest humiliation, when the 'stake' (or 'thorn', as it is called in our Version) is driven far into his quivering flesh, when he feels helpless and all but hopeless, he casts himself unreservedly upon Christ. And he receives an answer: 'My grace is sufficient for thee, for my strength is made perfect in weakness. Therefore', he adds, 'I take pleasure in infirmities, in reproaches, in necessities, in persecutions, in distresses for Christ's sake: for when I am weak then am I strong'. His spirit is at once exalted and humble. The most commanding energy does not make him proud. The most unconquerable fortitude does not make him hard. Though he had 'laboured more than they all', he yet counts himself less than the least. He knows how to be abased as well as how to abound.

Paul is himself the best commentary upon his own theology. His life was inspired by his theology, and his theology is the reflection of his life. It is no scholastic system, worked out in the cold atmosphere of the study. It is the fruit of an intense religious experience, the victorious result of prolonged inward conflict. We seem to trace at almost every step in it how the old has been fused into the new. But the fusion is complete. Unseen forces have been at work upon it. Never was there a soul that might so truly be said to be 'baptized with the Holy Ghost and with fire'.

Chapter 15

ST PAUL'S EQUIVALENT FOR THE 'KINGDOM OF HEAVEN'*

There is a broad contrast between the Gospels and the epistles which
strikes the eye at once: the one simple, pellucid, profound with the
profundity that comes from elemental ideas and relations and that is
quite consistent with great apparent artlessness of expression; the other
involved and laboured, only at times emerging into real simplicity of
language, often highly technical, and if profound, not seldom also
obscure.

This contrast, as I have said, strikes the eye from the first. It represents
not only two styles of writing but two distinct types of thought.

From the point of view of criticism the distinction of these two types
is important. There is no better guarantee of the generally authentic
character of the Gospel record. The older Tübingen criticism spoke of
Pauline and Petrine elements in the Gospels. And the very first thing we
should expect would be that some such elements would enter into them.
But the wonder is that the extent to which they are actually present
should be so small. When the Gospels are examined the really intrusive
Pauline and Petrine elements (in the Tübingen sense) are found to be
quite insignificant. The distinctiveness of type is hardly affected. There is
exceedingly little running of the one type into the other. All this we may
take as proof that the teaching of our Lord as it is recorded in the
Gospels has been preserved substantially as it was given. We have by the
side of it later types of teaching of marked individuality. These later
types in one form or another covered nearly the whole Christian world.
And yet they have not encroached upon the earlier. They have not
obliterated its sharpness of outline. There is practically no confusion of
type. The teaching of the Gospels has not been corrupted by the
theology of the epistles. The teaching of the epistles has not been mixed

*   This chapter originally appeared as W. Sanday, 'Some Leading Ideas in the
Theology of St Paul', *The Expositor* 8 (1878), pp. 40-58.

up with that of the Gospels. The two types stand out clearly marked off from each other.[1]

But this state of things leaves us with a problem which has been, I cannot but think, as yet insufficiently faced. What is the relation of the two types to each other? The one, as we can see, passed into the other; but how did it pass? Can we trace a continuity between the leading conceptions of each? How far is there a real identity of substance underlying the difference of form?

A wide field of investigation is opened up which I believe needs more working out than it has received either in England or on the Continent. This we may hope will not be wanting.

For the present I propose to take only one leading conception of the Gospels, but that perhaps the most central of all—the doctrine of the Kingdom of God, or of Heaven. I propose to ask, What becomes of this conception in the epistles, and in particular in the earlier epistles of Paul? I propose to ask, first, if we find this conception there; and if we do not, what takes its place.

Now it is remarkable upon the face of it that we hear so little of the Kingdom of God in the epistles. Let us think for a moment of the way in which it is the one theme of a whole succession of our Lord's parables; and then if the very subordinate place, to say the least, which the conception takes with Paul. If we run over in mind the main trains of thought in all his epistles, and especially in the early epistles, it is conspicuously absent.

And yet the conception by no means disappears entirely. It occupies really just the sort of place that we might expect, if it were taken over from an earlier body of teaching—a body of teaching of which the Apostle himself had not been a hearer, but which came to him rather at secondhand and when his own mental habits had been largely formed.

There are a few familiar places where the phrase occurs. Five times over the Apostle speaks of 'inheriting the Kingdom of God'. Four times he reminds his readers that evil-doers will not inherit the Kingdom (1 Cor. 6.9, 10; Gal. 5.21; Eph. 5.5); once he says that flesh and blood cannot inherit it (1 Cor. 15.50). In all these places he has in view the Messianic Kingdom of the saints in glory. And it is in the same sense he encourages the Thessalonians with the hope of being 'counted worthy of the Kingdom of God', for which they were suffering (2 Thess. 1.5). This

---

1. On this subject see especially an essay by H. von Soden in the volume dedicated to Weizsäcker (Freiburg i. B.: Herder, 1892), pp. 113ff.

is the purified and spiritualized Christian form of the current Messianic expectation.

There are however two passages which go beyond this. One is in Romans (14.17), where it is said that 'the Kingdom of God is not eating and drinking, but righteousness and peace and joy in the Holy Ghost'. And the other is in 1 Corinthians (4.20), where the Kingdom of God is described as not being 'in word but in power'.

In both these cases the Apostle is thinking not of anything future but of the present, not of any catastrophic change, but of the actual experience of Christian men. Where were they to look for the coming of the Kingdom? What were to be the signs of its coming? The signs are— not any change in the Levitical order, a new list of clean and unclean, new regulations as to abstinence or the like, but a new spirit permeating the life, a new attitude and temper of mind, a new relation of the soul to God—righteousness and joy and peace in the Holy Ghost. What a beautiful description in those few strokes! What an advanced experience of the best gifts of religion! How undreamt of by Pharisee or Sadducee or Essene or Zealot! There was only one school of Jesus. If we had only that one verse it would suffice to tell us that the teaching of Jesus had really sunk into his soul.

And it is no less a direct reflection of that teaching when he says that the Kingdom of God is 'not in word but in power'. I shall have in a moment to say more of this aspect of the Kingdom.

We may think it strange that with so much insight into the mind of the Master, Paul did not fall more into his habitual language. He did fall into it; he did adopt it, in no lukewarm manner, but with his heart and soul. And yet is only on rare occasions that this particular mode of speech comes uppermost.

To change a whole vocabulary is not an easy thing. Paul had been brought up as a Pharisee. He was like one of us, trained in his own academic tradition. The language of that tradition was the mould into which his thoughts naturally fell.

Further, he was an ardent student of the Jewish Bible. The words of the Psalmists and of the Prophets lived in his memory. And they happened to be a different cycle of words from those which are most prevalent in the Gospels.

It is marvellous to see how Paul has recast the old phrases and reads into them a specifically Christian content. But the phrases are old; they are in great part phrases to which he had been accustomed before he became a Christian.

Let us once again then ask where the coincidence between the Gospels and the Pauline Epistles comes in. I said just now that Paul really knew what Jesus had meant when he spoke of the 'Kingdom of God'. He knew Jesus' innermost, distinctive, and characteristic meaning. Many times our Lord seems to speak—or half to speak—as his contemporaries might have spoken. The Kingdom of God was the Messianic Kingdom. But he infused into the phrase a larger as well as deeper meaning than it bore on the lips of the people. The Messianic Kingdom was for him the culmination, or bringing to a head, of a process that was always going on. It is probable that the phrase which we translate 'Kingdom of God' meant quite as much, as it is said to mean predominantly in the Talmud, 'reign' or 'sovereignty' of God.[2] It was nothing less than the sum of all those influences and forces that specially betoken the presence or manifestation of God in the world.

The world is energized by God. There are constantly streaming, as it were, down from heaven a number of currents which come straight from God. The Apostle's phrase expresses exactly the effects by which these divine currents are manifested. Where they are, there are 'righteousness and peace and joy in the Holy Ghost'.

But the Apostle knew quite well that these were the effects and not the cause. The cause lay in those mighty powers or energies put forth by God for the redemption of the world. To be within the range of those powers, to clasp them—so to speak—to the heart, was to 'enter into the Kingdom of Heaven'. It was to be really loyal to God as King—to let his sovereignty have its way, not to obstruct and oppose but to welcome it, to surrender the will to it, to open the soul to those divine influences and forces which flowed in its train.

This is the Kingdom which Jesus told his listeners was 'within them'.[3] Those influences and forces taken into the heart were the pearl of great price, the treasure hid in the field. Righteousness and peace were their natural fruit. And the consciousness of them brought with it an exceeding great joy.

2.   E. Schürer, *Geschichte des Jüdischen Volkes im Zeitalter Jesu Christi* (3 vols.; Leipzig: J.C. Hinrichs, 1898), II, p. 454 note (3rd edn, p. 539 note).

3.   For proof that this is the true sense of ἐντὸς ὑμῶν see especially F. Field, *Notes on the Translation of the New Testament being the Otium norvicense (pars tertia)* (Cambridge: Cambridge University Press, 1899), p. 71.

Such is the life-history of this work of God within the soul. It begins above in the highest heaven; it ends below in the hearts of men. It diffuses itself throughout the world. It sweeps individuals along with it, so that they gather into a society. And so another kind of figure becomes applicable to it. It is like a draw-net cast into the sea and bringing the fish which it encloses to land.

Where shall we seek an analogy for all this in the writings of Paul? The thought of the Kingdom is so central in the teaching of Jesus that we naturally look for its counterpart in the central teaching of the Apostle. Now by common consent that central teaching is contained in two verses of the first chapter of the Epistle to the Romans: 'I am not ashamed of the Gospel: for it is the power of God unto salvation to every one that believeth; to the Jew first, and also to the Greek. For therein is revealed the righteousness of God by faith unto faith' (Rom. 1.16, 17: RV has '*a* righteousness', but '*the* righteousness' is probably better).

We may put aside the mention of 'faith'. It is no doubt a term of great importance for the purpose of Paul; it is less important for ours. Paul has in view the psychological process by which the righteousness of God becomes actual for the believer. With this we are not concerned for the present, though if it were to be examined we should find the teaching of the Apostle on this head falls perfectly into its place.

For us the important term is 'the righteousness of God'. This expression, I think we may say, is better understood now than it was only a few years ago. At that time there seemed to be an almost established tradition in Protestant exegesis that was not so much wrong as one-sided and inadequate.

I cannot think that it was wrong to explain the words in Romans on the analogy of the more explicit language of the Epistle to the Philippians. Paul there in a well-known passage (Phil. 3.8, 9) speaks of his hope that he may gain Christ and be found in him, not having a righteousness of his own, 'even that which is of the law, but that which is through faith in Christ, the righteousness which is of God by faith' (τὴν ἐκ θεοῦ δικαιοσύνην ἐπὶ τῇ πίστει). The insertion of the preposition ἐκ makes the phrase explicit. The contrast of the two kinds of righteousness is decisive. On the one hand is the righteousness which he disclaims, the righteousness which he calls 'his own', the righteousness of Scribes and Pharisees, the product of a mechanical obedience to the law. On the other hand is the righteousness which he desires, the righteousness which is 'from God based on faith'. This righteousness, however much it begins with God, must at least end as a state or condition of man. It is as such that the Apostle prays that it may be his.

And yet it does begin 'from God'; and it is this beginning that has had less justice done to it. When Paul says, in the verse of Romans, that in the Gospel is revealed 'the righteousness of God', he means in the first instance the Divine attribute of righteousness, just as in the verse that follows he says that the wrath of God is also revealed. For him the whole Gospel is summed up as a revelation of the righteousness of God.

It is a very large conception, and one that is not easy to grasp at all adequately.

This is an instance that illustrates in a striking way how much we are at the mercy of language. We remember that the Latin- and Romance-speaking peoples have but a single word for 'justice' and for 'righteousness'. The almost inevitable consequence is to lose sight of the larger meaning in the smaller.

We are somewhat better off than that. We have the two words, and we can keep clear the two senses. We are not in so much danger of limiting our idea of righteousness to that of equal dealing between man and man. But even we must find it hard to rise to the full height of the conception as it was present to the mind of Paul.

Paul had behind him the whole weight of the Old Testament realized with a vividness and a force with which it is impossible for us to realize it.

Now there is perhaps hardly any word in the Old Testament that has so rich and full a meaning as this word 'righteousness', especially as applied to God.

Even as applied to man, even as applied to the Judge, it is still a good deal more than 'justice'. The righteousness even of the Judge is before all things tender care for the weak, the defence of those who cannot defend themselves—the poor, the fatherless, the widow, the stranger—vigilant protection of the oppressed. Hence it goes on to mean an ever-present and ever-active sympathy. We see this in the famous passage in the Book of Job (29.14-16), 'I put on righteousness, and it clothed me: my justice was as a robe and a diadem. I was eyes to the blind, and feet was I to the lame. I was a father to the needy: and the cause of him that I knew not I searched out.'

When this character is transferred to God it is of necessity enlarged and deepened yet further. We must never forget that for Israel everything was seen in the light of the special relation in which God stood to his own people. All that is tenderest, all that is most gracious, was concentrated upon this relation. And the word for it all—the word that describes the faithfulness of God to his people—was 'righteousness'. That one comprehensive word described the deepest workings of the Divine Mind as it went forth in lovingkindness and pity to the people of his choice. All the mighty acts of the Lord sprang from this motive and from this relation: 'In His love and in His pity He redeemed them; and He bare them, and carried them all the days of old' (Isa. 63.9).

All this we may be sure that Paul the Pharisee grasped intensely. In so doing he was not exceptional. The sense of the love of God for Israel, of the covenant relation between Jehovah and his people, was the very best side of Jewish religion. The Jew too often traded upon his privileges, too often let himself repose on them without making any strenuous effort really to live up to them. But that was the perversion of a feeling good in itself. The sense of intimacy between Israel and its God, the delighted response of the nation to its Benefactor, is one of the brightest strains in the Old Testament, but runs on into the Talmud, and is deeply implanted in the consciousness of the Jewish race.

Even Paul the Pharisee felt all this. But what of Paul the Christian? For him it was not lost, but transformed and indefinitely strengthened. We must remember that all the Jew felt for Israel as a nation Paul took over bodily, and claimed for the Church of Christ. The covenant relation of God and his people still subsisted, but with a nearness and with a sense of reality that could not attach to it before. The mighty acts of God the Lord which the Christian recalled and on which he placed his hope and his confidence were not far back in the distant past, but they centred in the life and death and resurrection of one whom the generation then living had seen and known, to whose words they had listened, and whom their hands might have handled. And further, the influence which we associate with the gift of his Spirit was one of which they had actual experience day by day.

Can we not understand the extraordinary vividness with which it all came home to the mind of the Apostle, and which he tried in his turn to convey to the outer world? His whole life was one prolonged effort to convey to the world outside what Christ had done for them that loved him.

It was but natural that Paul should throw his description of this into the forms supplied to him by the Old Testament. The Old Testament was saturated with the conception of the righteousness of God. The history of Israel was the expression of the working of that righteousness. And it lay very near at hand to regard the whole great Divine process which constituted Christianity as an expression of the same righteousness. It was the righteousness of God which set it in motion. Through the operation of that righteousness it became the power of God unto salvation to every one that believed, to the Jew first and also to the Greek. The righteousness of God showed itself in the desire to produce in man a righteousness which should be the reflection of itself. Justification and sanctification are the technical names for the process. We should try to think of them not as technicalities but as the actual living effects that men like Paul felt in themselves and say in the hearts and lives of the brethren around them.

And now let us compare this sketch of what the Apostle meant by the righteousness of God with the teaching of the Gospels about the Kingdom of God or of Heaven.

The righteousness of God, as we have seen, was not a passive righteousness, but an active energizing righteousness. It was simply God at work in the world. And the Kingdom of God also, if we try to express it in unmetaphorical language, was just the same thing—it too was *God at work in the world.*

Paul's phrase, borrowed straight from the Old Testament, lays stress upon the moral character of the process, which had its root in the moral character of God from whom it sprang. His essential righteousness was the moving cause and the active persistent force at work behind and through the whole.

The 'Kingdom' or 'reign of God' is slightly more neutral in form. It does not lay the same stress upon the moral nature of the Kingdom or reign. But this is implied, and implied close at hand, even if it is not expressed. It is enough to say that it is the Kingdom, or reign, *of God.* God asserting his sovereignty in the world must needs assert it in the form of righteousness. If we say that it is his love which impelled him, we have also seen that righteousness, as it was conceived in the Old Testament and as Paul conceived it, included a large element of love. And in like manner the Kingdom, realized among men, necessarily expressed itself in righteousness. 'The Kingdom of God is not eating and drinking, but righteousness and peace and joy in the Holy Ghost.'

The points of contact are evident. God may put forth his sovereignty either in the large scale or on the small. He may make it seen by broad movements in the world, by the founding and growth and spread of his Church, or by the working of his gracious influence in the hearts of individual believers. Parables like the Leaven or the Mustard-seed cover both at once. For the Divine seed may be as a germ in the heart, and the Divine leaven may work in the heart as well as in a society making its conquests in the larger world.

Then so far as that society reflects its origin it must do so by its righteousness, and as an instrument for the propagation of righteousness; while for the individual, righteousness is the wedding-garment in which all the guests of the Kingdom must be attired.

And in both cases, the fruit of the Kingdom as of the energizing righteousness of God is peace and joy. 'The Kingdom of heaven is like unto a treasure hidden in the field; which a man found, and hid; and in his joy he goeth and selleth all that he hath, and buyeth that field' (Mt. 13.44). Compare this with the description of the effects of righteousness by faith in the Epistle to the Romans:

> Being therefore justified [or put into this condition of righteousness, the righteousness which comes from God] by faith, let us have peace with God through the Lord Jesus Christ; through whom also we have had our access by faith into this grace wherein we stand; and let us rejoice [or exult] in our tribulations: knowing that tribulation worketh patience; and patience, probation; and probation, hope: and hope putteth not to shame; because the love of God hath been shed abroad in our hearts through the Holy Ghost which was given unto us (Rom. 5.1-5).

There we have a detailed description of the 'joy of the kingdom'.

The parallelism thus runs through all the stages. The greatest emphasis in both cases is on the point of origin. The energizing righteousness is the righteousness of God; the Kingdom is the Kingdom *of God* or of heaven; that means that it is God's sovereign power, the influences and forces that come from him, at work among men. Both express themselves as righteousness; both make their presence felt in a settled temper of exultant joy.

The language is different. That of the Gospels turns on a phrase that runs through all the Old Testament, beginning with the Books of Samuel and ending in the Book of Daniel, to be kept alive in the popular Messianic expectation. The language of Paul is based perhaps mainly on that of the Psalms and the second part of Isaiah. But the content of the two cycles of language and of thought is substantially the same; or it only throws into relief slightly different aspects of that which has a fundamental identity. The central and cardinal point of the Christian dispensation is the same, whether we call it the 'righteousness of God' or the 'Kingdom of heaven'. In either case it is the goodness and love of God, actively intervening to guide, redeem, sustain, and bless his people.

Chapter 16

ST PAUL THE TRAVELLER*

Professor Ramsay's new book and the commentary of Dr Blass,[1] taken together, mark an epoch in the study of the Acts. Once more it has become possible to approach the literature on that book without a feeling of utter weariness. For some years past it had seemed as though the criticism of the Acts was doomed to waste itself among the sands of sterile hypothesis. It all moved along a single channel, and that a channel which led nowhere. Because literary analysis has won its triumphs in the Old Testament, and because it was employed at least hopefully in the case of the Synoptic Gospels, it was assumed that it could be applied without further qualification, and it was applied with interminable hair-splitting, to the Acts. The first condition of successful literary analysis must be the existence of clearly marked differences of style and of ideas. But in regard to the Acts the differences of style throughout the book were less marked than the identity; and though it was often assumed, it was never proved that such peculiarities as existed in idea and mode of treatment were inconsistent with substantial unity of authorship. I am not concerned to deny the existence of sources—even written sources—in the Acts, but the attempts to discriminate them so far have ended only in failure; the various reconstructions have been each more artificial than the last; and, in fact, hardly a single step in the process has been made good to the satisfaction of any one beyond the critic by whom it was put forward.[2]

    *   This chapter originally appeared as W. Sanday, 'St Paul the Traveller', *The Expositor*, Fifth Series, 3 (1896), pp. 81-94.
    1.   W.M. Ramsay, *St Paul the Traveller and the Roman Citizen* (London: Hodder & Stoughton, 1895); and F. Blass, *Acta Apostolorum sive Lucae ad Theophilum liber alter* (Göttingen: Vandenhoeck & Ruprecht, 1895).
    2.   I find myself in much agreement with the estimate of recent criticism of the Acts by Dr O. Zöckler ('Die Apostelgeschichte als Gegenstand hoherer und niederer Kritik', *Greifswalder Studien theologische Abhandlungen Hermann Cremer zum 25*

The fundamental mistake has been that the critics—in different degrees and with proportionate degrees of ill-success—have approached the Acts in a spirit of suspicion. Here they have seen redaction in one sense, there they have seen redaction in another; the one hypothesis which they have often seemed least willing to entertain is that the author of the Acts meant what he said and had good reasons for saying it.

In this lies the significance, and, as I cannot but think, the conspicuous superiority of the methods pursued by Dr Blass and Professor Ramsay. They have begun by taking their author as he stands. They have approached him with the presumption that he was right and not wrong. They have looked hard at what he said and weighed thoroughly all the surrounding circumstances before they have had recourse to theories of redaction, interested statement, or fiction. In addition to this they have had advantages shared by none of their more recent predecessors. Dr Blass has had a long training in the severe school of classical philology, and in consequence he has given us a commentary which is before all things the work of a scholar—clear, concise, hitting off the main point in the fewest possible words, and supporting the interpretation adopted by well-selected parallels. I do not by any means always agree with him. I am convinced that the Acts was written after and not before 70 AD, and I greatly doubt the theory of two recensions of the text both issued by Luke himself. But opinions are always less important than the presentation of the *data*, and it is for the presentation of these that Dr Blass has earned our profound gratitude. His book will remain the commentary on the Acts for many a long day.

Professor Ramsay has much in common with Dr Blass. He too comes to his subject from the side of classical philology, but it is classical philology in its broadest sense, an intimate knowledge of ancient life. The one man whom he calls master is Mommsen,[3] and like Mommsen he brings to bear on the interpretation of his text a mastery, which is every day becoming more complete, of that which lies behind the text, the framework of the Roman Empire, the deeper roots of ancient civilization. Add to this familiarity with the actual soil which Paul trod,

jahrigen Professor jubilaum [Gütersloh: C. Bertelsmann, 1895], pp. 109ff.). I differ from him chiefly in the extent to which I am able to accept the textual theories of Dr Blass. He adopts them *en bloc*.

3. A like phrase is also applied to Bishop Lightfoot (W.M. Ramsay, *The Church in the Roman Empire before AD 170* [Mansfield College Lectures, 1892; London: Hodder & Stoughton, 1893], p. 8).

the actual roads by which he travelled, the actual sites of the cities in which he stayed; and add again a singular faculty for going to the heart of a problem, vigorous powers of reasoning, and a nervous, masculine style, and I think it will be agreed that Professor Ramsay brings to his task a very exceptional equipment.

Nothing could be easier than to illustrate this from the volume before us. It simply bristles with points of interest. There is not a page of it from the first to the last that is not fresh, independent, original, grappling with his subject at first hand. The writer's gifts perhaps sometime disturb the balance of his judgment. He sees his own points so vividly, they stand out from the canvas so boldly, that he cannot see anything besides. The considerations which weigh with others seem to him trivial by comparison. Sometimes, perhaps, they are trivial, but not, I think, always. There are times when I should be tempted myself to put in a plea for arrest of judgment where the case is stated so powerfully as almost to overbear opposition. I propose to give an instance presently. But this again rather enhances than detracts from my admiration for Professor Ramsay's book. It is not infallible any more than Dr Blass is infallible; but it shows an extraordinary faculty for bringing real questions to a real issue; and that is the surest means of the advance of knowledge.

Necessities of time and space—the time at my own disposal and the amount of space available in a single number of *The Expositor*—prevent me from going through the book, as I should like, point by point, and compel me to select a particular topic which seems most to need discussion. This topic shall be the one on which Professor Ramsay's views depart most widely from those generally current. The view which has hitherto greatly preponderated is that the visit of Paul to Jerusalem described in Gal. 2.1-10 was on the occasion of the Apostolic Council described in Acts 15. Professor Ramsay denies this, and identifies it rather with the mission of Barnabas and Paul to convey to Jerusalem the alms collected at Antioch, of which mention is made in Acts 11.30. This visit, Professor Ramsay thinks, took place in the year 45, or more probably 46; the Apostolic Council he would place in 49 or 50. Between them would intervene the whole of the first missionary journey (Acts 13, 14) and the founding of what Professor Ramsay would call the Galatian churches.

If this view holds good, it will no doubt greatly affect the chronology of the Acts, and not inconsiderably the chronology of the epistles. For this I am quite prepared, if it shall be necessary. So far as I can see no question of principle is involved. I am ready to be converted to Professor Ramsay's view if the balance of argument shall be found to lean that way; but he has not as yet succeeded in converting me, and it seems well that a case should be stated on the other side. I do not deny for a moment that Professor Ramsay's arguments are real arguments. The question only is whether they are decisive, and whether there are not real arguments to be set against them.

I will put in the forefront at once the one consideration which compels me (as at present advised) to adhere to the older view; and I will then try to weigh the minor arguments for and against the rival hypotheses.

The consideration which to me seems in the strictly Baconian sense 'crucial' is that Gal. 2.1-10 implies a stage in the controversy as to the terms of admission of Gentile converts which had certainly been reached by the date of Acts 15 but which had not been reached at the date of Acts 11.30.

On the visit of Gal. 2.1-10, the main point decided was the distinct spheres of labour of the Judean Apostles, especially Peter, and Paul.

> When they saw that I had been intrusted with the gospel of the Uncircumcision, even as Peter with the gospel of the Circumcision (for He that wrought for Peter unto the apostleship of the circumcision wrought for me also unto the Gentiles); and when they perceived the grace that was given unto me, James, and Cephas, and John, they who were reputed to be pillars, gave to me and Barnabas the right hands of fellowship, that we should go unto the Gentiles, and they unto the circumcision (Gal. 2.7-9).

We cannot resist the conclusion that by this time there is a cleavage, a great and deep cleavage, in the Church: the Christians of Gentile origin are on one side, those of Jewish origin on the other. Already there lies behind a period of vigorous mission work, in which the efforts of Paul for the Gentiles had been conspicuously crowned by the Divine blessing. This the Judean Apostles recognise, and they shake hands over the *fait accompli*. Henceforward they will keep for their own province the Jews, and they bid God-speed to Paul in the work that lies before him among the Gentiles.

Now this is exactly the state of things which we find in Acts 15. It is, I would venture to say, as clearly not the state of things which we find in Acts 11.30. At that time the preliminary conditions for it did not exist. The gospel had been preached to a few Gentiles, most probably all of them as yet in some degree of connexion with the synagogue; but no cleavage, no question of principle had as yet arisen. There is no watchword 'Jew' and 'Gentile', no antithesis of 'Circumcision' and 'Uncircumcision'. Professor Ramsay himself shows very skilfully how this antithesis arose in the course of the journey of Acts 13, 14, but on his theory that journey is still in the future. Hitherto there have been nothing but friendly relations between the Church at Antioch as a whole and the Church of Jerusalem as a whole. The visit of Paul and Barnabas to Jerusalem has for its object only to convey the gifts of the one Church to the other. If matters of larger moment had been at stake, I should expect, and from the opinions which he expresses I should have thought that Professor Ramsay would expect, the historian to take some note of them.

I am aware that in the August *Expositor* he has given a different version of the events in question. I venture to place my version side by side with it, and I know that Professor Ramsay himself will do it justice.

It seems to me, if I may say so, that Professor Ramsay minimizes too much the amount of friction to which the passage in Galatians bears witness. When he writes, 'This visit then belongs to a period before the question had actually come to the front; it was already imminent, but was not yet actually the subject of contention', I cannot recognise this as an adequate description. How, for instance, does it agree with this?

> But not even Titus who was with me, being a Greek, was compelled to be circumcised: and that because of the false brethren privily brought in, who came in privily to spy out our liberty which we have in Christ Jesus, that they might bring us into bondage:[4] to whom we gave place in the way of subjection, no, not for one hour; that the work of the gospel might continue with you.

Is there no contention there? And is there none in the impatient words that follow? 'But from those who are reputed to be somewhat (whatsoever they were, it maketh no matter to me: God accepteth not man's person)—they, I say, who were of repute imparted nothing to me', etc. True, the Apostle goes on to say how they shook hands and agreed to go different ways. He was a warm-hearted and generous opponent, and ready enough to close a threatened breach. The tension does not seem to have been directly with the Judean Apostles, but it is clear that their names had been thrown in his teeth. He stood his ground, and held it; but even as he writes the memory of the scene comes back to him, and something of the spirit of battle imparts itself to his pen.

---

4. Professor Ramsay proposes here a rather different translation and punctuation.

Surely there are a number of striking coincidences between this narrative and that of Acts 15. The 'false brethren privily brought in…to spy out our liberty which we have in Christ Jesus'—what are they but the 'certain men' who 'came down from Judea and taught the brethren, saying, Except ye be circumcised after the custom of Moses, ye cannot be saved'? The conflict (or at least the beginnings of it) must have been at Antioch, because the liberty spied upon was that of the Pauline congregations. The accounts I believe to be independent, and the points of view are different, but the situation is essentially the same.

That there was an openly conducted controversy is proved also by the case of Titus. It is not merely that Paul is appealing to a precedent drawn from a time of peace in a time of war. 'To whom we gave place in the way of subjection, no, not for an hour.' The epistle echoes the war-note as well as the history.

Not only was there controversy on the two occasions, but the course of the controversy was the same. It had the same subject: the Pauline gospel was concerned; and the question of circumcision was definitely raised. It had the same turning-point. In both cases the argument which carried the day was the appeal of Paul to the hand of God as seen in the success of his own missions (Acts 15.3, 4, 12, 26 = Gal. 2.7-9). The issue was the same: the fraternizing of the leaders, and the framing of a concordat which left to both sides all the freedom which they needed.

Against all these marked coincidences, what is to be quoted for Acts 11.30? The single point, 'only they would that we should remember the poor; which very thing I was also zealous to do'. Professor Ramsay lays stress on the aorist ἐσπούδασα, and he makes it refer to the alms which Paul and Barnabas had just handed over. But the proof that it does this is anything but stringent. Professor Ramsay points out the delicate courtesy of the Judean Apostles in selecting for their one condition the very thing that had brought Paul to Jerusalem: 'Make it your rule to do what you have been regularly doing'. In any case the request is courteously and delicately put, because in any case Paul had given proof of his willingness to do what was required of him. But to me it seems distinctly more natural that such a request should be made at a moment when the answer to it was less glaringly obvious. To ask Paul to do what he had done before, is one thing; to ask him to do the very thing which he came for the purpose of doing, is another. Action such as that supposed would hardly mark a high sense of what was graceful and fitting.

I confess that to me the coincidences between Acts 15 and Galatians 2 come with great force—with all the more force because the differences which accompany them show that they are wholly undesigned. On these differences Professor Ramsay would insist; and it is right that we should discuss them.

Before doing so I have one general criticism to make on Professor Ramsay's book which may come in here as appropriately as anywhere. I am reluctant to make it, because the point to which it is directed is so very much the opposite of the treatment accorded to the Acts of late by most other scholars. And my own sympathies are far more with Professor Ramsay than with them. I must in candour admit that his treatment of Luke as a historian seems to me too optimistic. Not but that I gladly and heartily join in his eulogies, but he seems to me not to allow enough for facts over which Luke himself had no control; that is to say, he does not allow enough for the limitations to which Luke was inevitably exposed from the nature of his sources.

He writes as if Luke had the whole of the facts fully spread out before him, and as if all that he had to do was to make a selection among them. Now I do not doubt that there is selection, and very skilful selection. Professor Ramsay has brought out this in a way for which we have much reason to be grateful to him. But I conceive that the selection was made within narrower limits, and that it was more largely conditioned by the available information. Let us think of the historian for a moment as he girds himself for the task of writing the two works which have come down to us, as Professor Ramsay and I believe (though all would not agree with us) about the years 75–80 AD. I should not, speaking for myself, suppose that he had conceived the idea of chronicling the history of the infant Church very much earlier. It would appear from the preface to the Gospel that Luke was set upon writing it by the existence of other narratives dealing with the subject. But I do not think that these narratives began to spring up copiously before the decade 60–70 AD. I believe that Paul was dead when Luke definitely planned the composition of the Acts. I want something more than selection to explain the historian's silences. I should find it hard to explain them if he had a first-rate authority always within reach. The materials used I take to be in part written (like the greater part of the sources of the Gospel, and very possibly the source of the early chapters of the Acts), in part oral collected chiefly during the two years that Paul was imprisoned at Caesarea, in part his own recollections and notes—such as those which perhaps lie behind the 'We-sections'. It is one thing to suppose that Luke had directed attention to the events which passed around him, to those before as well as after his own actual discipleship. So much seems to be implied in the παρηκολουθηκότι ἄνωθεν of the preface. But it is another thing to assume that Luke began with the intention of writing a history, and that he accumulated materials deliberately in view of this intention all through his career. If that had been the case, it seems to me that the narrative of the Acts would have been different from what it is.

We cannot say when or where or how Luke met the particular informant from whom he derived the narrative contained in Acts 15. But it seems to me, as I read that chapter, that this informant, whoever he was, gave him a plain, straightforward, consistent story, which differs indeed from that in Galatians 2, but for the single reason that it is told from a wholly different point of view. The person in question was one of the crowd, who saw what other outside spectators saw, and filled up the gaps with what he was told by others in the same position as himself. It was matter of common hearsay that disputes had arisen at Antioch, that these disputes were due to the presence of strict-minded Jews from Jerusalem, that it was decided to appeal to headquarters, and that a formal meeting of the mother-church had been summoned, that at this meeting the leading actors spoke—not at once, but after much discussion, which is expressly mentioned in Acts 15.7—summing up the position, and finally ending with a resolution which was carried without open dissent.

This is all that any one standing in the crowd could be expected to see and know; it hangs together perfectly; and, so far as it goes, we may accept it without hesitation. How strongly contrasted with this are the circumstances under which Paul is writing to the Galatians! That his account of what happened takes the form of narrative at all is an accident: it is all subordinate to his own purpose, which is to prove the independence of his own teaching. Where Luke's informant speaks from common knowledge of facts that might be seen from without, he writes from within, from the innermost of inner circles, of things perhaps in part known only to himself and God.

So long as this is borne in mind there is not a detail that does not seem to me to fall easily and naturally into its place. We do not know at all what the 'revelation' was which impelled Paul to take the action he did, or how it fits into the chain of events; but Professor Ramsay, I think, presses this ignorance of ours quite unduly when he takes it as excluding the statements of Acts 15.3.[5]

When I say 'unduly', I mean more than we can afford to do if we are to attempt to write the history of events for which the data are so scanty. The juxtaposition in Acts 13.2, 3, of Divine prompting with formal commission seems to me sufficiently parallel. Commission seems implied in the laying on of hands, if not in ἀπέλυσας.

In like manner as to the private intercourse which the Epistle to the Galatians implies as going on concurrently with, or perhaps as leading up to, the great public meeting recorded in the Acts. Any one who is acquainted with affairs knows that vital controversies are not settled in public meetings. But indeed on this head I need only quote Professor Ramsay's own language on page 57: 'Another purpose is said in *Epist. Gal.* to have been achieved on this journey, but Paul immediately adds that this other purpose was carried out as a mere private piece of business, and implies thereby that it was not the primary or official purpose of the journey'. If Professor Ramsay can find room for the events of Gal. 2.1-10 in Acts 11.30, I may claim to find room for them as well in Acts 15, where they stand indeed in much nearer relation to the main subject.

Weigh in opposite scales the coincidences and the discrepancies in the two accounts, and in my judgment at least there is no doubt which will fall and which will rise.

Only one really serious difficulty seems to me to attend the identification of the incidents in Acts 15 and Galatians 2. That is the one on which in pursuance of his argument Professor Ramsay naturally insists, that on this theory we identify a visit to Jerusalem which in Galatians is apparently the second, with one which in the Acts is quite indisputably the third. Is this too covered by the special purpose of the two writers? On the view which I am adopting that is the only outlet from the dilemma.

We have to remember that Paul in Galatians has nothing really to do with visits to Jerusalem. What he has to do with is the intercourse of Paul with the elder Apostles. And we observe that although it is true that the author of the Acts would certainly make the visit of his fifteenth chapter the third, he says nothing whatever which would make it the third occasion of intercourse with the other Apostles. Rather there is what may well be a significant silence in regard to them in the

5.   Ramsay, *St Paul the Traveller*, p. 155.

description of the second visit. What Luke says about this is compressed into a single verse: 'And the disciples [at Antioch]…determined to send relief unto the brethren which dwelt in Judea: which also they did, sending it *to the elders* by the hand of Barnabas and Saul' (Acts 11.30). I take this as a compendious expression implying not that the church at Antioch intended its contributions to be delivered to the elders, but that as a matter of fact it was so delivered. But if so, is it purely by accident that there is no mention here of 'Apostles'? that whereas elsewhere 'the Apostles and elders' are constantly bracketed together as though they formed a single body (Acts 15.2, 4, 6, 22, 23; 16.4; cf. 21.18), in this one place the Apostles drop out and the elders stand close? Professor Ramsay attaches value to the silence of the Acts, even where it extends only to a single word; and so do I attach value to it. I do not think that this marked omission of 'the Apostles' was without a reason. Shall we speculate what reason?[6] I had been in the habit of supposing that this mission of Barnabas and Saul to Jerusalem synchronised with Herod's persecution in the year 44. The graphic picture of Acts 12.12-17 shows that at this time the leading Apostles were in some sort of hiding. Now we note that the arrival of the two envoys is mentioned in 11.30, and their departure in 12.25; and between these two points comes the description of the Herodian persecution. So that the inference does not seem to be forced, that on this occasion the Apostles were not at hand, and the envoys from the church at Antioch returned without having seen them.[7] On this hypothesis the various statements seem to dovetail neatly into each other. But in any case there is no direct contradiction between the language of the Acts and that of Paul on the assumption that the latter is referring to his third visit; and, that being so, I do not feel called upon to manufacture one where we know so little; the whole chapter of accidents is open.

For these reasons I still adhere to the older view, substantially as it was presented by Bishop Lightfoot. It seems to me that in this instance Professor Ramsay has used the microscope which he has applied with such splendid effect elsewhere, but that he has turned one end of it

6.   Professor Ramsay explains the pointed mention of 'elders' as due to a nice sense of the duties of different officials.

7.   Professor Ramsay puts the visit in the year 45, or preferably 46. He thinks that the famine had begun, and that provisions were taken and not money. I believe it to be more probable that money was taken, on the faith of Agabus' prophecy, and that the Judaean church was left to lay in stores for itself.

towards certain of the arguments, and the other end towards others. Hence it is that he speaks with a confidence which the facts do not appear to me to warrant.

I am also inclined to go with Bishop Lightfoot in regard to the place which he assigns to the next section (Gal. 2.11-14). Professor Ramsay very ingeniously inserts the scene at Antioch in the series of events which led up to the council. According to him, it would correspond to Acts 15.1, 2, a position which is rendered possible by throwing back the previous verses, Gal. 2.1-10, to the latitude of Acts 11.30. For us this ceases to be tenable, because we cannot invert the order of the two sections, or make the intercourse with Peter at Antioch precede what is expressly said to be the second occasion of intercourse with him at Jerusalem.

Thus the one conclusion carries with it the other, and for my own part I must be content to follow in the beaten track instead of taking the devious, but tempting paths opened up by Professor Ramsay. Just this part of the book seems to me to miss the mark in its attempted reconstruction of the life of the Apostle. But even supposing that the verdict of others should go with me, it would detract but very little from the value of what is probably the freshest and most penetrating study ever made of that life in two of its aspects—'St Paul the Traveller and the Roman Citizen'.

Chapter 17

THE EARLY VISITS OF ST PAUL TO JERUSALEM[*]

I shall hope to be forgiven if, in offering a few words of reply to my friend Professor Ramsay's criticism in the last number of the *Expositor*, I say very little about that part of it which is personal to myself. If I were to go more fully into this, I should have to deduct much from my friend's praise, but I should also have to deduct something from his blame. I fear it is true that I had overlooked some points in his argument—not wholly, for I find most of them marked in my copy of his book, but at the time of writing my article. I did not intend this to be in any sense exhaustive, and I stated the case in the form in which it still held possession of my own mind. I shall do my best to repair omissions; and I hope that at least, after Professor Ramsay's own dear and incisive restatement, the readers of the *Expositor* will have had the data for forming a judgment sufficiently set before them.

I think that in some ways my friend expects rather too much. It is true that I am one of those who have given in adhesion to his view about the Galatian churches; that is, on a balance of the evidence, I believe it to be somewhat more probable than the view which is opposed to it; but I should not as yet be prepared to treat it as quite axiomatic. There must be an intermediate stage after the first acceptance of a new view in which it lies in the mind (so to speak) still upon its trial and in process of adjustment to other data.[1] I cannot claim to have got beyond this point; and I do not think that Professor Ramsay, who has for some time been giving concentrated attention to the subject, should expect the rest of us

*   This chapter originally appeared as W. Sanday, 'The Early Visits of St Paul to Jerusalem', *The Expositor*, Fifth Series, 3 (1896), pp. 253-63; in response to W.M. Ramsay, 'St Paul and the Jewish Christians in A.D. 46', *The Expositor*, Fifth Series, 3 (1896), pp. 174-90.

1.   Though complaining of me for not being at the level of his own latest arguments Professor Ramsay confronts me with quotations from a popular work which I wrote eighteen years ago, and have hardly looked into since. I should express myself now rather differently.

to keep quite even pace with him. In the present instance, however, this backwardness is of less importance, because the particular argument affected by it does not seem to me to be valid.

I have no wish to deprecate reasonable criticism, but my friend will allow me to say that I do rather deprecate some parts of his recent article. At the present stage of the inquiry we are, as it seems to me, concerned mainly with premises and data. I should have thought that these were fit subjects for the 'dry light' of judicial investigation. But my friend is like a hound who, when once he has got upon the scent, goes off at full cry. He hunts down the statements of his opponents into what seem to him to be their consequences; and as these are nearly always either morally or intellectually discreditable they are held up to ignomiy. It is not only I who have this fate, but Bishop Lightfoot, and, on certain hypotheses for which we are responsible, even Luke and Paul. I know that my friend does not think us quite so bad as would appear (p. 189). At the end of his paper he pronounces over me an absolution for which I am most sincerely grateful; but if he would ask himself rather earlier whether his opponents (for the nonce) really meant to do or to countenance all these wicked and stupid things, I believe that he would lower his note, and the process would be less harrowing. I would suggest, with all deference, that while we are still in the region of construing and comparing texts we can afford to keep our equanimity. We are as yet only sketching in the outlines of our picture in pencil: the colour can be put in later.

I take it that we are both, Professor Ramsay and I, not aiming simply to establish a thesis, but co-operating together in the attempt to find out the truth. I therefore gladly go over the ground again with my friend's renewed statement before me, and with the help of this I shall endeavour to revise my own.

There are two main questions on which it is necessary to make up our minds: (1) Is it possible to identify the visit of Paul to Jerusalem described in Gal. 2.1-10 with that of Acts 11.30, 12.25? (2) If these two visits are not to be identified and Gal. 2.1-10 corresponds rather to Acts 15.3-29, can any adequate account be given of the silence of Paul in regard to the second visit of Acts 11.30?

1. On the first point I took the broad ground that Gal. 2.1-10 implied a more advanced stage of the controversy with the Judaists than could have been reached at the time of the second visit, i.e., about the year 44 (46 Ramsay) and before Paul's Galatian journey.

In reply to this Professor Ramsay quite rightly calls attention to the attack made on Peter by 'them of the circumcision' for his dealings with Cornelius (Acts 11.2), and he also lays stress on the extreme sensitiveness of the Jews on any point connected with the religious status of those who had not undergone circumcision. Along with this he notes a coincidence of language in the description of the situation in Acts 11.3 and Gal. 2.12. Peter was accused in both instances of 'eating with Gentiles'.

By all means let these arguments have their due weight. I think it is true that I stated the case on the other side with rather too little qualification. But I am still some way from acknowledging that Professor Ramsay has proved his case, and that the situation of Galatians 2 could really have been reached by the years 44–46. I go further, and it seems to me that the language of Paul in his Epistle to the Galatians is satisfied by nothing short of the events of the first missionary journey.

Professor Ramsay makes it clear in his book that down to the departure of Paul on this journey the Gentiles who had been admitted to the Church were all drawn from the class of proselytes—of the second class, if not of the first.

Speaking of the case of Cornelius, he says: 'But this step, though an important one, was only the first stage in a long advance that was still to be made. Cornelius was a proselyte; and Peter in his speech to the assembly in his house laid it down as a condition of reception into the Church that the non-Jew must approach by way of the synagogue (10.35), and become "one that fears God".'[2] Again: 'The Church of Antioch...contained a number of Greeks,[3] who were in the position of "God-fearing proselytes", but had not conformed to the entire law; and the question was still unsettled, what was their status in the Church'.[4] It is not until the first journey that Paul takes the next step forward, and offers the Gospel directly to Gentiles. At Salamis, in Cyprus, Paul

2. W.M. Ramsay, *St Paul the Traveller and the Roman Citizen* (London: Hodder & Stoughton, 1895), pp. 42-43.

3. This would be still clearer if the reading of Acts 11.20 were, as I am inclined to think it should be, Ἑλληνιστάς and not Ἕλληνας (see especially F.J.A. Hort, *The New Testament in the Original: Introduction and Appendix to the Text Revised by Brooke Foss Westcott and Fenton John Anthony Hort* [Cambridge: Macmillan, 1882], *ad loc.*; and *Judaistic Christianity: A Course of Lectures* [Cambridge: Macmillan, 1894], pp. 59-60).

4. Ramsay, *St Paul the Traveller*, p. 44.

was appealing direct for the first time to the Graeco-Roman world as himself a member of that world. This is put plainly in [Acts 14:27] as the great innovation and the great fact of the journey. As soon as Paul and Barnabas returned to Syrian Antioch they made a report to the assembled Church 'of all things that God had done with them, and how He had opened a door of faith unto the Gentiles'.[5]

Of the two stages into which the preaching of the gospel to the Gentiles is divided, this is the second: 'and the historian fixes the psychological moment [of the change] precisely at the point where the Apostles faced the Magian in the presence of the proconsul of Cyprus'.[6] This is brought out by Professor Ramsay in a very striking way.

But then we have to ask ourselves, Which of these two stages is presupposed in Gal. 2.1-10? I cannot for myself have any hesitation in replying, the same later stage—the second. The turning point is already behind the Apostle not before. When he speaks of himself as laying before the leaders of the Church the gospel which he preached among the Gentiles (Gal. 2.2, ὃ κηρύσσω, 'what I am in the habit of preaching'), I can only understand this of Gentiles in the fullest sense of the word, and of a practice which the Apostle had begun and not was about to begin. A little lower down he tells his readers how the actual success of his preaching was accepted as proof of the genuineness of his commission:

> When they saw that I had been intrusted with the gospel of the uncircumcision, even as Peter with the gospel of the circumcision (for He that wrought for Peter unto the apostleship of the circumcision wrought for me also unto the Gentiles); and when they perceived the grace that was given unto me, James, and Cephas and John, they who were reputed to be pillars, gave to me and Barnabas the right hands of fellowship, that we should go unto the Gentiles, and they unto the circumcision (Gal. 2.7-9).

Surely this 'gospel of the uncircumcision' is something more than occasional preaching to proselytes; and surely the acceptance of it is the ratification of a success already gained. It seems to me to point as clearly as anything could point to the events of the first journey, the founding of the Galatian churches. As I said in my previous article, it corresponds exactly to the 'rehearsing of what God had done' through the instrumentality of the two Apostles among the Gentiles (Acts 15.4, 12). The conclusive argument in the narrative is the same as that in the epistle; the

---

5.   Ramsay, *St Paul the Traveller*, p. 85.
6.   Ramsay, *St Paul the Traveller*, p. 85.

promise of work still to do is based upon the retrospect of work done. And if words are to bear their natural construction, that retrospect can only, I think, be of the successes of the first mission.

On this ground I take my stand. If I am dislodged from it, then it will be time to consider Professor Ramsay's highly ingenious combinations. But, as it is, I am stopped at the threshold.

Professor Ramsay has, however, an argument on the other side which he appears to consider decisive. He thinks that if we adopt (as I do provisionally) his own South-Galatian theory and identify the churches founded on the first missionary journey with the Galatians of the epistle, it becomes an 'argumentative absurdity' for Paul to refer at all to his third visit to Jerusalem, on the ground that he is proving the independence of his gospel *as first preached* in Galatia, and this third visit did not occur until after that first preaching. 'On the South-Galatian theory the third visit to Jerusalem was later than the conversion of the Galatians, and it would therefore be not merely unnecessary but unadvisable to speak of that visit when he was discussing the origin of, and authority for, his original message to the Galatians.'[7]

All depends on the validity of this last phrase. Is it only the authority of the *original* message to the Galatians that is in question? In assuming that it is I believe that Professor Ramsay presses too rigorously the phrase used by Paul—not anywhere in the near context, but—in Gal. 1.10: 'I make known to you, brethren, as touching the Gospel which was preached by me, that it is not after man'. No doubt Paul begins at the beginning; he begins by speaking of his gospel as he first obtained it and as he first preached it. But his general argument has to do not merely with this initial step but with its authority in the abstract—its authority at the time at which he is writing, its authority at the moment when it was deserted by the Galatians. These later moments cannot, I think, be excluded; and in reference to them the experience of the third visit is as much in point as that of the second.

For these reasons—not to speak of others which he will find concisely stated in a source to which I will refer later—Professor Ramsay has neither removed the stumbling-blocks which prevent me from accepting his identification of the visit of Gal. 2.1-10 with the second visit of the Acts, nor overborne the difficulties in the way of this view by the statement of others still greater.

7.   Ramsay, *St Paul the Traveller*, p. 176.

2. But he will say, 'If the visit of Galatians 2 is the third visit of the Acts, then the second visit mentioned in that work must be passed over by Paul without mention—which is incredible'. There is, I am inclined to think, a better case to be made out for this proposition than for the other. It does not, however, in my opinion amount to anything decisive, and the ἀπορίαι raised in connexion with it seem to me to arise mainly from our want of knowledge. I took my stand here on the negative ground that whereas Paul's purpose in Galatians required him to mention—not all his visits to Jerusalem but—all the occasions on which he had had any substantial intercourse with the Judaean Apostles, there was nothing in the Acts to show that on his second visit he had such intercourse. In the two verses which alone are devoted to this visit (Acts 11.30; 12.25) there is no allusion whatever to the Apostles. It is natural to ask, Why is this? I offered as a possible explanation one put forward by Bishop Lightfoot, by myself years ago, and probably by others—I have not looked up the history of it—that the Apostles may have been absent from Jerusalem owing to the persecution of Herod Agrippa I, the account of which falls in the Acts just in the verses which intervene between that which describes the arrival of the mission and that which describes its departure. But this, no doubt, is pure conjecture. It is not conjecture to which I attach any importance. The most I would say for it is that there are one or two indications (the position of the account of the persecution in the Acts, the silence as to any contact of Paul and Barnabas with the Apostles, the traces of secrecy in the description of the meeting in the house of Mary, Acts 12.12-17) which seem to point in that direction. So it still seems to me; the insufficiency of the data prevent me from saying more. I sit loosely to this hypothesis, as I do to all hypotheses which have so little direct evidence to commend them. The last thing that I would do would be to pledge myself to a precise reconstruction of details.

Here Professor Ramsay strikes in. He has his own theory clear and sharply defined as usual. He will not allow it to be supposed that the mission of Paul and Barnabas was brief and hurried. Stress is laid on the accomplishment of a διακονία; and διακονία in the Acts means a prolonged and carefully conducted personal ministration. The gathering in the house of Mary was not a gathering of the whole church. There is nothing to show that the Apostles were in hiding (Acts 12.17 does not prove this). The persecution was not wide-spread or severe. To suppose that the Apostles fled from it would be a disgrace to them. On the other hand, the stay of Paul and Barnabas probably lasted some time; and into that time may be packed the events of Gal. 2.1-10.

There is much in this position which I should not care to contest. I never pretended—it would be wrong to pretend—that there is proof demonstrative of the flight and hiding of the Apostles. All I would say is that Professor Ramsay's arguments do not seem to me decidedly to disprove it. I think that he lays too much stress on Luke's use of διακονία. In the two Lukan writings together the word occurs in all but nine times. This is not enough to sustain a negative induction. Besides, there is a parallel in Rom. 15.31 so exact as, it would seem, quite to justify the opinion of those who would take it of a short visit. The Apostle there prays that on his approaching journey (AD 58) he may be delivered from his unbelieving countrymen in Judaea, καὶ ἡ διακονία μου ἡ εἰς Ἰερουσαλὴμ εὐπρόσδεκτος τοῖς ἁγίοις γένηται. The ministration in question is the presenting of the sums collected in Macedonia and Greece for the poor of the mother church, so that the word is in a sense rightly glossed by the Western reading δωροφορία.

An argument to which I quite assent is that the meeting in the house of Mary (Acts 12.12) is a private meeting for prayer, not a public assembly of the whole church. I never thought of maintaining the contrary; and I have never to my knowledge spoken of Luke as a 'rough narrator'. But though a private meeting, the house in which it was held would seem to have been an important Christian centre, both from what we know of the position of Mark, the son of its owner, and also from the fact that Peter, on his release, at once makes his way there. This may suggest that there was some significance in the absence of James, and in Peter's sending a message and not proposing to go to him. But these are of course mere trifles, and very far from stringent proof that the leaders of the Church were in hiding. The most I should say would be that they may have been.

As to the morality of retiring before persecution it is hardly worth while to argue. No doubt there were unreasonable ways of doing this as well as reasonable; but to suppose that the Apostles (if they withdrew) withdrew from cowardice would be most gratuitous. The Early Church had a deliberate policy in such matters which history has approved, and not condemned. Its leaders did not court martyrdom, though they met it cheerfully when it came. The instances of Polycarp, Cyprian, and Dionysius of Alexandria, will occur to every one.

I might go on in this strain for some time, partly accepting and partly rebutting Professor Ramsay's arguments; but I should take up more space than either the editor or the readers of the *Expositor* would care to give me. The result would, I freely admit, be inconclusive; just as I believe that Professor Ramsay's case on the other side is inconclusive against me. The building up of imaginary situations where the data are so slight seems to me not very profitable. The facts may have been so, but they may have been quite different. A grain of positive evidence would outweigh much speculation. But the grain is wanting.

What I do contend for is only that we have no sufficient reason either (1) to throw over the definite statements which Luke makes as unhistorical,[8] or (2) to desert the preponderating indications that the visit which Paul has in his mind in Gal. 2.1-10 is the third and not the second.

In conclusion I would venture to suggest to my friend and to others who may care to pursue the subject further, that they would find it worth while to consult the little commentary on Galatians by Dr James Drummond, principal of Manchester College. The preface is dated December, 1892; so that it was given to the world before the South-Galatian theory had been stated with so much force in Professor Ramsay's *Church in the Roman Empire*.[9] It therefore gives what is substantially the old view in regard to the epistle; but it gives this with conspicuous clearness, independence, and impartiality. The author is at least removed from the imputation, which neither Bishop Lightfoot nor I have escaped, of apologetic harmonizing; though, speaking for myself, my conscience is clear of having given to the sacred writers any different measure from that which I should have given them if they had been profane.

I think that I have said enough; and I shall leave it to Professor Ramsay, if he wishes it, to have the last word.

---

8.   Dr Drummond adopts this alternative as to the visit of Acts 11.30, and I should not refuse to do so if the arguments for it were stronger (*Galatians* [London: Sunday School Association, 1892]).

9.   W.M. Ramsay, The *Church in the Roman Empire before* AD *170* (Mansfield College Lectures, 1892; London: Hodder & Stoughton, 1893).

Chapter 18

PAUL'S ATTITUDE TOWARDS PETER AND JAMES[*]

Like Professor Ramsay, I had not thought to write any more on the subject in debate between us at present. But the invitation which he gives me is so friendly, and the opening which his article offers seems to me so satisfactory, and so really conducive to an understanding, not only between our two selves, but among those who are interested in the subject generally, that I have not hesitated to take him at his word, and I have asked the editor to allow me to append a few remarks to his paper.

It has unfortunately happened—I hardly know how—that besides the necessary and inevitable differences between us in regard to the interpretation of this section of Church History, others had gathered round them which did not seem to me so necessary, and which I am afraid must have encumbered our discussion to the reader. These, I am glad to think, have now nearly all been cleared up, and the one that remains may, I hope, soon be removed.

I can assure Professor Ramsay that I had no wish to stand in the way of the full consideration of his case. If I proposed to restrict our discussion to certain lines, my motives in doing so were quite on the surface. Partly, they were a very prosaic desire to economize time and space, and partly a certain mental habit which impels me whenever I can to simplify a complicated question by going straight to what seems to me the most vital part of it, where a decision once taken carries with it all the rest. Of course, I may have been wrong in singling out the part I did as vital. There are other considerations which I should myself have liked to take up when that had been disposed of. But as the question stood it seemed to me sufficient to deal with the one main point at once. That was all I meant by putting in my plea as it were *in limine*; it was a

*   This chapter originally appeared as W. Sanday, 'Paul's Attitude towards Peter and James', *The Expositor*, Fifth Series, 4 (1896), pp. 56-64; it is a response to W.M. Ramsay, 'Paul's Attitude towards Peter and James', *The Expositor*, Fifth Series, 4 (1896), pp. 43-56.

short cut to a decision, such as I am afraid one is obliged to have recourse to in this crowded life of ours, and nothing more.

I hope there was nothing unjust in this. It seemed to me that the particular question did admit of being isolated, that it did admit of a definite answer Yes, or No, and that the one general answer carried with it other subordinate answers. I am quite open to correction, and merely state my case for what it is worth.

However this may be, Professor Ramsay has now been good enough to meet me on the ground of my choosing. I thank him for it, and I thank him for bringing to bear his unique power of giving to the details of a question definiteness and reality. There can be no doubt that his article is calculated to advance our debate a long step forward. I shall have no reason to complain if, when I have said my say, the votes are taken and the decision goes against me.

Professor Ramsay has stated his case, and I will say at once that I do not think it could be better stated. The view which he takes of clause after clause of the crucial passage seems to me (on his premises) the most reasonable that could be taken. If he should end by making a convert of me, I should myself take the same view. But I cannot say that as yet the argument, as a whole, seems to me convincing.

It is important that we should have the text of the passage (Gal. 2.6-9) before us; and as some exception has been taken to my renderings (which I believe were usually those of the Revised Version), it may be most satisfactory if I adopt the paraphrase given by Professor Ramsay himself:[1]

> But from the recognised leaders—how distinguished soever was their character is not now to the point; God accepteth not man's person—the recognised leaders, I say, imparted no new instruction to me; but perceiving that I throughout my ministry am charged specially with the mission to foreign (non-Jewish) nations, as Peter is with the Jewish mission—for he that worked (ὁ ἐνεργήσας) for Peter to the Apostolate of the circumcision worked (ἐνήργησε) also for me to be the missionary to the Gentiles—and perceiving [from the actual facts] the grace that had been given me, they, James and Cephas and John, the recognised pillars of the Church, gave pledges to me and to Barnabas of a joint scheme of work, ours to be directed to the Gentiles, while theirs was to the Jews.

1.	W.M. Ramsay, *St Paul the Traveller and the Roman Citizen* (London: Hodder & Stoughton, 1895), p. 56.

Professor Ramsay thinks that these verses have reference to a point of time corresponding to that of Acts 11.30 (the mission of Paul and Barnabas to Jerusalem with succour against the famine). This he would date in the year 46. I would rather place the events described in the epistle in the longitude of Acts 15., i.e., about the year 50. The great difference between us is that on Professor Ramsay's view the first missionary journey and the founding of the Galatian churches (Acts 13.14) are subsequent to the situation implied by the epistle, whereas on my view they precede it. I have maintained that Paul makes a direct appeal to the successes of the Galatian mission, and this Professor Ramsay denies. The issue between us is, therefore, as clear and simple as possible, and it should not be difficult for the reader to make up his mind about it.

Professor Ramsay rests his case mainly on the force of ἐνήργησε, which—as he rightly urges—is subjective rather than objective. When Paul says that God 'worked for' him towards the Gentiles as he 'worked for' Peter towards the Jews, the Greek lays stress rather on the powers implanted, the gifts and energies bestowed upon the two Apostles, than upon the results which they obtained. The inference drawn from this is that when we are told that James and Peter and John 'perceived the grace' that was given to their colleague, they perceived it rather through their private intercourse with him—and their 'sympathetic insight into the qualifications of men', than through the witness of events. Their confidence in Paul is prophetic rather than in retrospect of work done.

I should not think of contesting the perfect tenability of this as an interpretation of the Greek. At the same time I am a little surprised that Mr Boys-Smith, who has expressed his adhesion to Professor Ramsay's view, should think it 'conclusive' as against my argument. I note by the way that Professor Ramsay can hardly have so regarded it at the time when he wrote his paraphrase. He inserts there the words which I have placed in square brackets (in the original they are in smaller type) 'perceiving [from the actual facts] the grace that had been given me'. Perhaps his view has developed since the paraphrase was written. I do not mean to press the words against him further than to show how very naturally they are introduced, and how entirely the Greek admits of my construction of the history as well as of his. The words chosen no doubt lay stress on the God-given energies of the Apostles. But these might be inferred either directly or indirectly, either by personal contact and insight into character, or by the news of effects produced; the context leaves both methods open, and I should not wish to exclude either.

One little phrase at least makes for the wider reference. If Paul had written no more than 'he who worked for Peter worked also for me', the working might well have been only inward. But then he adds 'he who worked for Peter *to the apostleship of the circumcision* worked also for me *towards the Gentiles*'. The appeal is transferred from the inward to the outward. It was the actual success of Peter among Jews, and the actual success of Paul among Gentiles that supplied proof of their endowment and fitness for their respective missions.

It thus appears that Professor Ramsay was not wrong in inserting 'from the actual facts', and that I am (so far) not wrong in following him. The next question that comes up is, What are these facts? The context seems to show that they are facts upon a certain scale, facts upon a considerable scale. When Paul ascribes to his brother Apostle 'the apostleship of the circumcision', he implies, though he leaves the word to be understood, that 'the apostleship of the Gentiles' had fallen to himself. What evidence had he of this?

Professor Ramsay insists on a point which I had waived. He claims that the right reading in Acts 11.20 is Ἕλληνας, and not Ἑλληνιστάς; he thinks that this proves the presence of Greeks (Gentiles) in some numbers in the church at Antioch, and that Paul had exercised his ministry among these.

It is a dangerous thing in textual criticism to take at once the reading which seems to give the best *prima facie* sense, especially where that sense is required by a particular theory. Has Professor Ramsay weighed the reading as a question of such difficulty ought to be weighed? The mass of manuscripts, including B, the Laudian Acts, and the important cursive 61, has Ἑλληνιστάς; a small but important group, the third hand of ℵ, the first hand of D and A, have Ἕλληνας. The first hand of ℵ has the clerical error εὐαγγελιστάς. It is commonly assumed that ℵ is really a witness for Ἑλληνιστάς, the first syllables being evidently due to the influence of εὐαγγελιζόμενοι which follows. It may, however, be urged that a substantive suggested by εὐαγγελιζόμενοι could only be εὐαγγελιστάς.[2] The evidence of ℵ* has to be taken with so much reserve, which in a case like this is not without importance. On the other

---

2. As it was by Professor B.B. Warfield, 'The Readings Ἕλληνας and Ἑλληνιστάς, Acts xi. 20', *Journal of the Society of Biblical Literature and Exegesis* 3 (1883), pp. 113-27, esp. p. 114.

hand, one of the two leading witnesses on the other side, A, is discredited by reading Ἕλληνας for Ἑλληνιστάς in 9.29, where D is not extant, and therefore cannot be tested.

Into the scale in favour of Ἑλληνιστάς must be thrown the strong temptation to editor or scribe to substitute an easy and familiar word for one which was by no means familiar. There is no like temptation to set against this, so that the argument drawn from it seems to me a strong one. Generally speaking, textual considerations in the strict sense tell decidedly for Ἑλληνιστάς.

Are they overthrown by considerations of exegesis? I greatly doubt it. The words 'Hellenist', 'Hellenistic', etc., are with us in constant use; they occupy a convenient place in the language of scholarship, and a meaning has been attached to them which is well understood. This is apt to make us forget that the case was very different in antiquity. The three places where the word Ἑλληνιστάς occurs in the Acts, and certain comments upon the Acts, are said to be the only instances of its occurrence. It is not, I believe, found in the whole of Josephus, or in the whole of Philo. Hence the meaning of it is really far from certain. I suspect that it is to be taken strictly of the Jews who habitually used the Greek language. In the places where they are mentioned the Hellenists always seem to be in a minority. Even at Antioch they would be, although it is described as 'a Greek city'; the main body of the Jews would use their own Aramaic, which did not differ greatly from that of the native Syrians. We may suppose that only a few synagogues were set apart for the Jews who were in the stricter sense 'Hellenists'.

The Jews in these synagogues would doubtless be in closer touch with Gentiles; and I am ready to believe that there may have been at Antioch a certain number of proselytes or inquirers who had embraced Christianity as Cornelius did. But I am not prepared to think that these existed at Antioch in such numbers by the date of Acts 11.30 that Paul could speak of himself as holding an ἀποστολὴν εἰς τὰ ἔθνη. I cannot think that as yet there was a clear demarcation of spheres between himself and Peter. It seems to me an anachronism to speak at this date of τὸ εὐαγγέλιον τῆς ἀκροβυστίας. All these expressions would be perfectly in place after the first journey. I cannot think that they could be in place before it.

There are three great steps in a steady and gradual ascent. The handful of converts of Gentile birth at Antioch and Paul's dealings with them is the first; the scene before Sergius Paulus (Acts 13.8-12) is the second;

the third and greatest is the definite turning to the Gentiles at Antioch in Pisidia (Acts 13.46ff.). This is the real turning-point. 'It was necessary that the word of God should first he spoken to you. Seeing ye thrust it from you, and judge yourselves unworthy of eternal life; lo, we turn to the Gentiles.' With these words Paul announced his assumption of the true 'apostleship of the Gentiles'. From this day onwards he may be said to preach a real 'gospel of the uncircumcision'. To use either of these phrases at any earlier period seems to me to antedate them; it seems to me to introduce confusion into a history the main lines of which stand out with wonderful clearness.

The two phrases, ἀποστολὴ εἰς τὰ ἔθνη and τὸ εὐαγγέλιον τῆς ἀκροβυστίας, both seem to me to imply a certain scale in their contents—deliberate preaching, systematically directed over a considerable extent of time and with considerable results. I still fail to see that these conditions are satisfied by the view put forward by Professor Ramsay.

I will only add a word of explanation in reference to the discrepancies which seem to arise if my view is adopted. Professor Ramsay thinks that I minimize these, though I quite understand that the charge is not pressed, as my error is set down as a natural and pardonable consequence of my position as a teacher. 1 am grateful for the indulgence, but I am afraid that I cannot avail myself of it. What Professor Ramsay would call a minimizing of discrepancies is with me a matter of deliberate principle, applicable equally to secular writing as to sacred. I would formulate the principle thus: Where we have reason to think that two writers are each singly deserving of credit, discrepancies between them are more likely to be apparent than real: even where the discrepancies may seem to be serious, and the methods suggested for resolving them are open to some objection, it is still better to accept the testimony than to discard it, because our knowledge is almost sure to be too limited to exhaust the possibilities of reconciliation. *Subtilitas naturae subtilitatem sensus et intellectus multis partibus superat.*[3] I sometimes wish that a lawyer with competent knowledge would collect for us instances in which verdicts more or less confidently given had been afterwards, by the confession of the real culprit, or by the production of new evidence, proved to be wrong. I believe that if this were done, and if the instances in question were duly weighed, our ideas as to the possibilities of things would be considerably enlarged.

3. F. Bacon, *Novum Organum*, 1.10.

In the particular case before us I have little doubt that, as conceived by Professor Ramsay, they are really too narrow.

As at present advised, the sum total of the difficulties on my reconstruction of the history seems to me less than on his. I do not pledge myself to the whole of the reconstruction, but I think that there are certain fixed points in it; the filling up between those points is only put forward as speculative and conjectural. For the first I should contend somewhat strenuously; for the second I do not much care to contend. But I hope that Professor Ramsay will believe that, even while I am arguing against him, I am weighing his case as well as I can, and that no mere obstinacy in debate will prevent me, if I am satisfied with it, from coming over to his opinion.

Chapter 19

THE TEXT OF THE APOSTOLIC DECREE (ACTS 15.29)[*]

Two recent articles in *The Expositor* for March and July of this year help to bring home to us that there is one important and in some respects fundamental group of readings in the Book of Acts in regard to which, in this country at least, opinion is still wholly unsettled. And, as it happens that in regard to this particular group of readings my own opinion is clear, I will venture to re-state the case as it seems to me at the present moment. I speak of 're-statement' because I have once before set forth at some length my views on the subject, but in a volume which is not likely to be in the hands of many in England. I had the honour of contributing to the volume of essays presented to the veteran scholar Dr Theodor Zahn on his seventieth birthday.[1] The subject which I took was 'The Apostolic Decree'; but the essay, though known to Professor Kirsopp Lake,[2] has not, so far as I know, attracted the attention of others of my countrymen. And I cannot help just asking myself whether Professor Lake—although he has discussed fully and satisfactorily a single point in the case as I presented it—has considered as carefully as I should like him to do the effect of that case as a whole. At the same time I quite admit that in the article and the appendix to which I have referred

---

   *   This chapter originally appeared as W. Sanday, 'The Text of the Apostolic Decree (Acts xv 29)', *The Expositor*, Eighth Series, 6 (1913), pp. 289-305; it responds to M. Jones, 'The Apostolic Decree in Acts xv: A Compromise or a Triumph?', *The Expositor*, Eighth Series, 5 (1913), pp. 242-55; E.H. Eckel and S.A. Devan, 'The Question of the Apostolic Decree: A Reply', *The Expositor*, Eighth Series, 6 (1913), pp. 66-82.
   1.   W. Sanday, 'The Apostolic Decree, Acts xv (20-29)', in N. Bonwetsch, G. Nathaniel, *et al.* (eds.), *Theologische Studien, Theodor Zahn, zum 10. Oktober 1908, dargebracht* (Leipzig: A. Deichert, 1908), pp. 317-38.
   2.   See K. Lake, 'The Judaistic Controversy, and the Apostolic Council', *The Church Quarterly Review* 71 (1910–11), pp. 345-70, and his *The Earlier Epistles of St Paul: Their Motive and Origin* (London: Rivingtons, 1911), pp. 48-60.

he has covered the whole ground and offered an alternative construction which by inference excludes mine.

I shall not attempt to repeat the substance of all that I have already written, but will confine myself mainly to the text of the decree (Acts 15.29) and the two connected verses (15.20 and 21.25), with a few further remarks pointing backwards and forwards. For the sake of clearness I will divide what I have to say into separate heads.

1. *The Present Situation*

I had in view more especially, on the one side Zahn;[3] and on the other, Harnack,[4] and Gotthold Resch.[5] Since that time I observe that things have taken a rather different course in this country and in Germany. On this side of the North Sea, there has been something like a drawn battle, with the honours rather on the side of Harnack and Resch than otherwise. On this side, besides the article in the July *Expositor* must be set Dean Furneaux's edition of the Acts[6] and the two writings already referred to by Professor Lake. These may be set against the older works of Rackham,[7] Knowling (that best of all English Commentaries on the Acts)[8] and Bartlet (in the Century Bible).[9] In Germany, on the other

3.   T. Zahn, *Einleitung in das Neue Testament* (2 vols.; Leipzig: A. Deichert, 3rd edn, 1906–1907), II, pp. 344-46, 349, 353-54.

4.   A. Harnack, *Beiträge zur Einleitung in das Neue Testament*, III (3 vols.; Leipzig: J.C. Hinrichs, 1908).

5.   *Das Aposteldekret nach seiner ausserkanonischen Textgestalt, untersucht von Gotthold Resch* (Texte und Untersuchungen, 28.3 [Neue Folge, 13.3]; Leipzig: J.C. Hinrichs, 1905).

6.   W.M. Furneaux, *The Acts of the Apostles: A Commentary for English Readers* (Oxford: Clarendon Press, 1912). In referring to this book I cannot help regretting that Dr Furneaux should write so dogmatically and on such very imperfect data ('Harnack has shown conclusively that three things are forbidden all of them moral—idolatry, fornication and murder... The words "and from what is strangled" are an early gloss written in the margin by some one who misunderstood the "blood", etc.).' Dr Furneaux has command of a clear and vigorous style, and might have done good service in helping to make the Acts more generally understood; but, to say the truth, his book required at least three times the work and thought that have been actually given to it. It is much to be hoped that readers will not be carried away by his confident assertions.

7.   R.B. Rackham, *The Acts of the Apostles: An Exposition* (Westminster Commentaries; London: Methuen, 1901).

hand, all the recent books that I can think of are against Resch and Harnack; so (e.g.) Wendt, in the new edition of his Commentary;[10] Rudolf Knopf (in the series edited by J. Weiss);[11] Erwin Preuschen (though he places in square brackets 'things strangled' in the text of 15.20, 29, and the whole verse 21.25);[12] and above all, Freiherr Hermann von Soden in his new text.[13] The last-named should carry special weight with Professor Lake, as he is not only a specialist of great experience (should we not say, in view of his *magnum opus* now completed, *the* leading specialist?) in textual criticism, but also shares with him the general principle 'that our most famous uncials only represent an Alexandrian recension of the third or fourth century'. Taking the two countries together and considering all the circumstances, I think I may claim that the balance of authority is in favour of the older view. I would not, however, lay stress upon authority, but should wish the question to be decided strictly on its merits.

2. *The Problem at Issue*

And yet I cannot be surprised that Professor Lake's book, and in particular his statement of this question, should have attracted the attention that it has both on other points and on this; he writes with such bright intelligence and in such a genuinely scientific spirit that his views deserve full discussion. For several reasons I should be glad to be allowed to state the problem in his words. It cannot be better stated— either with less of pedantry or with more lucidity—and I should be glad to mark the point up to which we can travel together. It should be said that Professor Lake writes (by inference) collectively of the three related

---

8.   R.J. Knowling, 'The Acts of the Apostles', in W.R. Nicoll (ed.), *The Expositor's Greek Testament* (5 vols.; London: Hodder & Stoughton, 4th edn, 1912), II, pp. 3-554.

9.   J.V. Bartlet, *The Acts* (Century Bible; London: Henry Frowde, 1900).

10.   H.H. Wendt, *Die Apostelgeschichte* (Kritisch-exegetischer Kommentar über das Neue Testament, 3; Göttingen: Vandenhoeck & Ruprecht, 9th edn, 1913).

11.   R. Knopf, *Die Apostelgeschichte* (Die Schriften des Neuen Testaments, 3; Göttingen: Vandenhoeck & Ruprecht, 1906).

12.   E. Preuschen, *Die Apostelgeschichte erklärt* (Handbuch zum Neuen Testament, 4.1; Tübingen: Mohr Siebeck, 1912).

13.   H. von Soden, *Die Schriften des Neuen Testaments in ihrer ältesten erreichbaren Textgestalt: Hergestellt auf grund ihrer Textgeschichte von Hermann Freiherr von Soden*, IV (4 vols.; Göttingen: Vandenhoeck & Ruprecht, 1913).

verses, but primarily of the actual text of the Decree (Acts 15.29). He opens his case as follows:

> The text of all the manuscripts which represent the dominant Greek tradition ℵ A B C P, etc.—supported by the Alexandrian Fathers Clement and Origen, states that the Apostles told the Gentile converts to keep themselves from things offered to idols, from blood, from things strangled, and from fornication. Thus there is a four-clause text of which the first three clauses seem, when united in this way, to give a food law, to fix, as it were, the conditions of intercourse between Jewish and Gentile Christians, while the last clause—against fornication—seems to have nothing to do with food, but to belong to a different category altogether.
>
> Over against this reading is the evidence of D, the Latin version, Irenaeus (in Greek as well as in the Latin translation), Tertullian, Cyprian, and other Latin writers, who omit 'things strangled', generally insert after the reference to fornication, 'and do not do to others what you would not that they should do to you', and at the end of all add, 'Ye shall do well, being carried along by the Holy Spirit'. Thus it is plain that a widely received text of the decrees ran somewhat as follows: ἀπέχεσθαι εἰδωλοθύτων καὶ αἵματος καὶ πορνείας, καὶ ὅσα μὴ θέλετε ἑαυτοῖς γίνεσθαι ἑτέρῳ μὴ ποιεῖν· ἀφ' ὧν διατηροῦντες ἑαυτοὺς εὖ πράξετε [or πράξατε?] φερόμενοι ἐν τῷ ἁγίῳ πνεύματι, and was opposed, ultimately successfully, by a rival form which ran ἀπέχεσθαι εἰδωλοθύτων καὶ αἵματος καὶ πνικτῶν καὶ πορνείας· ἐξ ὧν διατηροῦντες ἑαυτοὺς εὖ πράξετε.
>
> Now, the evidence of Irenaeus and Tertullian on the one hand, and of Clement on the other, shows that both these readings are very old. Moreover, the history of exegesis confirms them. For in Alexandria the Apostolic Decrees were always interpreted as a food law, but in Africa (up to the time of Augustine) and in Europe as referring to the three deadly sins. Irenaeus and Tertullian were, it is true, acquainted with a food law, but they did not connect it with the Apostolic Decrees.
>
> Nevertheless, the three-clause text, in its entirety, cannot be maintained. Among modern critics there is an almost complete agreement that the additions of the negative form of the golden rule, and the reference to the Spirit cannot be original; partly because the former introduces a very harsh parenthesis or change of thought but chiefly because, if the golden rule had been in the text from the beginning, the interpretation of the decrees as a food law would have been impossible.

Down to this point my critic and I are in complete agreement, and I shall venture to use the statement thus made as if it had been my own. But from this point onwards there is usually some little change that I should like to see made in most of the paragraphs which affects the inference that I should draw from them. It will, however, be better just to indicate these changes as we go on, and then to endeavour to draw the threads of the evidence together.

Professor Lake continues:

> This consensus of opinion had prejudiced critics against the omission of 'things strangled', which is supported by much the same witnesses, and Dr Sanday in particular has argued that as D and Irenaeus have made a mistake in adding the golden rule, they ought not to be trusted where they omit 'things strangled'. His view is that the same people left out 'things strangled' and inserted the golden rule [not to do to others what one would not have done to oneself] in order to change a food law into a moral enactment.
>
> Against this argument serious objections can be brought. In the first place, it is not the case that the evidence for the golden rule is quite the same as that for the omission of 'things strangled'; Tertullian omits 'things strangled' but does not insert the golden rule. There is, therefore, important if not extensive evidence that the two readings are independent of each other. In the second place, there is no historical evidence whatever that the circles which can be shown to have read a text which omitted 'things strangled' had any objection to a food law.

It was not so much the modern consensus of opinion that led me to my conclusion as the common elements that ran through the ancient authorities for the text. Nor did I at all slur over the difference in regard to the 'golden rule' in Tertullian's version of it. I will come back to this in more detail when we have the evidence more fully before us. In regard to the omission of 'things strangled', I would not say that the circles responsible for that omission 'had any objection to a food law'. I do not dispute the evidence which Professor Lake brings forward to show that they had no such objection. I will explain later just what I believe to have been their attitude on the subject. The sentences that follow are an argument in favour of looking for a reading which will explain the divergences on either side. That is no doubt quite in order as a rule of critical procedure. But it is another thing to say that 'such a text would be excellently provided by the reading of Tertullian, which omits "things strangled", but does not insert the golden rule'. I understand the reasons which have led to this remark; but we must reserve the discussion of them until we come to speak of the evidence of Tertullian as a whole. Before we do this it will be well to have before us a concise statement of the critical attestation of the different clauses.

3. *The Textual Phenomena*

The alternatives lie between two connected groups of what are technically known as 'Western' and 'Eastern' readings. It will be enough to set out in full the evidence for the first of these (the Western group). It may be assumed that the mass of the other authorities, including the leading Greek manuscripts and the versions, is on the other side. I shall not hesitate to use the recognised critical symbols; because to do so makes the statement much more compact and it is easier to get a synoptic view of the whole. It is not important that all the symbols should be understood. They may be simply taken as so many pawns in the game; the main point on which we have to fix our attention is their tendency to recur.

I proceed then to give the commonly accepted texts, with the Western readings represented as variants. I omit a few secondary details of evidences that would only confuse.

Acts 15.20: ἀλλὰ ἐπιστεῖλαι αὐτοῖς τοῦ ἀπέχεσθαι ἀπὸ τῶν ἀλισγημάτων τῶν εἰδώλων καὶ τῆς πορνείας καὶ τοῦ πνικτοῦ καὶ τοῦ αἵματος ('but that we write unto them that they abstain from the pollutions of idols, and from fornication, and from what is strangled, and from blood').

> *Omit* καὶ τοῦ πνικτοῦ ('and from what is strangled'). D, g, Latin Irenaeus, *add at end* καὶ ὅσα μὴ θέλουσιν ἑαυτοῖς γίνεσθαι ἑτέροις μὴ ποιεῖν or the like ('and what they would not have done to themselves not to do to others'), D, Sahidic (Egyptian) version, Latin Irenaeus, Eusebius.

Acts 15.29: ἀπέχεσθαι εἰδωλοθύτων, καὶ αἵματος, καὶ πνικτῶν, καὶ πορνείας· ἐξ ὧν διατηροῦντες ἑαυτοὺς εὖ πράξετε ('that ye abstain from things sacrificed to idols, and from blood, and from things strangled, and from fornication; from which, if ye keep yourselves, ye shall prosper').

> *Omit* πνικτῶν ('things strangled'), D, Latin Irenaeus, Cyprian, Pacian, Ambrosiaster, Jerome, Fulgentius.
> *Insert* (after πορνείας, 'fornication') καὶ ὅσα μὴ θέλετε ἑαυτοῖς γίνεσθαι ἑτέρῳ μὴ ποιεῖν or the like, D, Harclean (Syriac) version with an asterisk, Sahidic (Egyptian) version, Ethiopic, Latin Irenaeus, Cyprian, Eusebius, Ambrosiaster (nearly) and others.
> *Add at end,* φερόμενοι ἐν [τῷ] ἁγίῳ πνεύματι, D, Latin Irenaeus, Tertullian.

Acts 21.25: φυλάσσεσθαι αὐτοὺς τό, τε εἰδωλόθυτον καὶ αἷμα καὶ πνικτὸν καὶ πορνείαν ('that they should keep themselves from things sacrificed to idols, and from blood, and from what is strangled, and from fornication').

Omit καὶ πνικτόν, D, g, Ambrosiaster (nearly), Augustine.

We observe that D (Codex Bezae, the leading authority for the Western text) enters into the testimony for every one of these readings; the Latin Irenaeus also enters into every one where the verse is quoted by Irenaeus. A single verse is quoted by Tertullian; and there Tertullian agrees with Irenaeus except in the insertion of the golden rule. This one reading (with the corresponding insertion in 15.20) stands rather by itself, and must be considered separately. It too is Western, resting primarily upon D, Irenaeus. The other readings are not only Western, but belong definitely to the Latin branch of the Western Text. In regard to the golden rule, we note (1) that the absence of Tertullian and the presence of a small group of early versions gives the reading a rather special character. The 'Harclean Syriac with an asterisk' requires a word of explanation. Thomas of Harkhel (Heraclea) in the year 616 published a revised form of an earlier version of 508 AD, as he expressly tells us, with a careful collation of two (or three) 'accurate Greek manuscripts'. This edition was made in a monastery nine miles from Alexandria. The Greek manuscripts referred to were remarkable, and contained a number of very ancient readings. This (the insertion of the golden rule) was one of them, and the asterisk in the manuscripts denoted that the reading was an addition to the current text. Strictly, this authority was Greek rather than Syriac; but it is Greek that was closely bound up with the Syriac tradition. The readings of this witness are characteristically Western, and it is in close alliance with D. Its presence here, along with two other ancient versions, also Western in character, shows that the reading which they attest had a wider diffusion and was earlier in date than those for which the authorities are purely Latin. It must have originated before the point at which the Latin branched off from the Syrian (primitive Western Greek) and Egyptian.

(2) I should therefore regard it as practically certain that, whether Tertullian had or had not in his copy the reading 'do not do to others what you would not have done to you', that reading is at least of considerably older date than his own. To my mind the probabilities are that he had it before him, because in any case he had the other admittedly secondary reading *vectante vos spiritu sancto*. But it would

not follow that, because he had it in his text, he would therefore include it in his quotation. It has always, in modern times as well as in ancient, been held to be permissible to drop a clause of the original that was not directly relevant to the purpose for which it was quoted. Tertullian could not, even if he had wished, have quoted this clause, because it would have made havoc of the rest of the quotation: *a quibus observando recte agitis* (the authenticated text, Reifferscheid's reconstruction is certainly wrong, but does not affect the point), links on naturally to *a quibus necesse est abstineri, a sacrificiis et a fornicationibus et sanguine,* but would make nonsense if preceded by the golden rule. A careful modern writer would call attention to the omission by printing ... where the clause should occur, but the ancients did not adopt these niceties.

(3) If we do not follow this reasoning, then we can only say that through some accident of transmission Tertullian has in this verse two readings of his group but not the third. Anomalies of this kind are frequent: for instance, of the seven Western non-interpolations in Luke 24 the Old Syriac (apparently) supports three, does not support three, and has part of one.

For these reasons it seems to me that Tertullian is at best a precarious foundation to build on, as Professor Lake builds upon him. But I would waive this point, if there were not weightier considerations in the background.

4. *Antecedent Probabilities*

We may follow the example of Professor Lake in propounding to ourselves the question which is more likely to have been the decision of the Council—the three-clause group (in the main of moral precepts) or the four-clause group (of ceremonial observances).

In any case neither group is strictly homogeneous. On the one hand, 'things sacrificed to idols'—i.e., meat from a victim portions of which had been sacrificed on an idol altar—must be ceremonial. On the other hand, 'fornication' is no less clearly moral. But the leading aspect in which it is regarded in this context is as presenting a contrast between Jew and Gentile. To the Gentile it was a thing indifferent; by the Jew it was to be avoided at all costs. But that condition does not apply to 'homicide'. The prohibition of homicide was really common to Jew and

Gentile. In this context it is a moral commonplace, which is flat and pointless; it is indeed so pointless as to be incredible.[14]

It is otherwise with what is called the 'food-law'. In regard to this we are not left to vague possibilities; we have the best of evidence to show that discussions precisely of this kind were actively going on at the time and place indicated. It is rather surprising to me that more has not been made of this point, and that I myself did not make more of it. The scene at Antioch in Gal. 2.11-14 presents a graphic picture of the urgency of such questions and the sharp controversy to which they were liable to give rise.

> But when Cephas came to Antioch, I resisted him to the face, because he stood condemned. For before that certain came from James, he did eat with the Gentiles; but when they came, he drew back and separated himself, fearing them that were of the circumcision. And the rest of the Jews dissembled likewise with him; insomuch that even Barnabas was carried away with their dissimulation. But when I saw that they walked not uprightly according to the truth of the gospel, I said unto Cephas before them all, If thou, being a Jew, livest as do the Gentiles, and not as do the Jews, how compellest thou the Gentiles to live as do the Jews ?

For those who identify (as I am still disposed to do) the Council with the events referred to in the preceding verses, the scene thus described would be in near proximity to it and would naturally throw back a light upon the circumstances which led up to it. It will be remembered that some scholars, including Mr C.H. Turner,[15] have raised the question whether it is necessary to suppose that the events alluded to in the two paragraphs of Galatians 2 are in strict chronological order, and whether the events of the second paragraph may not have really preceded those of the first, or (in other words) fall before the Council rather than after it. It would simplify the whole story to suppose that they did; and I too lean to the same hypothesis, which however, of course, cannot be verified. But whether the relation of this incident to the Council is nearer or more remote, in any case it illustrates aptly the nature of the controversy between the Judaizing party and their opponents. With this scene in our minds the debating of questions of food loses any semblance of inappropriateness. In fact such questions were really among the burning

14. This would not exclude the possibility that αἵματος was in some sense ceremonial; but that sense is much clearer in conjunction with πνικτοῦ-τῶν).

15. C.H. Turner, 'Chronology of the New Testament', in J. Hastings (ed.), *A Dictionary of the Bible* (5 vols.; Edinburgh: T. & T. Clark, 1898), I, pp. 403-25, esp. p. 424.

practical issues of the day; and practical issues are apt to take precedence of theoretical.

All that is to be said on the other side is contained in the argument that if 'the Council enacted a food law, it would be hard for St Paul to say that the Apostles had made no additions to his gospel'.[16] But what reason is there to suppose that Paul would ever have thought of connecting such things with 'his gospel'? That was surely concerned with very different matters.

There is one small confirmation of the view just taken that may easily be overlooked. Preuschen has rightly pointed out that ἀλίσγημα in v. 20 is properly used of defilement through food. The word is not classical, and the noun does not occur in the LXX, but the cognate verb occurs there four times and always in connexion with pollution by food.

> Daniel 1.8. Daniel would not defile himself with the king's meat.
> Malachi 2.7. Ye offer polluted bread.
> Malachi 1.12. The table of the Lord is polluted.
> Ecclesiasticus 40.29. He will pollute his soul with another man's meat.

This shows at least that the writer of this chapter had the idea of pollution through food strongly before his mind.

It is interesting to notice that the Latin translator of Irenaeus misses this point, where the bilingual manuscripts retain it. Irenaeus renders ἀλισγημάτων by *vanitatibus,* d, e (Latin columns of D and E), with g (cod. *gigas*), by *contaminationibus.*

5. *Origin of the Readings*

It is then, I submit, proved that in the near neighbourhood of the time and place to which the decree is assigned there was a real interest in questions relating to food, due to the prominent part which such matters played in the Mosaic Law and in Jewish practice. It was an incident in the inevitable controversy as to the terms of intercourse and communion between Jewish and Gentile Christians. It comes in most naturally when that controversy was at its height. And it certainly was at its height in the first age of the Gospel, in what we may call the Pauline period. We know how rapidly the controversy subsided, not so much through the victory of Paul in argument—though we have no doubt that he was victorious in argument—as through the shifting of the balance between the Jewish and Gentile parties, the one contracting and drawing into its

16. Lake, *Earlier Epistles of St Paul*, p. 54.

shell, while the other was as fast expanding in growth and increasing in influence. As this process went on, and as the old controversy receded into the distance, the points on which it turned became less intelligible. Professor Lake seems to me rather to miss the mark here. He speaks of the circle which omitted 'things strangled' as not having 'any objection to a food law' (p. 50), and again of such a law becoming 'repugnant or obsolete' (p. 59). He has indeed proved (and we welcome the proof) that a food law was recognised by Tertullian and in the churches of Vienne and Lyons which were under the government of Irenaeus. If I were merely arguing for a thesis, I might quote the two leading supporters of the Western text as witnessing to the Eastern readings in spite of themselves. But I do not think that they really do this. The evidence really points, not to the continued influence of the Apostolic Decree, but to the survival down to this date in the churches of Africa and Gaul of practices derived from the Levitical Law. When Tertullian refers to the abstention of Christians from things strangled and from the flesh of dead beasts, he is clearly thinking of Lev. 17.13-16. 'Whatsoever man there be...which taketh in hunting any beast or fowl that may be eaten, he shall pour out the blood thereof and cover it with dust... And every soul that eateth that which dieth of itself or that is torn off beasts...he shall wash his clothes, etc.' This rule was obviously regarded as still unrepealed. Tertullian knew his Bible, and the martyr Biblis also knew her Bible, but the rule came by degrees to be more or less ignored. From the first the special abstention from 'things strangled' must have been a puzzle in the West, where no such usage existed; and it is not strange that among the scribes to whom we owe the origin of the Latin branch of the Western Text there should have been one or more to whom allusions to such a practice were a stumbling block. That is all we have to assume in order to account for the Western readings. Nothing could be more simple, or more natural in view of the course of historical development. The Eastern readings are really Eastern, and reflect a condition of things that we know to have existed in the middle of the first century. The Western readings reflect, no less naturally, conditions which obtained away from Syria and Palestine (or from the districts where Jewish Christians were thickest) in the first half of the second century.

There is clearly a close interconnexion between all the members of the two groups of reading; but it is not necessary to suppose that they all came in at once. For me, the Eastern readings represent the genuine text; and therefore the *onus* on my side is to explain the origin of the Western. For the advocates of the Western text, this relation is inverted. And here I cannot help thinking that the task is beyond what they are able to perform. It is never a very serious matter to explain an easy reading out of a difficult one; but the reverse process is likely to prove troublesome. I will give my sketch of what I conceive to have been the origin of the Western readings first.

I have argued above, from the distribution of the authorities, that the first link in the chain was the insertion of the negative form of the golden rule. This was probably in the first instance a gloss written in the margin. Some scribe who was interested in the substance of what he was writing, took the decree as containing the essentials of Christian practice.

From this point of view it seemed to him somewhat external and deficient, and he jotted down by the side a current summary of duty to one's neighbour. Then came a copy in which by accident the clause about 'things strangled' was omitted. Such accidents are very common, especially where there is a string of clauses like one another in meaning. Professor Lake aptly refers to two examples in connexion with this same decree. He notes that both Origen and Methodius (though Origen at least was familiar with the ordinary four-clause text) quote it in a three-clause form, omitting 'blood' instead of 'things strangled'. There was nothing deliberate or intentional in this. But, with 'things strangled' omitted and the golden rule inserted, and with 'blood' an ambiguous term and 'fornication' certainly ethical, it was natural that a scribe— especially one of those masterful scribes who are almost as good as 'editors'—should consider with himself whether the whole decree ought not to be mainly ethical. He decides that it ought; and then, in order to harmonise all three verses, he strikes out 'things strangled' (which indeed he only half understood) in 15.20 and 21.25. There must have been deliberate action somewhere, because the three passages have all been brought into agreement; but on this view we should have that combination of accident and design which is so common in human affairs, and especially in the vagaries of textual criticism.

The difficulty on the other view is to account for the insertion of 'things strangled'. Omissions, as I have said, are easy; but, insertions always require an explanation of the special nature of the insertion. Professor Lake's hypothesis is, I think, the best that can be suggested. He thinks that there were two lines of exegesis of the ambiguous 'blood', and that those who took the ceremonial side inserted 'things strangled' to make the meaning clear. The question is, from what quarter in the Church could an impulse in this direction come? There was no longer an interest in these old Jewish scruples. If there had been, as perhaps there was in some Palestinian community on a very small scale, it would never have possessed itself of the great mass of Greek uncial manuscripts, with the single exception of Codex Bezae. That is where the explanation seems to me to break down. The four-clause text, with its appurtenances, belongs to the great main stream of Greek tradition; and to obtain command of this before the time of Clement and Origen, a reading or group of readings must have proceeded from a very central and authoritative quarter indeed. It is much easier to suppose that this particular group of readings was original.

6. *Subsequent History*

We have hitherto spoken of the 'Apostolic Decree', and that is the common designation. But I am by no means sure that 'Apostolic Rescript' would not be a better name. No doubt a rescript proceeding from 'the apostles and elders with the whole church' of Jerusalem would be as authoritative as if it were called a decree. But the point brought out would be that it was a direct answer to a limited local question arising out of limited local circumstances. The reason why we bear so little of this answer later was because there were so few churches in which the conditions were the same. The apostles and their colleagues evidently knew that they were legislating for a region in which the Jewish and the Gentile elements in the Church were more or less evenly balanced. Their object was to consult as far as possible the susceptibilities of the Jews, sharpened by long ages of exclusive practice. It is a matter of experience that questions affecting social relations of this kind lead to more acute controversy within their range than others of far greater theoretical importance. But when Paul carried his missionary labours further westwards, when the Jews definitely rejected his preaching while Gentiles freely joined his newly founded communities, the problem that arose was of a different kind. It was only what was right and seemly in itself; there was no longer need to provide against Jewish sensitiveness. Hence the so-called 'food law' practically reduced itself to the question of meats 'offered in sacrifice to an idol'. In regard to those Paul gave the wise advice, not to ask too many questions, but in case attention were called to the origin of the meat set before you, to abstain in order not to offend tender consciences. The whole atmosphere of this decision is different. It could easily and simply be placed upon a basis of Christian principle. There was no need to invoke the Levitical law. Paul had too much insight and tact to do this where it was not necessary. He had more important things to bring home to his converts than to explain to them the Levitical system; and it was probably more prudent, and more likely to keep discussions of this sort in their proper place, if he treated them just by the way and without any appeal to authority at all. When we consider what Paul was and what his converts were, I fail to see that there is anything improbable in the treatment of food questions in his epistles, or anything really inconsistent with the special instructions laid down to meet a special case in Acts 15. It is not likely to have been ever forgotten that in these the church of Jerusalem was addressing the churches of Antioch, Syria and Cilicia, and that it had no thought of 'binding' or 'loosing' the whole Christian Church for all time.

On such a general view, the events of the middle of the first century seem to me to fall into their places, and the evidence of the end of the second century also falls into its place; it also seems that a reasonable bridge of hypothesis has been constructed between them. But in any event I very much hope that we in England shall not be in too great haste to commit ourselves to a theory which as a whole is losing ground in Germany, and which I believe to be fundamentally wrong and misleading.

INDEX OF ANCIENT SOURCES

OLD TESTAMENT

NEW TESTAMENT

CHRISTIAN AUTHORS

OTHER ANCIENT AUTHORS

JOURNAL FOR THE STUDY OF THE NEW TESTAMENT
SUPPLEMENT SERIES